A TOPOLOGY OF
EVERYDAY CONSTELLATIONS

Writing **Architecture** series
A project of the Anyone Corporation; Cynthia Davidson, editor

A TOPOLOGY OF EVERYDAY CONSTELLATIONS

GEORGES TEYSSOT

THE MIT PRESS

CAMBRIDGE, MASSACHUSETTS

LONDON, ENGLAND

MIT Press books may be purchased at special quantity discounts for business or sales promotional use. For information, please email special_sales@mitpress.mit.edu or write to Special Sales Department, The MIT Press, 55 Hayward Street, Cambridge, MA 02142.

This book was set in Filosofia and Trade Gothic by the MIT Press. Printed and bound in the United States of America.

Library of Congress Cataloging-in-Publication Data

Teyssot, Georges, 1946–
A topology of everyday constellations / Georges Teyssot.
    pages   cm — (Writing architecture)
Includes bibliographical references and index.
ISBN 978-0-262-51832-1 (pbk. : alk. paper) 1. Space (Architecture) 2. Spatial behavior. I. Title.
NA2765.T49 2013
720.1—dc23
                                                        2012028541

10   9   8   7   6   5   4   3   2   1

CONTENTS

ACKNOWLEDGMENTS

Bernard Cache of Objectile in Paris generously shared his unpublished manuscripts, including his 2009 PhD thesis on "parametric" Vitruvius. Francis Strauven, whose body of work introduced me to the contradictory issues of "structuralism in architecture," was very generous with his advice. My gratitude also goes to Dirk van den Heuvel, who invited me to the biannual peer-review colloquia for PhD researchers at the Department of Architecture of Delft Technical University, and was a gracious and outstanding guide to the Dutch landscape, figuratively and literally. Research for this volume was carried out while I was a visiting scholar at the Institute for the History and Theory of Architecture (GTA), Department of Architecture, at the Swiss Federal Institute of Technology (ETH), Zurich, in 2009. A special debt of gratitude is owed to Marc Angélil (D-Arch), Christophe Girot (MLA), and Laurent Stalder (GTA). Chapters of this book were presented in lectures and seminars with colleagues, including: Martin Bressani and Aaron Sprecher, School of Architecture, McGill University, Montréal; Jean-Louis Déotte, Maison des Sciences de l'Homme–Paris-Nord, Saint-Denis; Antoine Picon, Graduate School of Design, Harvard University; Paulo Providência, University of Coimbra, Coimbra; Dominique Rouillard, École Nationale Supérieure d'Architecture, Paris-Malaquais, Paris; Nasrine Seraji, Institute for Art and Architecture, Akademie der bildenden Künste, Vienna. Discussions with the hospitable colleagues of the School of Architecture, University of Montréal, have been ongoing, including Georges Adamczyk, Jean-Pierre Chupin, Anne Cormier, and Alessandra Ponte. Moreover, I want to express thanks to the colleagues of Laval University's School of Architecture, Québec, who helped set up a creative environment. The contribution of Marjorie Bradley-Vidal and Ariane Ouellet-Pelletier, as copyright assistants, extends throughout this volume. Gregor Harbusch was very helpful in providing images from the Archives of Sigfried Giedion at the GTA. Access to the amazing collection of Werner Nekes (Mülheim/Ruhr) was crucial, as was the permission to publish rare items. At the FRAC Centre, Orléans, Marie-Ange Brayer kindly provided stunning images from the collection. Many thanks to Dirk de Meyer at Ghent University for arranging a visit to the Hôtel Max Hallet in Brussels. In addition, I thank Tess van Eyck, who liberally granted the permission to publish items from the Aldo van Eyck Archive. My gratitude also to Jurriaan van Stigt (son of Aldo van Eyck's student, Joop van Stigt), who gave me access to, and permission to publish from, the *Forum* archive. I thank Didier Faustino (Bureau des Mésarchitectures, Paris) for making available examples of his "mis-architecture." I want to express my gratitude to Hiroo Iwata at the University of Tsukuba, Japan, for the photo of his prosthetic contraption. For the generous help she provided, I am grateful to Eva Neumann, daughter of Alfred Neumann. I thank the various galleries, archives, libraries, museums, private collections, architects, artists, and institutions who kindly provided help, advice, and permission for this publication. At the MIT Press, Roger Conover was always encouraging and patient. Cynthia Davidson was very supportive, and without her confident optimism and editorial skill, much of this work would have remained on various computer screens. Lastly, for her enthusiasm, intelligence, and vast expertise on the subject, I am, as ever, indebted to Alessandra Ponte, whose unflinching support has sustained the making of this book.

SOURCES

The texts published here are either newly conceived or have
been thoroughly rewritten, sometimes translated anew by the
gifted writers Pierre Bouvier and Julie Rose. An abridged version of chapter 2 appeared as "Norm and Type" in *Architecture
and the Sciences*, a collective volume edited by Antoine Picon and
Alessandra Ponte (2003) Parts of chapter 3 were published as
"A Topology of Thresholds" in *Home Cultures* (vol. 2, no. 1, 2005)
and as "Mapping the Threshold" in *AA Files* (no. 57, 2008). The
text here has been wholly reworked and retranslated. Chapter 4
appeared as "The Wave" in *AA Files* (no. 61, 2010), and, in a preliminary form, in the collection *Experiments: Architecture between
Sciences and Arts*, edited by Ákos Moravánszky and Albert Kir-
chengast (Berlin, 2011). Chapter 5 was published in *Log* 11 (2008),
then revised for the anthology *Structuralism Reloaded*, edited by
Tomáš Valena, with Tom Avermaete and Georg Vrachliotis (London, 2011). Chapter 6 was originally written in French for the
2003 catalogue *Architectures expérimentales. 1950–2000*, edited by
Marie-Ange Brayer and published by the FRAC Centre in Orléans; however, it appears here as a newly written essay. A version
of chapter 7 appeared as "Architectural Embodiment" in the collection *Perspective, Projections and Design*, edited by Mario Carpo
and Frédérique Lemerle (Abingdon, UK, 2007). Chapter 8 was
first published (abbreviated) in *ARCH+* (no. 191/192, 2009), an
issue edited by Laurent Stalder, then in *Log* 18 (2010), and appears here in a revised form.

1 A TOPOLOGY OF EVERYDAY CONSTELLATIONS

Research into that serious disease, hatred of the home. Pathology of the disease. Progressive growth of the disease.
Charles Baudelaire, *My Heart Laid Bare*[1]

[T]hat's what I feel, an outside and an inside and me in the middle, perhaps that's what I am, the thing that divides the world in two, on the one side the outside, on the other the inside, that can be as thin as foil, I'm neither one side nor the other, I'm in the middle, I'm the partition, I've two surfaces and no thickness . . .
—Samuel Beckett, *The Unnamable*[2]

In the *Arcades Project*, Walter Benjamin invoked a history that dispensed with the reverence accorded to great names and the political, artistic, and individual heroes of older histories.[3] By opening the "trash can" (*der Abfall*, waste), he directed history toward new objects: the horizon of technological civilization, the crowd of unknown figures, and the effects of repetition within long series. Reading Benjamin today is still to rethink the possibility of history as a constellation saturated with tensions. So, too, the ambition of the studies in this book is to open up a series of paths cutting across the tangled thicket of everyday life, with its burden of miseries, perpetual bad habits, repressed desires, ineffable longings, and untold melancholies—but a gloom relieved by the animated chatter of gossip, the cozy reassurance of mainstream opinions, and the uncanny comforts of familiarity.

The essays collected here examine the nature of spaces, public or private, at the moment they become part of the innumerable series of devices and technical equipment that control the movements of people and things. Inhabited spaces in society present themselves as institutions that open a place for life, offer shelter and refuge, command the precepts of domesticity, set the rules of hospitality, and prescribe those of hostility.[4] Such spaces are also places where the law is inscribed and human technics and technology can mature, as well as locations where one can rest or linger, stay or dwell. In a way, to be hospitable, and to accommodate life, the "house" (that is, wherever one dwells) has to be fully equipped with appliances, with devices in their modern, ultratechnological forms. Because the house is a place saturated by different, overlapping institutions (ownership, sexuality, kinship, family, lineage, technics, servitude, repression, civilization, privacy, intimacy), it might be effective to define the household itself as an "equipment." To define "equipment" in this context, it is not only necessary to consider the architectural and technological features of the houses themselves, but also to introduce a "genealogy" of equipment in modern societies.

Equipment

Between the nineteenth and the twentieth century, architects were using various notions, such as program or type, taken from the vocabulary of criminology, anthropology, and sociology. It should be recalled that "types" are not only determined by institutions, prescribed by ideology, or guided by circumstances, but have their own "regularity," logic, and strategy. Michel Foucault called such regularity "regimes of practice," which he defined as "programs of conduct that have at the same time prescriptive impacts in relation to that remaining to be done ('jurisdictional'

1.1
Julius Jacob, *Stair in the New Friedrichstrasse*, Berlin,
1887, watercolor and tempera. Courtesy Stiftung
Stadtmuseum Berlin, Landesmuseum für Kultur und
Geschichte Berlins, Fotothek.

impacts) and impacts of codification in relation to that remaining to be known ('truthfulness' impacts)."[5] Planning, building, and housing cannot be conceived as an effect of domination and constituent division except genealogically. Use is secondary. No functional or programmatic needs fed this compelling desire; it was merely the effect of strategies imposed by the modern State, as well as by corporate interest. In other words, it was not social needs that were the "cause" of public and private equipment created by the State (and/or corporations), but the State itself, in its role of offering services and assistance through its various entities, those that imposed instruments determining specific needs. Although these needs had existed, they were warped by this very provision of social mechanisms, the subject thus becoming molded to the dominion and existing only for the State. There is, of course, no single strategy, nor do these strategies always produce the desired effects. Nor does the State necessarily succeed in conferring positive value and functionality when configuring and forming what Gilles Deleuze has named the "Social," composed of different, intertwining lines, whether "conjugal, philanthropic, hygienic, industrial."[6] It is possible to draw the map of the social as a Modern Hybrid, a chart that would show how "desires and powers, the new demands for control but also the new abilities for resistance and liberation are organized and confront each other on these lines."[7] Virginia Woolf's possession of *A Room of One's Own* (1929)—that is, having access to a room to oneself—is a desire but also an instrument of control. Deleuze reminds us that "a regulatory mechanism is haunted by what overflows it and makes it burst from the inside."[8] Nevertheless, the social is determined by means of multiple strategies, which include the division of space (town-suburb-country), the system of ownership (public-private), the forms of consumption (individual-collective), or the categories in the population (child-adult, normal-abnormal, masculine-feminine, citizen-alien).

There is nothing paradoxical in this description of the dominating State. Friedrich Nietzsche had shown, in his *Genealogy of Morals*, that "the actual causes of a thing's origin and its eventual uses, the manner of its incorporation into a system of purposes, are worlds apart; that everything that exists, no matter what its origin, is periodically reinterpreted by those in power in terms of fresh intentions."[9]

Those who dominate will always present their interpretations as truth, and for Nietzsche: "No matter how well we understand the utility of a certain physiological organ (or of a legal institution, a custom, a political convention, an artistic genre, a cultic trait) we do not thereby understand anything of its origin."[10] It is clear, then, that any history or theory of the dwelling wishing to analyze it in terms of a response to needs, to seeing the house as the rational planning of spaces as a response to new ends, new functions, and new uses, must also take into account the role of power (of industry, capital, and the State) in controlling the interpretation and definition of those needs. "[A]ll pragmatic purposes," continues Nietzsche, "are simply symbols of the fact that a will to power has implanted its own sense of function in those less powerful."[11] To address the issues of planning and building by focusing only on processes of rationalization or mechanization and its increasingly functional character and instrumental essence is, while fascinating, a problem: it would confuse indexes and symptoms with the actual and multiple processes of subjection. As Nietzsche warns, "While forms are fluid, their 'meaning' is even more so."[12]

Borrowing, for a moment, from Foucault's heterotopias and from Giorgio Agamben's apparatuses as instruments of governance,[13] one might begin with the notion that a piece of equipment is first an economic device that, in his words, "produces a production." That is, it not only produces goods or merchandise, but also creates a sector of activity and structures for its control that entail new administrative services and institutions. Second, a piece of equipment also produces new "needs"—that is, it opens a void space that must be filled by new demands. For instance, the development of a new product concurrently produces a consumer who comes complete with new needs and requests for assistance. Finally, a piece of equipment imposes a regime of normalization, adjusting the "production of production" to the "production of demand," classifying things and objects, and regulating flows and fluxes of money, goods, and information. This normalization works by establishing limits (of property, for example) and exclusions (between the forbidden and the permitted). In order to make the history of "inhabited spaces" meaningful, a post-Foucauldian approach situates the history of places within the genealogy of larger axiomatics in modern society, with the verbal and nondiscursive apparatuses that tend to some collective needs. These axiomatics include such notions as "free time," as distinct from a more classical idleness (Latin, *otium*); "lodging," which is no longer poetic dwelling; schooling, a space for the normalization of knowledge and not one for children's humanistic education; and "social hygiene," which is a biopolitic, a technology of health implemented on the population, not a specific guarantee of the health of every individual.

Type

Of course, there are other methods and procedures that allow for alternative analyses of the history of inhabited spaces. Among these, the ethnology of social space, such as that undertaken by Émile Durkheim, Marcel Mauss, and Claude Lévi-Strauss (limiting oneself to French writers), must be cited, acknowledging, however, that nearly every school in the world was based on the German-American Franz Boas's pioneering work in anthropology. (Boas, the so-called father of modern anthropology, died in 1942 of a stroke, literally in the arms of Lévi-Strauss, at the

Columbia University Faculty Club.)[14] In *Structural Anthropology* (1958), Lévi-Strauss states that "structural studies in the social sciences" should also find inspiration in the new "hard" sciences. He refers to the outstanding achievements of John von Neumann and Oskar Morgenstern's *Theory of Games* (1944), Norbert Wiener's *Cybernetics* (1948), and Claude Shannon's *Theory of Communication* (1948), and insists that "soft" sciences should get their insights from the rigorous approaches of topology and group theory.[15] Lévi-Strauss attempted this in his own theory of the group, which he thought should lead to a precise definition of a social morphology. Through the tools of sociology, ethnology, linguistics, and structural anthropology, Lévi-Strauss tried to explain space as a social construct. The object of social structure studies is to understand social relations with the aid of models. However, one cannot construct social relations outside a common framework: "Space and time are two frames of reference we use to situate social relations, either alone or together. These space and time dimensions . . . have no properties outside those which derive from the properties of the social phenomena which 'furnish' them. According to their social structure, human societies have elaborated many types of such continuums," he writes.[16] Later, Lévi-Strauss was more precise with his definition of the house, establishing a connection between household, generation, families, and kinship: the house is "a moral person which possesses a domain that is perpetuated by the transmission of its name, its fortune and titles, along a real or fictive line, held as legitimate on the sole condition that this continuity can be expressed in the language of kinship or alliance, and more frequently, of the two together."[17] But there was peril present in structuralist method, residing in what Pierre Bourdieu defined as the "realism of the structure" through which systems of relations could be rendered "hypostatic," transformed into an abstract totality already constituted outside of the history of the individual and the group. Durkheim's professions of faith in the "collective conscious," or the notion of "collective memory," coined by philosopher and sociologist Maurice Halbwachs, attest to this danger.

To be specific, the act of habitation consists in grasping routines that help to organize life, and in rethinking and transposing customary modes of action in response to the need to adapt to unfamiliar circumstances. The structuralist theory of the habitat was historically to construct something found in the "practices" of everyday life of the inhabitants (or any other agent in a society), rather than their "consciences," which led to what Bourdieu calls a "theory of practice." This theory was dependent on the reconstruction of the method of generating those practices—that is, their genealogy. To achieve such an endeavor, Bourdieu, inspired by Durkheim and Lévi-Strauss, and himself a follower of structuralism, reintroduced the Latin and medieval (especially Aquinian) philosophical notion of *Habitus* as an ensemble of unconscious patterns able to generate practices and representations.[18] *Habitus* refers to social status, style, and uses or practices, and is formed by *habi-*, which comes from *habere*, to have or to hold, and *-tus*, the suffix of verbal action. The archaic meaning of *Habitus* referred to the action of dwelling in, which explains why the Latin *habitare*, the frequentative of *habere*, refers to inhabiting. In late-nineteenth-century medicine, *Habitus* referred to the physical characteristics and constitution of a person, especially regarding susceptibility to disease. The term was singled out by sociologists to define a structure of the mind distinguished by a set of acquired schemata, dispositions, and tastes. In addition, historians and human geographers employed *Habitus* to define the dispositions that shape the actions, bodily behaviors, and experience associated with a particular social class or group. As Bourdieu noted, *Habitus* is improvisatory, operating through human practice rather than through prior conscious thought.

Peter Sloterdijk writes: "Not by chance the Latin and German languages have deduced the concept of habitude (*Gewohnheit*) or of *habitus* from the sojourn within the primary *living* space, that is to say, from the habitat (*Wohnen*)."[19] In addition, these languages always interpret the acquisition of new habits as a response to the emergence of something new or unexpected. In this view, the act of inhabiting would consist in the production of regimes of habitudes, as well as in the transposition of these regimes when in contact with extraordinary situations or noncustomary events, such as an invasion of other humans, a change of climate, or the spread of unusual diseases. Inasmuch as the notion of disease refers to malady, a word that derives from the Latin *male* (ill) and *Habitus*, the idea of *Habitus* also relates to states of illness, whether endemic or epidemic, as well as to conditions of acquiring habits, whether bad or good. *Habitus*, then, is a social construction that generates cultural practices, which are regulated without being directed by any force, power, or authority.[20] With Lévi-Strauss, and later with Bourdieu, attempts to rewrite the notion of *Habitus* from an ethnological view tended to overcome the difficulty of previous historical, social, or anthropological analyses, which were constituted through concepts such as social norms, theoretical models, rules, or principles immanent in practice. It is well known that Bourdieu's sociology was opposed to Foucault's analysis of discursive (and nondiscursive) practices, but in a paradoxical way, despite the struggle in which they were enmeshed, Bourdieu's *Habitus* approached the notions of "regularity" and "regime of practices" later defined by Foucault. However, Foucault would make the valid point that Bourdieu's theories underestimated the role of power mechanisms.

In the history of Western architecture since the eighteenth century, it is difficult to recognize where and how the polarization developed between, on the one hand, "cultural models," "regimes of practice," or "types," which were more or less forcefully applied as norms to various social groups, and, on the other, *Habitus*, or systems of habitation historically located in specific regions, sites, or traditions. For many, the habitat—defined as the inscription of sets of practices, rites, hierarchies, and symbols—constituted a "truth" of inhabiting. From the 1960s on, these critical instruments, for the most part borrowed from the armament of the human sciences (type and typology, the cultural model, the regularity of practice, *Habitus*, and so on), had seemingly secured a firm and "objective" foundation for the definition of "type" in architecture, determining its anthropological, ethnological, and sociological "structure." Type in architecture was thereby presented as the combining of spatial-symbolic relations derived from cultural models in the form of a distributive typology of sites of practice. However, even in contemporary anthropology, Lévi-Strauss's notion of "house-based societies" (*sociétés à maison*) is widely discussed and questioned, and the notion of types of houses derived from cultural anthropology is thought to raise as many problems as it solves. As two critics write, "While houses may receive indigenous emphasis in many societies, their cultural and geographic diversity suggests that the 'type' will always be far too heterogeneous to constitute an analytical model."[21]

Combining consciousness with stereotypes while promising a psycho-logical, secure place to live in was explored by Gaston Bachelard in *Poetics of Space* (1958); he said that the space of the house can be depicted as the "topography of our intimate being."[22] Bachelard investigated the house, inhabited not just in daily life but in the imagination—that is, through ideas of the "nest," the "shell," the "cave," the "corner," the "drawer," the "attic," and the "cellar."[23] Such an analysis diluted and exploded the "regularity" of the complex topography of polarity found in such oppositions as inside and outside, dirty and clean, full and empty, front and back, exposed and hidden, near and far, and so on. This investigation of the "poetics of space" would be insufficient, however, if not supported by a history of spaces, or, to use Benjamin's terminology, a topology of the complex "everyday constellations" of society. In other words, it is necessary to investigate, as the philosopher Michel Serres writes, "The accidents or catastrophes of space and the multiplicity of spatial varieties. What is the closed? What is the open? . . . What is the continuous and the discontinuous? What is a threshold, a limit? Elementary program of a topology." Today there is no longer a mythology that reassuringly recounts all possible myths: "From now on there is the space, or the spaces, that are the condition of the old stories. The spaces by which I have the chance of acquiring a new knowledge. And myths are written on them."[24] In this way, a historical project might reconstruct the genealogy of organizational charts ("those of language, of the factory, of the family, of political parties, and so forth"),[25] the means of generating regimes of cultural and social practices, the hermeneutics of the intimacy of interior spaces, the topo-analyses of the secret and the hidden, the stylistic classifications of built form, and the cartography of the connections and linkages that the body must practice in this large family of spaces.

In his entry "Type" for the *Vocabulary of Modern Architecture* (2000), Adrian Forty is careful to differentiate between the classical, Neoplatonic notion of (arche-) type as exposed by Antoine-Chrysostome Quatremère de Quincy, the anthropologization of type accomplished by Gottfried Semper, the concept of *Typisierung* defined by Hermann Muthesius as a normalization of industrial products, and Aldo Rossi's idea of typology, a theory of formal permanencies to be found in an urban context.[26] What binds the different approaches is one common aim: to determine either societal continuums or underlying forms, or the connection between the two. Relying principally on Quatremère de Quincy, the revival of the notion of type and its extension into a "typology"—that is, a science of types—was achieved largely by the Italian historian Giulio Carlo Argan in his 1960 article "Tipologia," which was republished many times and translated into English by Joseph Rykwert for a 1963 issue of *Architectural Design*.[27] Along with Argan, one could add to Forty's list the revival of Platonic archetypes (à la Rudolf Wittkower) attempted by Colin Rowe, which he developed in parallel with the structuralist inspiration of several critics in the 1960s and 1970s, including Alan Colquhoun, Anthony Vidler, and Rafael Moneo. Colquhoun's "Typology and Design Method" (1967) begins with a lengthy quotation from Lévi-Strauss's *Structural Anthropology* (1963) that stresses the predominance of cultural meaning over biological matters. Afterward, the British critic suggested that "types" could provide the means through which structuralism could be translated into architecture: "[T]hrough the persistence of earlier forms . . . the system can convey meaning."[28] However, while the structural anthropologist was reading domestic space like a book, for the architect the question was how to inscribe the model in space. Between the 1960s and the 1980s, the reflections of Colquhoun and others attempted to reestablish the conventions of the architecture of the dwelling, which were to be understood as a common language that had to be restored. In this sense, "truth" stood in conformity with, and as an adjustment to, a common sense of inhabitation and a conventional means of production.

Such a lofty project did not succeed, to say the least. During this period, every socially agreed-upon consensus was increasingly excluded by nearly everybody (some designers, but especially customers and occupants), and any kind of authority defining a communal sense of habitation was doomed to be condemned. Nevertheless, the determination of the "common sense," or shared meaning, of habitation was entrusted to an anthropological realism capable of adapting the *Habitus* of the inhabitants, making their own "regular" habits spatially concrete and taking into account "cultural models," or patterns, and means of production. The model, or convention, acquired significance not so much through "truth" as through a verisimilitude that conferred on it the dignity of reproducibility, repeatability, and imitability (for what is a model, if not something to imitate?). The conventional role of the model was to take on the function defined by the sociologist Talcott Parsons as "pattern maintenance"—that is, the conservation of cultural and institutional models that constitute the heart of a social system and thereby assure the cultural continuity necessary to the functioning of society.[29] Influenced by Durkheim, Parsons thought that "the function of pattern maintenance refers to the imperative of maintaining the stability of patterns of institutionalized culture defining the structure of the system. . . . Overall, systems do show a tendency to maintain themselves (inertia)."[30] For Parsons, culture did not surround one as a vapor or an atmosphere, nor was it a veneer applied to the self; instead, culture penetrated one at every moment of life, and this happened precisely because of pattern maintenance.

Habit

Anthropologists, architects, and thinkers were condemned to be squeezed between two kinds, or two stages, of the philosophic repetition: that of habit and that of memory. One doesn't live without habits. The human being acquires habits and then is molded by habits: on the one hand he gains something, and on the other he loses, because there is always a risk of numbness in routine. The phenomenon of habit presents this singular ambiguity that amazed the French philosopher Félix Ravaisson,[31] who wrote in 1838: "An acquired habit is the consequence of a change. . . . All change is realized in time; and what brings a habit into being is not simply change understood as modifying the thing, but change understood as occurring in time. Habit has all the more force when the modification that produced it is further prolonged or repeated. Habit is thus a disposition relative to change, which is engendered in a being by the continuity or the repetition of this very same change."[32] The French metaphysician, who was read by Henri Bergson, Marcel Proust, Gilles Deleuze, and Jacques Derrida, concludes with this paradox: "Nothing, then, is capable of habit that is not capable of change; but everything capable of change is not by that fact alone capable of habit."[33] For instance, the mere movement of a body does not entail contracting a habit, inasmuch as "habit implies more than mutability . . . it supposes a change in the disposition, in the potential, in the internal virtue of that in which the change occurs, which itself does not change."[34] Habit is not the result of just any repetition. In *Difference and Repetition* (1968), Deleuze points out this paradox of repetition, which lies "in the fact that one can speak of repetition only by virtue of the change or difference that it introduces into the mind which contemplates it[.] By virtue of a difference that the mind *draws from* repetition[.]"[35] This difference is related to the fact that repetition creates an aptitude for change.[36] And Deleuze insists: "Habit *draws* something from repetition—namely, difference."[37] For both Ravaisson and Deleuze, habit is not the product of some mechanical routine but the actual law of being. Recalling the forgotten meaning of the Greek *hexis* (usually translated in Latin as *Habitus*), habit is a disposition or a "virtue," a constitution developed as the result of change, without which the finite being could not live.[38] Proust, a contemporary of Bergson, remarked: "Habit!—that skillful but very slow housekeeper who begins by letting our mind suffer for weeks in a temporary arrangement; but whom we are nevertheless happy to find, for without habit and reduced to no more than its own resources, our mind would be powerless to make a lodging habitable."[39] Habit puts the person in a paradoxical situation: one is lessened by it, and by it one is elevated. Nietzsche writes: "I love brief habits and consider them an inestimable means for getting to know *many* things and states, down to the bottom of their sweetness and bitterness. . . . The good things part from me, not as something that has come to nauseate me but peacefully and sated with me as I with it. . . . That is what happens to me with dishes, ideas, human beings, cities, poems, music, doctrines, ways of arranging the day, and life styles."[40]

In *Difference and Repetition*, Deleuze defined three temporal syntheses that create a line investigating our relation to time. The first, a passive synthesis, Habit (*Habitus*), was buried in the present. The second, again a passive synthesis, Memory (*Mnemosyne*), was concerned with the virtual past in an absolute state. The third, an active synthesis, was geared toward the prospective future, that of the "eternal return" that opened on an unforeseeable new condition. Sedentary distributions, good sense, and common sense were all based upon one particular, passive synthesis of time, that of habit.[41] Deleuze noted that Memory is the passive synthesis of time as pure past, organizing repetition according to a cycle of remembrance and forgetfulness, while *Habitus* is the passive synthesis of time as living present, and therefore the memory of practices in space and time. For Deleuze the true meaning of repetition is opposed to both the ancient category of memory (or reminiscence) and the modern category of *Habitus*.[42] *Habitus* resolves repetition in a contemporary present through the cycle of custom, or "a customary cycle."[43] Instead, Deleuze proposes to overcome the overly simple cycles, both the one followed by the habitual present (customary cycle) and the one described as pure past (memorial or immemorial cycle). To do so, he hypothesizes that the world is dominated by a condition characterized by "a completely other distribution which must be called nomadic, a nomad *nomos*, without property, enclosure or measure."[44] For Deleuze, the question is no longer the distribution of things and the division of persons in sedentary spaces, "but rather a division among those who distribute *themselves* in an open space—a space which is unlimited, or at least without precise limits. . . . To fill a space, to be distributed within it, is very different from distributing the space."[45] From sedentary structures of representation to nomadic distribution, a leap has taken place, leading to unsettling difficulties, transcending all limits, deploying errant and delirious distribution.[46] Nomadic structures lead to "mad repartitions . . . mad distribution—instantaneous, nomadic distribution, crowned anarchy or difference,"[47] a state which physics had described in thermodynamics as entropy.[48]

In his book on *Life and Habit* (1877), Samuel Butler questions the notion of personal identity, which he argues is made of an aggregation of many components, some of them depending on time.[49] One obvious constituent of a person is its body, although it goes through various modifications and, eventually, destruction. Even inside the body there are components in continuous mutation, dying and being born again. To live we need to eat food, drink water, and breathe air. So where is the limit between the organic and the inorganic? Is the air surrounding us already part of our body? And are clothes and habitation also part of the body? Butler recalls that man's clothes are "a kind of food which warms him and hatches him."[50] The life of a person is an accumulation of habits: "For even the corn in the fields," Butler writes, "grows upon a superstitious basis as to its own existence, and only turns the earth and moisture into wheat through the conceit of its own ability to do so, without which faith it were powerless."[51] Deleuze, who read the French translation of Butler's volume, argues in *Difference and Repetition* that acquisition of habit is built upon an organic synthesis during the passage of time, and this happens because the person has to satisfy "needs." Our *corpus* of habits helps read the "signs" of need, both internally, from the organism (perception, synesthesia, sensory awareness, reflection, and contemplation), and externally, from the environment. For Deleuze, "In essence, habit is contraction,"[52] because we are not born with our habits. There is no continuity apart from that of habit, and we have no other continuities apart from those of our thousands of components, which form within us so many superstitious and contemplative selves, so many claimants and satisfactions.[53]

For Butler, wheat is the contraction of earth and humidity, and this miracle is to be contemplated. But not forever: when the duration of faith, superstition, contemplation, or questioning is excessive, it leads to fatigue, at which point the soul can no longer contract what it contemplates. The need has been nurtured, and satiety follows. Hence, the process of repetition that orders our lives. The present time extends between two eruptions of need, between which there is the interval of contemplation. This repetition of need shapes time, but need is not properly understood in relation to a negative state, such as lack. Repetition is essentially inscribed in need, and this gives form to various aspects of duration in a person's life: rhythms (of the body), reserves (of energy), reaction times, intertwinings (of relationships).[54] It is tempting to extend this notion of habit to the house itself, conceived as a receptacle of practices, routines, and customs.

As a passive synthesis of time, as habit, the experience of repetition can be discerned in the images of the *intérieur* in customary rituals that Samuel Beckett described as a perpetual compromise with the environment. Having recalled that "[t]he laws of memory are subject to the more general laws of habit," Beckett writes: "Habit is a compromise effected between the individual and his environment, or between the individual and his own organic eccentricities, the guarantee of a dull inviolability, the lightning-conductor of his existence. . . . Breathing is habit.

Life is habit."[55] Habit organizes the time of our daily life and can eventually impose on it a dismal invulnerability. "The creation of the world," Beckett continues, "did not take place once and for all time, but takes place every day. Habit then is the generic term for the countless treaties concluded between the countless subjects that constitute the individual and their countless correlative objects."[56] Describing these "treaties" Beckett uses the term *pact*, which must be continually renewed. For Beckett, analyzing the poisonous, lethal effect of time in Proust's literary equation, any second that passes is an abstract future that drips endlessly into a vivid past: "The individual is the seat of a constant process of decantation, decantation from the vessel containing the fluid of future time, sluggish, pale and monochrome, to the vessel containing the fluid of past time, agitated and multi-colored by the phenomena of its hours."[57] As exposed in Beckett's dissection of habits, any alteration of this routine brings some danger: "The periods of transition that separate consecutive adaptations . . . represent the perilous zones in the life of the individual, dangerous, precarious, painful, mysterious and fertile, when for a moment the boredom of living is replaced by the suffering of being."[58] Habit reassures, but it also anesthetizes; it ignites ennui and calls for boredom, the most intolerable of diseases, since it is the most durable.[59]

Benjamin defined *modern* as "the new in the context of what has always already been there."[60] In the capitalist production of commodities, the new and the novel stimulate demand by reintroducing meaning. At the same time, the process of repetition, organized for commodity production, imposes "the eternal return of the same" (*immer gleich*).[61] In a world of stereotypes, the question becomes knowing how to tear the new from the always-the-same. "It is the inherent tendency of dialectical experience," Benjamin writes, "to dissipate the semblance of eternal sameness, and even of repetition, in history."[62] As a preliminary act, then, this dissipation, or dissolving, that Benjamin asks for in historical work would implicate "'human sciences,' from so-called habitus, from style, and the like."[63] For both Benjamin and Deleuze, it seemed that the humanistic category of *Habitus*, defined as the embodiment of conventions, concordance, and style, should be led toward its own dissolution, to force "the foundation of habit into a failure of 'habitus,'"[64] making it the thought and the production of a new kind of repetition, which becomes "difference in itself." Custom and regularity are concretized in habits, which, combined with needs, produce the form of the house. Today, "house" means anyplace one actually lives, resides, dwells, or travels, including one's bed, sofa, office, or vehicle. Accordingly, the form of the dwelling includes the contemplative pause between needs, inscribing those needs, and the lack of needs, into our floors and walls, as well as onto our screens.

Debris

Benjamin followed the path set up by the Goncourt brothers, themselves a source of inspiration, who said: "The anecdote is the indiscretion of history."[65] In an 1852 entry in their *Journal*, the Goncourts announced a novel field of study: "The bed where man is born, reproduces himself and dies: we should do something on that, one day."[66] Later, Remy de Gourmont called for a method that involved creating history "with the very detritus [*der Abfall*] of history."[67] Quoting such sources, Benjamin writes: "The constructions of history are comparable to military orders that discipline the true life and confine it to barracks. On the other hand: the street insurgence of the anecdote."[68] Comparable to an inopportune event or to an ill-timed irruption, "[t]he anecdote brings things near us spatially, lets them enter our life."[69] To write history one must accumulate minutiae, including ephemeral items, discarded paraphernalia, useless gadgets or outmoded gizmos. Far from drawing a large fresco with the illusion of giving a full picture of an epoch, those trivial details must keep their fragmentary nature. Moreover, in a general shift toward miniaturization, everything reduces and diminishes within the nineteenth-century city, because, as Honoré de Balzac lamented in *Lost Illusions* (1843): "Soon it will be a formidable problem to house one's library. . . . One can no longer find space for provisions for any sort."[70] Benjamin writes: "Perhaps there is a connection between the shrinking of residential space and the elaborate furnishing of the interior."[71] A historical approach based on the collection of trivia is at the heart of Benjamin's *Arcades Project*. Borrowing from the surrealists, Benjamin adopted "the principle of montage into history,"[72] as a means of writing and thinking. Out of such a strategy, he hoped "to assemble large-scale constructions out of the smallest and most precisely cut components. Indeed, to discover in the analysis of the small individual moment the crystal of total event."[73] He returned to this method elsewhere: "Method of this project: literary montage. I needn't *say* anything. Merely show. I shall purloin no valuables, appropriate no ingenious formulations. But the rags, the refuse [*die Lumpen, den Abfall*], these I will not inventory but allow, in the only way possible, to come into their own; by making use of them."[74] The only possible way to do the rags justice is to recycle them.

Benjamin was influenced by surrealism in general, including Max Ernst's collages and Louis Aragon's *Paris Peasant* (1926), particularly the "Preface to a Modern Mythology," which was published separately in 1923.[75] For Aragon, the "mythology" of the modern included negative experiences in a very precise sense. "Each day the modern sense of existence is modified," he wrote, "a mythology ravels and unravels. It is a science of life, which belongs only to those who have no experience of it."[76] Thus, modern mythology is knowledge, a "science of life" deferred in time and space, which illuminates only those who are already outside of, or feel removed from, or dispossessed by, this experience. In this way, myth is defined as the glimpse of an experience (for example, that of the Parisian arcades) at the moment of its disappearance, through death, destruction, or disuse.[77] Given that this mythology is defined by its instantaneous, ephemeral character, "no one is allowed to stop for more than an instant,"[78] in the midst of these awakened dreams and fantasies.[79] The past becomes a dialectical overturning, an unexpected eruption, and the sudden discovery of the awakened perception. Through the notion of the always-the-same, and by plunging into the deepest dream, things, immersed in a continuous flow, came to meet him. In this way, rather than remaining merely a series of notes, Benjamin managed to construct something closer to a surrealist montage out of his citations. A collector and *flâneur* of the library, as much as Aragon (or André Breton) was a street pedestrian, he gathered together fragments in order to build a history. Montage and assemblage of debris led to an aestheticization of the fragment, a process that, since the early German Romantics, has been at the basis of a modern project. The assemblage of such fragments revealed the historical mode of every collected fragment. For Benjamin, history must arise in a moment of condensation of reality, as a chemical precipitate, which will lead to "the increasing concentration (integration) of reality, such that everything past (in its time) can acquire a higher grade of reality [*Aktualität*] than it had in the moment of its existing."[80]

In contrast to a traditional history of design, punctuated by the continual production of new objects (objects which are more or less successful in aesthetic terms, and more or less well received by the market), studies in the history of the house require that one take into consideration longer periods of time. The sources of such a history are extraordinarily vast and necessarily hybrid. The material is heterogeneous, concerning as it does aspects of the histories of taste, mentality, culture, technology, and "lifestyle,"

as well as more specific aspects related to the concerns of territory and the city, construction and architecture. The history of
the "home," to use a traditional term, is particularly well suited
(as is the history of the city) to the "the long term" (*longue du-
rée*), defined by such historians as Marc Bloch and Lucien Febvre
before the Second World War, and by Fernand Braudel, Philippe
Ariès, and Paul Veyne, and labeled as the French *Annales* School
of historical writing, which gives priority to long-term historical
events.[81] Parallel to that trend, Norbert Elias wrote his two-volume *The Civilizing Process*, first published in Switzerland in 1939,
tracing the historical development of European *Habitus*, molded
by social attitudes and polite imperatives in the postmedieval
era, regulating the standards for violence, table manners, bodily
functions, sex, and so forth, all components that would become
part of the court etiquette. Developed independently from the
Annales and characterized by a sociological bent, Elias's work is
also placed in the long term.

Paradoxically, in this new history, the importance assumed by
"the long term" seems to coincide with a plunge into a limitless
forest of details. Elias referred to this at the close of a colloquium,
organized by Philippe Ariès, devoted to the conceptual problem
raised by the project of writing a "history of private space."[82]
Confronted by an abundance of research topics, one risks the
dissemination of objects: "Once one abandons the paths of older
types—shall we say of political, economic, and social history—
one can no longer see quite clearly the unity of it all . . . one perhaps has to ask himself: what is the unity?"[83] Given the confusion
resulting from the multitude of details, Elias proposed that these
be concentrated in a tightly fitting container, the historical development contained in the "private room."[84] It follows, at least
in theory, that to the extent that the history of living spaces and
cultural modes of inhabiting can be told as a narrative, or a meta-
narrative,[85] it would develop in two different registers that are

only seemingly contradictory: on the one hand, the accumulation of disseminated, almost pulverized details, monads defined over a relatively long period; and on the other, an operation of filtering and concentrating this multiplicity. The plurality of micro-events, the series of individual and social habits, repeated over the course of time, seems to hammer spaces with tiny, repeated blows, molding or forging, as it were, an "environment," that of everyday life. Not surprisingly, difficulties arise from this ambition to create a "macro" dimension of the long term, out of the "micro" context of particular subject matter.

The French philosopher Alain observed that a traditional house would evolve organically and grow naturally "from the inside"[86] to the outside. Edgar Allan Poe's *The Philosophy of Furniture* (1840) was a plea for elegance and simplicity, condemning the American parade of costly appurtenances. In his 1836 *Confession*, the writer Alfred de Musset deplored the accumulation of furniture of all periods and all countries: "Our century has no forms. . . . Eclecticism is our taste. . . . So we live surrounded by debris, as if the end of the world was approaching."[87] In a text published on the occasion of the 1855 Paris World Exhibition, the philosopher Ernest Renan compared such recurring events with Greek festivals and Olympian games, noting that the former lacked poetry: "Our century tends toward neither the good nor the bad; it tends toward the mediocre,"[88] he said, and "the progress of art is [far from being parallel] to that made by a nation in the taste for comfort."[89] He continues: "The epochs and the countries in which comfort became the public's principal attraction have had the least talent for art. . . . Convenience excludes style."[90] Noting the practical superiority of British kitchenware and pots, for him it is an incontestable fact that "nowhere in history is the progress of industry in any way parallel to the progress of art."[91] In *The Philosophy of Money* (1900), Georg Simmel complained about the combined effects of industrial production, eclectic taste, and quick changes in fads: "First, the sheer quantity of very specifically formed objects make a close relationship to each of them difficult. . . . This is expressed in the housewife's complaint that the care of the household becomes ceremonial fetishism."[92] Then, "changes in fashion disrupt that . . . process of . . . assimilation between subject and object. . . . [In the third place, there is] the multitude of styles that confront us when we view the objects that surround us."[93]

As quoted by Benjamin, the writings of Poe, Renan, and Simmel express a state of unhomely (*unheimlich*) malaise felt in facing industrial objects, the (more or less) durable goods and universal commodities. Benjamin noted: "Etuis, dust covers, sheaths . . . were so many measures taken to capture and preserve traces."[94] In *The Philosophy of Money*, Simmel distinguishes between money and all other consumer goods: only money is safe from disappointment, which threatens all possessions.[95] This distancing effect of things can also be explained by the high potential for disappointment where durable goods are concerned. As some economists explain, our everyday life is governed by a very unstable balance between necessities linked to comfort and stimulations that provoke pleasure.[96] Our disappointment in the face of things arises from the fact that the durable goods furnishing our living spaces bring a balance between pleasure and comfort—a balance leaning toward comfort, to the detriment of pleasure.

Interpenetration

The history of the house, oscillating between an ideal of transparency and the need for establishing certain forms of opacity, manifests a double, sometimes contradictory, ambition. The same ambiguity is perceptible in architecture, literature, and the visual arts. For example, in *Pot Luck* (*Pot-Bouille*, or "stew pot"), an 1883 novel set in a Parisian apartment building, Émile Zola describes the distasteful characters lurking behind the elegant façade and the mingling of lives that generates the heady, mildly distasteful mix suggested by the title. A more daunting image of such ambivalence appears during the destruction of some habitations. As Victor Hugo noted in his *Journal*, the pulling down of many houses in Paris created an awkward, grotesque spectacle: "Someone is demolishing, at this moment, on the boulevard du Temple, the Fieschi house. The roof trusses are stripped of their tiles. The windows without glass and without frames let one see the inside of the rooms. . . . Wallpaper strewn with a delicate greenish figure covers the walls and ceiling. . . . The ceiling is, like the rest, already broken up and amply cracked by the pickaxes of the masons."[97] On these disturbing ruins are inscribed all of the miseries and small pleasures of life. The same effect is well rendered in *The Notebooks of Malte Laurids Brigge* (1910) by Rainer Maria Rilke:

> *Houses? But, to be precise, they were houses that were no longer there. Houses that had been demolished from top to bottom. . . . Near the bedroom partitions still remained, along the whole length of the wall, a grayish-white streak; across this there crept up in worm-like spirals that seemed to serve some unspeakably disgusting digestive function. The gaping, rust-covered channel of the water-closet pipe. . . . The stubborn life of these rooms had not allowed itself to be trampled out. It was still there. . . . One could see it in the colors which it had slowly changed, year by year: blue into a moldy green, green into gray, and yellow into a stale, drab, weary white. . . . And from these walls once blue and green and yellow, framed by the tracks of the disturbed partitions, the breath of these lives came forth—the clammy, sluggish, fusty breath, which no wind had yet scattered.*[98]

Residues and traces left by inhabitants can be fetid and disgusting. As in Gordon Matta-Clark's *Splitting* (1974) series, or following Georges Perec's *Life: A User's Manual* (1978), a novel about the interwoven stories of the inhabitants of a fictitious Parisian apartment block, one wants to undo the structure of the building, observe all its components, inspect its every detail, and read the hundreds of stories that are discernible in lingering vestiges.

Benjamin, in the famous text "Naples" (1925), written with Asja Lacis, evoked the permeability of the city, which is as porous as *tufo*, the volcanic stone used in its Neapolitan construction: "Building and action interpenetrate in the courtyards, arcades, and stairways. In everything, they preserve the scope to become a theater of new, unforeseen constellations. The stamp of the definitive is avoided. No situation appears intended forever, no figure asserts it 'thus and not otherwise.' This is how architecture, the most binding part of the communal rhythm, comes into being here."[99] In such a city, public and private spaces are continuously amalgamated, as if made of a permeable substance: "Similarly dispersed, porous, and commingled is private life."[100] There is a continuous interpenetration of communal and single life: "Just as the living room reappears on the street, with chairs, hearth, and altar, so . . . the street migrates into the living room."[101] What characterizes this city is that porosity is the topological determinant. Apartment and street are in a continuous mode of exchanging status, either to privatize the street or to publicize the dwelling. Moreover, hidden from the street, the Neapolitan churches are out of sight, and no one notices their entrances. For the unaware visitor, "A single step takes him from the jumble of dirty courtyards into the pure solicitude of a lofty, whitewashed church interior. His private existence is the baroque opening of a heightened public sphere."[102] The church offers a baroque estuary of calm, and thus is privatized, at least for a moment. The place of devotion is also the place for a private refuge, and there is an unremitting reversal between sacred and profane spaces. In search of the right temperature, there is also a substitution between where one sleeps (outside), and where one lives (the living room during the day, but rarely): "There is interpenetration of day and night, noise and peace, outer light and inner darkness, street and home."[103] Even the activities of a holiday invade the ordinary day, while every day is also a festive day. Every wall is reversible, and its surface is like a membrane: "Buildings are used as a popular stage. They are all divided into innumerable, simultaneously animated theaters. Balcony, court- yard, window, gateway, staircase, roof are at the same time stage and boxes."[104] Here the membrane acts as a place of exchange. The whole city is porous, and allows for multiple penetrations, offering unique opportunities of interchange and transaction. Such porosity is what architecture could and should offer.

During the twentieth century, for Benjamin, a new era arises "with its porosity and transparency, its tendency toward the well-lit and airy, [which] has put an end to dwelling in the old sense."[105] Now, one inhabits a nontraditional world, a milieu in which, for ethical as much as for political reasons, one must cancel all traces. Following Sigfried Giedion's enthusiasm, he believes, with Le Corbusier, that "Air becomes a constitutive factor!"[106] He then connects the nineteenth-century metal con- struction with the aerial transparency of the new architecture (*Neues Bauen*): "The intoxicated interpenetration of street and residence . . . has prophetic value. For the new architecture lets this interpenetration become sober reality."[107] The sober reality began with the Victorian blocks of flats, the Parisian apartment blocks at the time of Baron Georges-Eugène Haussmann, the *Mietskasernen* in Berlin, the furnished hotels in Paris, the various workers' *Cités* in France; were fully developed with the *Siedlungen* in Germany, the Viennese *Höfe*, and all the varieties of tenement houses and blocks in New York City; and continued with Le Corbusier's Marseilles Unité d'Habitation (1947–1952), Alison and Peter Smithson's Robin Hood Gardens housing complex in East London (1969–1972), Piet Blom's The Kasbah housing estate at Hengelo in the Netherlands (1969–1974), and now BIG's (Bjarke Ingels Group) 8-House at Ørestad, at the edge of Copenhagen (2009–2010). Articulated as great complexes of cells, these organic and, in some cases, porous honeycombs offer selective hospitality according to class, gender, age, or origin.

Monads

In the *Arcades Project*, Benjamin establishes the quasi-identicalness of dream and truth, revealing the mechanism of dream architecture: "The true has no windows. Nowhere does the true look out to the universe."[108] The panoptic view is "a manifestation of the total work of art."[109] The universalism of the nineteenth century looks out to the whole world, which displays itself like some global spectacle: "Panopticon: not only does one see everything, but one sees it in all ways."[110] As with panoramas, theaters, arcades, "what stands within the windowless house is the true."[111] Such dream architecture thus has the structure of a monadological world. For Benjamin, "The monad has no window but carries within a miniature of the whole."[112] Monads are characterized by their discontinuity, but each one expresses all the others, just like panoramas, which constituted a reduced model of the whole universe as it was known in the nineteenth century. In the same way, arcades convert into miniature the whole mercantile world of the nineteenth century.

Beyond styles and epochs, the arcades of Paris could turn into objects of interpretation, as "baroque" spaces of a specular world, for they offer an expansion of the spaces created by the half-veiled reflection of dirty mirrors. These plays of mirrors plunge the passerby into a disturbing multiplication of perspectives, putting him through the troubling experience of a labyrinth. To this are added posters, signs, billboards, public notices, and so on. The set of these inscriptions produces the effect of allegory, for images accompany texts as writing that has then to be deciphered. The polyvocal nature of images is eccentric; it leads to a sort of between-fold, or folding between different conditions: inside/outside, lit/dark, private/public, hidden/revealed. In the *Arcades Project*, the monad sheds light on the structure of the thought images (*Denkbilder*). The arcade's infinitely polyvocal situation gives rise to the dialectic image: the "image is that wherein what has been comes together in a flash with the now to form a constellation. . . . Image is dialectics at a standstill."[113] In one of his last texts, "On the Concept of History," Benjamin starts with the search for a "constructive principle" with the aim of building a new kind of historiography: "Thinking involves not only the movement of thoughts, but their arrest as well. Where thinking suddenly comes to a stop in a constellation saturated with tensions, it gives that constellation a shock, by which thinking is crystallized as a monad."[114]

For Leibniz, the individual substance bears the name "monad." Union of body and soul, Leibniz's monad consists of a folded membrane, an elastic skin, able to record things (simple and complex) and capable of vibrating like a musical instrument. An organ acting as a receptor of the world, the folded membrane, to some extent, is also an enveloping substance. Each multiple monad perceives the whole of the world of which it is the mirror. For Leibniz, in their comprehensiveness, monads have no windows. Today, as Deleuze suggested in his book *The Fold* (1988), one issue remains: the question of how to live in the world. The "topological" condition of contemporary living does not allow the difference between inside and outside to survive. It has erased, or at least shifted, the limits between private and public: "What has changed now is the organization of the home and its nature."[115] In concluding *The Fold*, Deleuze writes that in the future, we will need "to overtake monadology with a 'nomadology.'"[116] The current paradoxical situation—one in which a closed space restores to us the outside of our interiority—describes the condition of our screens, those baroque, black boxes that are now part of our ever more interactive environment. Confronted by what has been defined as the "global screen,"[117] what appears on our screens today forms what we might call a virtual space of ghostliness.[118] Crisscrossed by hundreds of streams and constantly thought from an outside location, never properly deeper than any interior milieu but never actually further than any exterior milieu, the topological space of the network is, for Foucault, "never in things or in people, but in the impossible verisimilitude of what lies between them: encounters, the proximity of what is most distant, the absolute dissimulation in our very midst."[119] In Foucault's words, such a fictive space therefore "consists not in showing the invisible, but in showing the extent to which the invisibility of the visible is invisible."[120] Universal tools of work, but also devices supporting percepts and affects, the screens that populate our dwellings and houses function only by means of the topological torsion of a virtual space, whose closure allows contact with an absolute exteriority that acts like infinite folds, successive interlockings that cannot help but unfold, allowing us to plug in, not to the outside itself, but to the outside of any proper interiority. As Deleuze writes,[121] between the two stages of the monad, which are folded twice (body and soul), there is a between-fold, a folding, a zone that acts like a hinge, surface, interface, crease, or seam. The inner voice in Samuel Beckett's *The Unnamable*, pulsating between inside and outside like a diaphragm or a membrane, utters: "perhaps that's what I feel, myself vibrating, I'm the tympanum, on the one hand the mind, on the other the world, I don't belong to either . . ."[122]

2 FIGURING THE INVISIBLE

It is characteristic of architecture to press towards standard types
[Typischen]. Typology [or typification; Typisierung], in its turn,
spurns the abnormal and seeks the normal.
—Hermann Muthesius, "Die Werkbund-Arbeit der Zukunft" (The
Future Work of the Werkbund), 1914[1]

During the 1960s in Europe and the United States, the idea of
a "typology"—as opposed to the neoclassical "type"—was applied
to the plans of buildings, and the term *morphology* was used in
relation to the forms of the city.[2] Both terms were borrowed from
the biological sciences. The new use of *typology* was problematic,
since it was unrelated to the concept of type used in architecture during the eighteenth and nineteenth centuries. Architects,
in fact, appeared to be unaware of this disciplinary difference,
which has resulted in a terminological confusion between type
and typology. While the revival of the notion of type through Antoine-Chrysostome Quatremère de Quincy corresponded with a
return of architectural theory to Platonic ideals, the introduction
of the term *typology* put into circulation ideas that originated in
nineteenth-century ethnography and criminology.

In the second half of the nineteenth century, beginning with
Gottfried Semper, architects began to look for a "scientific" foundation for the origin of architecture. The classical notion of archetype

(developed, for instance, by Quatremère de Quincy) referred to original ur-forms such as the Greek temple or the Roman basilica. Semper extended those ur-forms to include the different activities of "primitive" man, such as weaving, pottery and ceramics, and carpentry. Semper was one of the most prominent architectural scholars to investigate the regional production of domestic architecture in Europe, connecting medieval buildings of northern and southern Germanic countries to a number of primitive, and vanished, archetypes. In his work *Der Stil* (1860–1863), Semper developed an interest in framework construction (*Fachwerk*)—half-timbered edifices that combine *Gezimmer* (structural carpentry) and *Gemäuer* (masonry, either stone or brick), which he illustrated with the example of a mill at Effretikon, near Zurich.[3] This inquiry into "primitive" architecture was pursued further in Eugène-Emmanuel Viollet-le-Duc's *The Habitations of Man in all Ages* (1875), in which the author maintained that the first houses were those of the "Aryas" (by which he meant the Aryans), who built walls and roofs using logs and then stones.[4] From the second half of the eighteenth century, travelers like the Frenchman Abraham-Hyacinthe Anquetil-Duperron (1731–1805) and the English poet and jurist William Jones were able to trace the affinities between Parsee and Sanskrit—the focus of their studies—and Greek and Latin.[5]

This work would slowly lead to the creation of a new genealogy of the European nations, allowing, for instance, an historian like Henri Martin (1810–1883) to think of "the great Indo-European family . . . of which Ariya, that holy land of the earliest ages, appeared to have been the cradle."[6] It was in France, through the work of the paleontologist Baron Georges Cuvier (1769–1832) and, later, the historian Jules Michelet (1798–1874), that the difference between the Semitic world and the Indo-Germanic world was cast in terms of struggle.[7] In Germany, one of the most influential promoters of the "Indo-German," or Aryan, myth was Jacob Grimm (1785–1863), who included in his classic *History*

The Primitive House of the Arya.—FIG. 3.

2.1
The primitive log house of the Aryas; in Eugène-
Emmanuel Viollet-le-Duc, *The Habitations of Man in
All Ages* [*Histoire de l'habitation humaine*, 1875],
trans. Benjamin Bucknall (Boston: James R. Osgood
and Co., 1876). Private collection of the author.

of the German Language (1848) a chapter titled "Immigration," which gave an account of the successive invaders of Europe from the East.[8] This opposition, presented as a scientific thesis, was confirmed by the writings of other "Indomaniacs" like Ernest Renan (1823–1892), the official ideologist of France's Third Republic.[9] This dangerous mixture of history, linguistics, and archaeology would build, via Herbert Spencer's reading of Charles Darwin, the long-lasting myth of the Aryan archetype.

New Archetypes

In his *Histoire d'un dessinateur* (*Story of a Draftsman*) (1879), Viollet-le-Duc dedicated two chapters to what he called "lectures on comparative anatomy," similar to those of Cuvier.[10] His organic concept of architecture in *Dictionnaire raisonné de l'architecture* very much resembled Cuvier's anatomic notion of the correlation of the organs,[11] in which an organ existed only in relation to the whole, and each form could be explained only through its place in the system. Cuvier believed that for classification purposes each animal could be represented by an ideal "type" that would include all of the characteristics distinguishing it from other types, and would not change from generation to generation. He classified all animals into four main branches (*embranchements*) according to the construction of their nervous systems. Less important, or subordinate, systems of characteristics were used to create classificatory subdivisions within the four branches. He called this method of classification the principle of the subordination of characters.[12] For Viollet-le-Duc, there was an initial formal principle in art, comparable to the one that the crystallographer René-Just Haüy had discovered in relation to minerals, and that Johann Wolfgang von Goethe had imagined in relation to an original or archetypal plant (*Urpflanze*). It is not known whether Viollet-le-Duc knew the work of Étienne Geoffroy Saint-Hilaire or his colleague Henri Dutrochet, who thought that vegetables and animals had the same cellular structure within their different tissues.[13] They believed cells are agglomerated through pressure, which confers on them a polygonal form, a form similar to that which Viollet-le-Duc thought made up Gothic architecture. In *Histoire d'un dessinateur*, Viollet-le-Duc published an image of compressed rubber pipes that are hexagonal in section.[14] This is exactly the cellular law of compression discovered by Dutrochet. While architecture was seen as organic, it still remained to be discovered how dwellings were to be constructed.[15] In fact, Viollet-le-Duc's argument is based on both organic ideas and ethnographic notations.

For Viollet-le-Duc, the primitive type of architecture in the West was the *chalet*, the rural Alpine dwelling that Jean-Jacques Rousseau first described in *Nouvelle Héloïse*.[16] An obvious source for the suburban and resort villa, the Swiss chalet in France and Germany was the equivalent of the cottage in England. In his article "House" in *Dictionnaire de l'architecture*, Viollet-le-Duc stated that the Western dwelling was the expression or visual identity of a distinguished or peculiar family as well as a symbol of modern individualism, hence his term *individual edifice*.[17] He added: "Everyone desires their own house." Having established a specific equation between individuals and the house, he drew a peculiar genealogy of the chalet as the structure nearest, in Europe, to the primitive abode.[18]

It is possible to postulate the influence on Viollet-le-Duc of the self-proclaimed "Count" Joseph-Arthur Gobineau's *Essay on the Inequality of Human Races* (1853–1855), which offered a genealogy of Aryan migrations and a theory of the superiority of the German Nordic races.[19] Viollet-le-Duc suggested that the nomads' wagons (traveling homes that at a certain point settled in a particular region or site) provided the archetype for the Swiss chalet, the Muscovite cabin, and the Norwegian peasant's hut.[20] He extended this genealogy to include the rural houses of Normandy

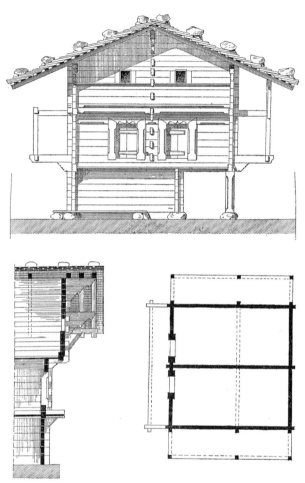

Fig. 245. — Chalet suisse (style ancien).

2.2
A "Swiss chalet (ancient style)"; in Julien Guadet,
Éléments et théorie de l'architecture, 3rd ed. (Paris:
Librairie de la Construction Moderne, 1909), volume 1.
Courtesy Prof. Martin Bressani, McGill University.

and the Vosges, which were still built of wood during his life-time. In addition to writing about these structures, he also built his own version of this nomadic hut, a chalet in Lausanne he called "La Vedette" (1874–1876).[21] The architectural myth of the chalet was also a political myth, probably one of the strongest in the nineteenth century, because it collapsed the diverse sources from biology, ethnography, and history into a single image.[22]

Meanwhile, in other parts of Europe and in the United States, the idea of type was presented as a scientific truth, derived from scholarly research associated with archaeological excavation. German cultural history (*Kulturgeschichte*) would extend some of Semper's and Viollet-le-Duc's assumptions. For example, Fried-rich von Hellwald, one of the developers of cultural history, re-produced many plates from Viollet-le-Duc's *Habitations of Man* in his *Der Vorgeschichtliche Mensch: Ursprung und Entwicklung des Menschengeschlechtes: für Gebildete aller Stände* (The Primitive Man: Origin and Development of Mankind, for the Cultivated Public of all Classes, 1879).[23] The idea of an ur-type for the German house was revealed by Franz Carl Müller-Lyer's *History of Social Development* (1912): "The house of wood was typical of the early Aryan culture. . . . [T]he Germans only built of wood, hence the connection of the word *bauen* = to build, and *Baum* = tree."[24] In Germany, an original genealogy was "scientifically" traced, connecting culture with civilization—that is, the Aryan culture with the (German) wooden house. Thus, an archetype, wrapped in the authority of the academy, was born.

At the end of the 1880s in Paris, the Committee for Scientific and Historical Works in the Ministry of Education decided to conduct an inquiry into the condition of dwellings in France. A questionnaire was sent to local administrators in every region and province asking for a description of "typical houses" (*mai-sons-types*) in order to determine the living habits in different parts of the country: "In nearly all regions, there are, for the use

2.3
The Aryan wagon; in Eugène-Emmanuel Viollet-le-Duc,
The Habitations of Man in All Ages. Private collection
of the author.

of farmers (whether they are owners or not), hundreds, thousands of houses, more or less similar, and it is this typical house, this characteristic unity, which it is necessary to study in order to define its elements."[25] For Alfred de Foville, who edited the findings, "each region showed a characteristic type, repeated a thousand times." The important question, however, was whether the milieu influenced the house, or the inhabitants influenced their dwellings. De Foville writes:

> Man makes his house and in doing so, he must put into it something of himself. However, through the passage of time, the house makes man too, through the particular fold [pli] that it impresses on his daily life. Our house, for us, and above all for the laborers of the city and the fields, is therefore more than a mirror: it is also a mold, and our existence partly owes to it the form and the direction that it takes.[26]

De Foville's hypothesis is one of reciprocal influences of milieu and inhabitant. In concluding his discussion of the contemporary housing situation, he remarks that "each household wanted its own 'home,' its separate lodgings," bearing witness to a unanimous desire for independence. Only the autonomy of a self-supporting household will guarantee its moral standards, its hygiene, and its social usefulness. "The more individual the house, the easier it is to modernize."[27] De Foville begins with a factual inquiry and survey, builds a theory, and concludes with a normative dictate, following precisely the method of the engineer and sociologist Frédéric Le Play (1806–1882), who had written a history of family types and a theory of "place-work-folk." Years later the young Charles-Édouard Jeanneret became an avid reader of de Foville's inquiry, which he studied before World War I at the National Library in Paris.

Human Typology

At the beginning of the nineteenth century, physiologist Xavier Bichat articulated the hypothesis that all men can be divided among three different classes related to three different realms of human behavior: acting, thinking, and feeling. This resulted in three different psycho-physiological types, which led to a human typology that comprised the practical, the rational, and the emotive. Included in the first type were administrators, workers, and engineers; in the second, scientists; and in the third, moralizers, artists, and poets.[28] These divisions influenced Henri Saint-Simon (1760–1825), who derived from Bichat's types his own classifications: first, the *artiste* as creator; second, the *savant* as critic and scholar; and, third, the *industriel* as executive. Later in his life, Saint-Simon would slightly modify his classification. A new aristocracy of talent was proclaimed, led by men of sensibility who showed Platonic abilities, including artists, poets, religious leaders, and ethical teachers, which replaced the old orders of nobility and clergy. Individuals with motor skills formed the second, or industrial class. Last came the scientists, who revealed Aristotelian faculty and belonged to the cerebral type.[29] To fight the malady of the modern age—an age of specialization dominated by self-centered, egotistical, isolated individuals—one had to return to a principle of synthesis, transforming society into an organic whole. The means for this metamorphosis was a social physiology.[30]

The sociology of Vilfredo Pareto (1848–1923) in Italy, of Max Weber (1864–1920) in Germany, and of Le Play and Émile Durkheim (1858–1917) in France were all answers from the European universities to the challenge raised by Marxism.[31] Both Le Play and Durkheim shared the belief that the science of society, or "social science," should be a normative science. Le Play, a conservative Catholic, wanted to defend private family life from the encroachments of public bureaucracies, but Durkheim and

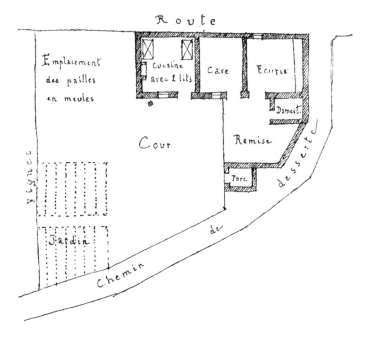

2.4
Elevation and plan of a traditional house in the
Beaujolais region (France); in Alfred de Foville,
Enquête sur les conditions de l'habitation en France.
Les Maisons-types (Paris: E. Leroux, 1894–1899),
2 vols. Private collection of the author.

his followers, at home in the French academic system, expected families to cooperate with the State in order to promote a kind of organic solidarity. One of Le Play's followers was Henri de Tourville (1842–1903), a founder of the periodical *La Science Sociale*. He accepted the principle of direct observation and the use of classificatory devices, but criticized what he thought was the overly quantitative aspect of Le Play's monographic method, and discarded Le Play's three types of family: the patriarchal, the stem, and the unstable.[32] De Tourville instead created a broader nomenclature, which became an instrument of social dissection, a kind of sieve, which permitted him to sift all elements of a social type and to classify them according to their qualities. This new method, which emphasized quality over quantity, was used by another follower of Le Play, Edmond Demolins (1852–1907), who studied the migratory routes of the nomads of the Asian steppes, and the manner in which migration had determined the development of new types of families and societies. In his two-volume *Les grandes routes des peuples* (1901–1903), Demolins rejected Le Play's "three ages of work" (the age of pastures, of machines, and of coal) and proposed that the history of the people of the steppes was the key to understanding the origin of Western civilization.[33] These nomads, first settling in the western part of Scandinavia, evolved into "particularized families," which then migrated to England, America, Australia, and New Zealand. "Particularized families"—that is, parents and their children—were autonomous, mobile, and capable of quick adaptation to the "modern" market economy and to a kind of individual housing type. This was in contrast to Mediterranean societies, which he claimed had retained the patriarchal family type: providing a home anchored in land and traditions for the extended family, with all its relatives, including employees, servants, cooks, craftsmen, cultivators. For Demolins, the correlation between nomadism and individualism created the norm, or type, that modern society should practice. Thus, he provided a "scientific" basis for the sanitization and modernization of the family. Only a particularized family could be acted upon by reformers, doctors, hygienists, philanthropists, nurses, priests, and judges. Not by chance, Demolins wrote a book that was immediately translated into English as *Anglo-Saxon Superiority: To What It Is Due* (1899).[34] The new, ideal "type" of family and household was to be North American: unconstrained by tradition, individualistic and nonconformist, self-governing and self-sufficient, and entrepreneurial.

Meanwhile, another kind of architectural typology originated in France. The Municipal Council of Paris decided, in December 1893, to create a "sanitary file" (*casier sanitaire*) of houses, similar to the criminal record of an individual. The idea had been announced in 1849 by Sir John Simon (1816–1904), London's medical officer, and developed by John Snow (1813–1858), who drew maps of the city in 1855 showing the addresses of those who had died from cholera.[35] In Paris, the job was given to Paul Juillerat (1854–1935), chief of the Bureau of Sanitation, who organized the files by collating various kinds of data: administrative (house plans), technical (drainage plans), statistical (demographics), and scientific (quality of drinking water).[36] In what would become a new urban ecology, the French administration, between 1894 and 1904, compiled 80,000 files representing all of the residential buildings within the walls of Paris.[37] Juillerat joined the traditional descriptions of buildings with medical files, creating records of unquestionable facts.[38] His method of collecting data in many ways resembled the one created for the study of criminal types compiled by Italian criminologist Cesare Lombroso in *Homo delinquens*, published in Milan in 1876. It was also analogous to the idea of creating a photographic archive for use by the police as irrefutable evidence in identifying suspects.[39] In all of these examples, the issues at stake are related

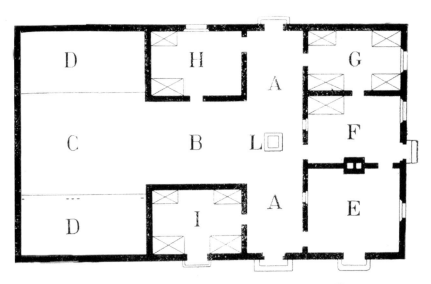

A, salle commune de travail (*flett*) **B**, aire **C**, grange (*dehle*); **D, D**,
étables **E**, salle commune de la famille (*dunzen*) **F**, chambre des
grands-parents (*kahmer*) **G**, chambre des enfants et des servantes
H, chambre de l'héritier-associé (*anerber*) **I**, chambre des céliba-
taires et des domestiques; **L**, foyer.

2.5
Frankish and Saxon dwelling types: plan of the
settlement of Luttershof, at Lüneburg near Celle in
northern Germany; in Edmond Demolins, *Comment
la route crée le type social* (Paris: Firmin-Didot,
1901–1903), 2 vols. Private collection of the author.

to the establishment of an archive, be it of diseased houses or of individuals. Making an archive through such rational, scientific procedures permitted the elaboration of the typical, and thus authorized the application of the normal.

Photography had been employed for judiciary purposes since 1860, but photographic portraits of a single person could often appear completely different. This problem was explored by Alphonse Bertillon (1853–1914), the creator of anthropometrics between 1883 and 1889. Bertillon was chief of judicial identity for the Paris police and the brother of Jacques Bertillon (1851–1922), chief of the Office of Statistics in Paris.[40] According to the younger Bertillon, the photographic portrait could be used for identification purposes only if the photographer, in the process of archiving the image, named the principal traits of the person photographed. Those singularities had to be described in words. One would "recite" the details of a face, hence the importance of what Bertillon called "speaking photographic portraits," or "speaking likenesses" (*portraits parlés*), in which language did not define the ever-changing particularities of real beings, but only peculiar elements revealed by the photograph. The "speaking likeness" was a commentary not on a real face, but on its photographic representation. To overcome the fact that photography could not reproduce the multiple phases of an aging face, Bertillon developed a "signaletic anthropometric"—that is, the measurement of the characteristic and invariant traits of a living individual, devoid of the envelope of the flesh and reduced to its structural nakedness. Man was now a combination of lines and measurements that could be compiled in a catalogue or displayed on a chart.[41]

Bertillon's archive attempted to associate images with words. Traditionally, the device used to couple images with words was called an emblem (a pictorial image epitomizing a concept) or an allegory (a visual device expressing an idea). However, emblem and

2.6
"Specimen of description card" and "Measurement of right ear"; in Alphonse Bertillon, *Signaletic Instructions Including the Theory and Practice of Anthropometrical Identification*, trans. from the latest French edition (Chicago and New York: Werner Co., 1896). Western Americana Collection. Rare Books Division. Department of Rare Books and Special Collections. Princeton University Library.

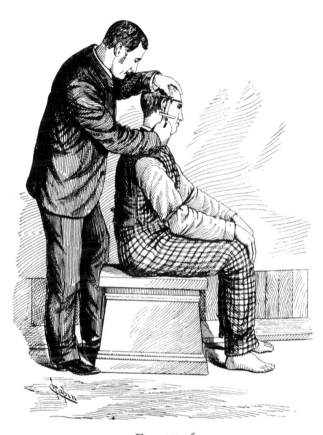

FIGURE 16.

RIGHT EAR.

FIRST MOVEMENT.—The operator gently touches the upper rim of the ear with the stationary branch, keeping it immovable by pressing the upper extremity firmly against the head with his left thumb, his fingers resting on the top of the subject's head.

SECOND MOVEMENT.—The shank of the compasses bring in a position parallel to the axis of the ear; the operator pushes forward the sliding branch until it touches very lightly the lowest point of the lobe. He then satisfies himself that the bell of the ear has not been compressed by the instrument, and reads the indication.

allegory could easily lead to universal condensation of meaning (such as justice, strength, danger), which was too general or abstract for police identification. What Bertillon attempted instead was a procedure connecting each individual to a general system of representation capable of recording the diversity of the type.

Morphological Types

Bertillon's method was derived in part from Franz Joseph Gall's work on the physiology of the brain and craniology. Gall (1758–1828) affirmed that the moral qualities and intellectual faculties of man are innate and that these depend on cerebral morphology. By collecting craniums and casts, which he compared and classified, the German physicist and biologist invented a kind of psychophysiology. He no longer attempted to define a common denominator for all humans, as had been undertaken in the eighteenth century, but instead tried to connect the twenty-seven faculties that he had defined to a system belonging to a particular individual.[42] Gall's work was expanded by his pupil, Johann Caspar Spurzheim (1776–1832), who became fashionable for detecting the character of individuals by reading the bumps on one's cranium.[43] In coining the term phrenology, Spurzheim's ambition was to affirm the universal value of the physiological principle according to which form corresponds to function.[44] Following in Spurzheim's footsteps, in the 1830s Orson Squire Fowler (1809–1887) opened a "Phrenological Cabinet" in New York and gave character readings by mail.[45] By way of the theory that function creates form, Fowler invented the concept of a "home for all," convincing more than one thousand Americans to build a house with an octagonal plan, the figure closest to the perfection of the circle.[46]

Another curious connection between architecture and science was the "Familistère," built between 1858 and 1879 by industrialist and philanthropist André Godin (1817–1888) on the outskirts of Guise in northern France.[47] Godin was a follower of Charles Fourier (1772–1837), who had dreamed of and designed a "phalanstery," a vast edifice housing an industrial "phalanx" that would be the foundation of a model community. Set in a pastoral landscape, its units would have housed people living in harmony through cooperation, with each individual following his or her own passions. Fourier believed there were twelve common passions that resulted in 810 character types, thus the ideal phalanx would have exactly 1,620 people. Godin, an industrialist who produced cast-iron coal stoves and furnaces, had joined the *École sociétaire* formed by Victor Considérant (1808–1893), a leader among Fourier's followers and author of many publications, including the book *Social Considerations on Architectonics* (1834; 1848).[48] Godin rejected the notion of Fourier's phalanx, however, and attempted instead to adapt it by building a "family-stery," a kind of monastery for working families organized around three rectangular courtyards, each with a glazed ceiling.[49] Like many during this period, Godin thought that human needs resided in a precise location in the body's organs—the sphenoidal part of the cranium, for instance, housed the needs for open space, light, and pure air. Because the Familistère responded to the requisites of human life, it improved its inhabitants. Godin maintained: "Intelligence is proportionate to the way in which light illuminates the house."[50] In a certain way, the Familistère was a phrenological construction.

The drive to compare craniums and brains was also pursued by the Turin-based scholar Cesare Lombroso (1835–1909), who analyzed the remains of Immanuel Kant, Alessandro Volta, Ugo Foscolo, and Carl Friedrich Gauss in his widely translated book *Man of Genius* (1864; English translation 1891).[51] Using Gall's principle of organology, Lombroso defined, through statistical methods, the frequency of the criminal type within a population of convicted perpetrators and honest people. The "delinquent

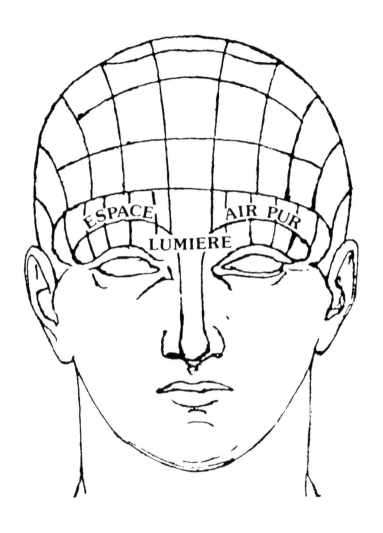

2.7
Localization of human needs in the cranium; in
André Godin, *Solutions sociales* (Paris: A. le
Chevalier, 1871). Courtesy of ETH-Bau Library,
Zürich, Switzerland.

type" was defined by "stigmata degenerationis," the stigma of the degenerate. Within his system of criminal anthropology, each stigma of the criminal contributed to the makeup of the criminal type. The criminal is such by nature, and, like a savage in a civilized country, he is an anachronism; by carefully isolating these types, society might free itself of them.[52]

The very notion of human type—the idea of a physiological mean in which the ideal would be deduced from the observation of the ordinary—was made possible by the Belgian sociologist Adolphe Quételet (1796–1874). In his *Treatise on Man* (1835), Quételet provided the statistical tools for the definition of a common type of human, proposing the concept of the "average man" as a "fictitious being."[53] Individual singularities were now to be observed only in light of the physiological mean or average. This was a reversal of the classical, Neoplatonic notion of type based on the ideal. The new anthropology defined singularity only as a quantitative type, defined by statistics and means. This prosaic type, which erased the individuality from any human being, concretized the exemplary figure of the "everyman." Thus, Quételet showed that the extreme varieties of individuals conformed, beyond their obvious appearances, to a general and invariable law. Two consequences arose from this philosophy: the body was now seen as an impersonal envelope, and every body was considered commensurate to a norm. This improved methods of identification, as it was now possible to measure identity by the degree of departure from the statistical norm.[54]

As seen in the discussion above, by selecting the principal traits of the face through words, Bertillon, a great admirer of Quételet, connected image with language. Beyond the encyclopedic purpose of Cesare Ripa's *Iconology* (the first illustrated edition, 1603); and long before Aby Warburg's atlas of images (*Bilderatlas*), Fritz Saxl's iconography, or Erwin Panofsky's essays in iconology, such an identity procedure was, literally, an "iconology." Rather than attempting to characterize a person's identity by broadly defining its whole picture, or by tracing a unique, particular icon, Bertillon's method is based on clues offered by minute details. Under his system, only a divergence from the mean can produce notation, since the mean, or the norm, is unutterable and ineffable. Identity is defined by the measurement of invariant traits of the living body. The living being is reduced to segments, which are themselves reduced to the essence of geometrical lines. This combination of lines, weaving the organic with the geometric, no longer imitates, but figures the invisible.

This geometricization, which was also explored in the chronophotographs of Étienne-Jules Marey,[55] gave theorists and artists the opportunity to analyze the various morphological types of the human being. In France, for instance, Paul Richer (1849–1933), in his *Canons of Proportions of the Human Body* (1893), provided a renewed basis for the study of human morphology, organized into types.[56] In Italy, the connoisseur of Italian Renaissance art Giovanni Morelli (1816–1891) devised a method for attributing paintings based on "signature motifs" (*motivi sigla*), the insignificant details such as the representation of hair, nails, or ears that permit one to recognize the hand of a specific artist.[57] With his medical background, Morelli was trained to recognize signs through symptomatology; thus his method is based on clues offered by trifling details, not by the identity of the whole composition, or by the subject matter. The identity of the artist is best expressed in details that, at first glance, escape attention. This geometricization would eventually lead to the rectangular division of the human body by Oskar Schlemmer (1888–1943), producing a "box man" (*Schachtelmensch*).[58]

It was Quételet's reduction of the body to a measurable type that permitted architects to think of the dwelling as a place that could be defined statistically, allowing the idea of normalization

to be established. By reducing the analysis of the house to measurable data and a diagrammatic scheme, Juillerat's sanitation
cases created morphological domestic types that could be used
in a policy of intervention. Used to track the path and origin of
disease, house by house, this sanitary file recorded the moment
of an encounter between medicine (the germ, the bacterium, the
bacillus) and sociology (the insalubrious dwelling), thereby defining a new housing type based not on a fictional narrative (the
Aryans, for example), but on numbers. The aim of the files was
to help eradicate "walls that kill." From then on, the authority of
evidence established the "evidence" of authority, meaning that
the authority had become conspicuous through the use of real
data and facts available as proof. This redefined authority was no
longer moral but scientific; as in a criminal trial, it presented
legal evidence, instituting a new semiotics of the house.

Following the creation of the sanitary files, a proposal was
made to hang a plaque on each house indicating its sanitary condition. Interestingly, the owners, a group highly represented in
Parliament, opposed and defeated this idea because they considered the hygienic State equivalent to the collectivist State.[59] Unlike other northern European countries, which attacked disease
(tuberculosis, for example), the French government preferred
to organize a hunt against the diseased—the infected persons. It
demolished entire neighborhoods, moving its inhabitants into
overcrowded hospitals or dispersing them to the farthest edges
of the cities. This process of exclusion based on disease could, of
course, be easily extended to a "hygiene of race."[60]

Organic Household

The idea to imbed and wed the history of a nation with the history of a people (*Volk*) can in part be credited to Wilhelm Heinrich Riehl (1823–1897) and his *The Natural History of the German
People*, written largely between 1851 and 1855.[61] The original title,

Natural History of the People as the Foundation of German Social Policy, showed that Riehl's sociology and anthropology of folklore (*Volkskunde*) was a conservative ideation of rural life, championing the virtues of neocorporatist social organization. In the first three volumes he presented German society as an organic totality, a natural work of art, and the connection between the physical and cultural topographies inscribed in the landforms. In the tradition of Johann Gottfried Herder (1744–1803) and Friedrich Schelling (1775–1803), Riehl exalted the Germanic folk ethos—found in villages, guilds, and social estates—as a bulwark against bureaucratic socialization and an antidote to revolutionary egalitarianism. Stressing the traditional German opposition between culture and civilization, Riehl writes: "I raise my voice on behalf of the rights of forests over fields, of mountains over plains, of a natural popular culture over a homogeneous civilization."[62] His enemy was what he called the "estate of the estateless," which included factory workers, day laborers, bureaucrats, commercial travelers, commodity speculators, wholesale merchants, intellectuals, journalists, Jews, and gypsies. An academic authority in Germany, Riehl presented the family as both the model and the metaphor for society at large, yet the very idea of family, he thought, had been disintegrated by modern life in Germany, by cosmopolitanism in France, by the nomadism of gypsies in the rest of Europe, and by the absence of roots in North America, where family life had almost completely disappeared "in the stampede to earn money."[63]

To resist the degeneration of the family—for Riehl, the origin of the decadence of modern society—suggested the revival of a traditional setting, that of the "entire household" (*das ganze Haus*), which tended to disappear when individual members of a family divided into separate groups. The site of the household, both its architecture and its landscape, contained the extended family—including relatives, servants, and agricultural workers—

and imposed a "domestic discipline" on each of its members. "This expanded household," Riehl wrote, "extends the benefits of family life to entire groups who would otherwise be without family. . . . For the social stability of the nation as a whole, such a practice is a matter of the most profound significance."[64] Claiming that the renewal of society depended on the renewal of the home, he dismissed modern residential architecture, which he described as "miniature versions of box-like urban tenements, designed to be as cheap and profitable as possible," and lamented the disappearance of large halls, huge family hearths, and ornamented galleries on each floor. Combining a medievalist resuscitation with an *avant la lettre* functionalist trend, Riehl claimed: "It is a fact of art history that the medieval house, castles, and churches were built from the inside out, that the exterior forms and proportions were freely arranged to suit the requirements of the interior, the practical uses of the building, whereas in our doctrinaire fashion we moderns routinely build from the outside in." As an example he referred to the models provided by "authentic" German farmhouses, and the so-called Swiss chalets, "which are constructed purely with a view to domestic utility, yet thanks to the instinctive aesthetic sensibilities of the common folk, are as lovely as folk song, as picturesque as peasant costume."

In his praise for the Swiss chalet, Riehl foreshadowed Semper and Viollet-le-Duc. All agreed (paradoxically, since Riehl despised the French attitude and manners) that the house of the future should be constructed "from the inside out." First, the family had to be reconstituted, so that it would build a house in its own image. "Once we have reestablished a solid domestic tradition," wrote Riehl, "a new and organic residential architecture will also emerge, and architects will be at a loss to explain precisely how it came about—for the style will have come to them, not the other way around."[65] For Riehl, the organic household had a name, grew like a plant, and was sung as a folkloric melody, while the modern house was changeable and temporary, mass-produced, and, even worse, rented. As such, it became a commodity, drawn into the maelstrom of urban capitalist society.

Riehl's work proved very influential in further studies of the household and its settlement (*Siedlung*). Inspired by Darwin's theory of evolution, the Austrian Friedrich von Hellwald (1842–1892) wrote *Culturgeschichte in ihrer natürlichen Entwicklung bis zur Gegenwart* (Cultural History in Its Natural Evolution, up to the Present,1876–1877), a history of civilization from an evolutionary perspective that was considered authoritative in the Germanic countries.[66] This work, which went through several revised editions and reprints, was dedicated to German evolutionary biologist Ernst Haeckel (1834–1919), a specialist in marine fauna and author of the bestseller *Art Forms in Nature* (1899–1904).[67] In *Culturgeschichte* von Hellwald presented a curious collection of oddities, such as a Wagnerian, Germanic warrior of the Iron Age, which he connected with a sealed funerary tumulus of the Stone Age at Waldhusen, near Lübeck.[68] Subsequently, von Hellwald published scores of successful volumes imbued with the racial beliefs common in that period, including one on the history of human settlements in 1888.[69] Riehl also influenced *The Prehistoric Man*, originally edited by Wilhelm Baer, but which von Hellwald reworked in an 1880 second edition that displayed peculiar imagery of "the Proto-German Family" (*urgermanische Familie*).[70] During the second half of the nineteenth century, every well-known authority in the Germanic countries agreed on the so-called superiority of the Aryans. One of the most eminent supporters of the myth was Ludwig Büchner (1824–1899), a materialist philosopher who wrote *Kraft und Stoff, Empirisch-naturphilosophische Studien* (Force and Matter, 1855),[71] in which he defended the thesis against the religious notion of free arbiter, arguing that since man is part of nature, he is, as such, not free, because he moves where his brain drives him. A convinced Darwinist, he expressed in an 1868 lecture a belief in the congenital incapacity of "primitives" to raise their minds to the level of abstract ideas. In his view, the lower classes—as well as women—could be compared to primitive peoples.[72] Riehl's presence can also be seen in the four-volume opus by August Meitzen, *Siedlung und Agrarwesen der Westgermanen und Ostgermanen, der Kelten, Römer, Finnen und Slaven* (Settlement and the Essence of the Agrarian in West and East Germans, the Celts, the Romans, the Finns and the Slavs, 1895), which was a cause of great concern for contemporary French scholars because it extended the Germano-Frankish housing type to half of France, denying the historical existence of the Gallo-Roman model.[73] In this way, it would seem that scholars were already preparing for the next war. Recent studies have shown how Hermann Muthesius's work on housing related to such trends, and have situated some of his publications, such as the celebrated *The English House* (1904–1905),[74] within the theoretical framework of German "cultural history," showing the intimate commonality of purpose with work such as Julius Langbehn's *Rembrandt als Erzieher* (Rembrandt as Educator, 1890), Paul Schultze-Naumburg's series of books titled *Kulturarbeiten* (Works of Culture, 1901–1917), or Paul Mebes's publication *Um 1800* (Around 1800, 1908), an originator of the so-called "circa 1800" movement that advocated a return to Prussian neoclassicism, circa 1800.[75] It is now possible to trace the genealogy, together with the mythology, of the "German house," which, starting from Meitzen's imperialistic affirmation and rewriting of history, as in his *Das deutsche Haus* (The German House, 1882), will lead to Schultze-Naumburg's theories on the German, organic type of houses, which will in turn lay the foundation for National Socialist ideas about "type," such as those exposed in Paul Schmitthener's multiple publications on the *German Dwelling House*. Together these investigations shed light on the debate about typology, or, more precisely, about "typification" (*Typisierung*), at the Deutscher Werkbund, founded by Muthesius, for instance—as well as its somewhat embarrassing connections with nationalistic trends and tendencies.

Hygienics and Eugenics

Superficially, one could argue that proposals for housing reform in France at the end of the nineteenth century were less nostalgic, or reactionary, than those in Germany, but such an assertion would not be accurate. The major influence at that time was the Arts and Crafts movement of William Morris (1834–1896), whose theories were disseminated in France by Dr. Henri Cazalis (1840–1909), a poet who belonged to the Parnassian group.[76] Cazalis's talent was not limited to literature, but extended to philosophy, history, the fine arts, and music. He was also a physician involved in psychiatry and eugenics.

Writing under the name Jean Lahor,[77] Cazalis published a booklet, *W. Morris et le mouvement nouveau de l'art décoratif* (William Morris and the New Movement in Decorative Art, 1897), in which he described ugliness and beauty as somewhat similar to "atmosphere," or the environment, possibly subject to contagion.[78] He referred to Gabriel de Tarde's book *Les Lois de l'imitation* (1890), a sociological analysis of repetition, adaptation, and imitation by the lower classes of the traditions, habits, and fashions of the dominant classes, which provided a vivid history of the arts as well as of luxury, courtesy, and civility. De Tarde argued that the eighteenth-century salon "would admit only equals, or equalized those it would admit," demonstrating that such instruments of civilization were also instruments of social leveling, producing democratic societies and a type of person governed by public opinion.[79] Picking up on de Tarde's idea, Cazalis believed that bad taste could be communicated, like

2.8
The "Sealed Site of a Stone Age Funerary Barrow (or,
Tumulus) near Waldhusen (Lübeck, Germany)";
in Friedrich von Hellwald, *Kulturgeschichte in ihrer
natürlichen Entwicklung bis zur Gegenwart*, 4th ed.
(Leipzig: Friesenhahn, 1896), between pp. 48 and 49.
Courtesy of Princeton University Library.

2.9
A "Germanic Warrior of the Iron Age"; in Friedrich
von Hellwald, *Kulturgeschichte in ihrer natürlichen
Entwicklung bis zur Gegenwart*, 4th ed. (Leipzig:
Friesenhahn, 1896), between pp. 200 and 201.
Courtesy of Princeton University Library.

2.10
The Proto-German family; in Wilhelm Baer, *Der
Vorgeschichtliche Mensch: Ursprung und Entwicklung
Menschengeschlechtes*, 2nd renewed edition by
Friedrich von Hellwald (Leipzig: O. Spamer, [1879]),
67. Courtesy of Princeton University Library.

good taste, through the powerful social instrument of imitation. For art to remain elevated and pure, it was necessary that the mediocre or vile contagion "from below" be barred from spreading to the highest sphere.[80]

Both the *Jugendstil* and Art Nouveau movements developed parallels between aesthetics and hygiene. The curves of the "natural" body were brought into the building, while the building curved to receive the imprint of bodies. At the 1900 Parisian Exposition, Cazalis praised the restraint of the French iron architecture of Paul Sédille, admired the work of Belgian architect Gustave Serrurier-Bovy, liked the "very modern" art of the Finn Eliel Saarinen, and commended Japanese craftwork, English sideboards and bathrooms, and American Tiffany lamps.[81] The doctor was particularly concerned about hygiene: "For the first time since antiquity, this new art gives to hygiene the place which it rightly deserves in the design and organization of the building or the house."[82] He went on to mention an exhibition on the hygiene of hotels and inns, praising the simplicity and cleanliness of the northern European countries and observing that aesthetics was obliged to occupy itself with this very humble virtue. Finally, quoting the experiments of the Lever Corporation at Port Sunlight, near Liverpool, and the House of Cure built by the Krupp factory in Bensdorf, which were exhibited at the Parc de Vincennes in Paris, Cazalis revealed his social and architectural program: "We want art to be distributed to everybody, like air and light, and we want it to be everywhere, in the house of the artisan, as in our own, from school to college, from those university barracks usually so ugly and always lugubrious, to hospitals, railway stations, and everywhere where human crowds, and especially popular ones, assemble."[83] Nothing in Cazalis's outline appeared to be written by a racist or extreme reactionary. This is because there was no contradiction between the racist agenda and the socialist program in Europe at that time. In both cases, the aim was unique: to target the human body through hygienics and eugenics.

The Aryan Dwelling

The reference to the "human crowds" in Cazalis's 1901 book *L'art nouveau . . . au point de vue social* (Art Nouveau . . . from the Social Point of View) was probably intended as an allusion to the right-wing theories of the physiologist Gustave Le Bon (1841–1931), who published a volume titled *Les civilisations de l'Inde* (The Civilizations of India) in 1887, and whose book *The Crowd: A Study of the Popular Mind* (1895) referenced Cazalis by name.[84] For Le Bon, the crowd was the receptacle of the unconscious and opposed to the conscious elite. An inferior part of contemporary society, it had to be controlled by medical strategies. Le Bon warned that the crowd, with its "herd mentality," could bring about the psychological decline of races because its irrationality was the cause of mental contagion and left the mind open to manipulation by leaders. In this regard, it should be noted that eighteen editions of *The Crowd* had been published by 1913, and it was carefully read by, among others, Georges Sorel (1847–1922), a theoretician of the political use of violence, and Benito Mussolini (1883–1945). "A crowd is a serial flock that is incapable of ever doing without the master," wrote Le Bon.[85] Men collected in a crowd are subject to "rapidly contagious" emotions, which explains not only the suddenness of panic, but also illnesses such as agoraphobia. An affirmation "sufficiently repeated," he thought, could lead, as in advertising and political campaigns, to a convincing truth by the "powerful mechanism of contagion"; the same powerful mechanism could enforce "not only certain opinions, but certain modes of feeling as well."[86]

Le Bon was likely influenced by the psychophysiologist Jules Soury (1842–1915), an ultranationalist who used evolutionary biology to justify racial, as well as social, inequalities. Both men wanted to found an official society similar to Francis Galton's Eugenics Society, established in London in 1867.[87] They believed in the new "science" of anthroposociology, which, through craniometry, could determine racial typologies. From 1875 to 1885, Rudolph Virchow (1821–1902), a prominent German liberal and physiologist, by arguing that Darwinism was more useful to socialists than to conservatives, launched a colossal inquiry, measuring the cephalic index of fifteen million schoolchildren in order to establish statistics of cranium morphology in all of Germany.[88]

In a similar exercise in 1891, the social anthropologist Georges Vacher de Lapouge (1854–1936), aided by the poet Paul Valéry (1871–1945), measured six hundred craniums extracted from an old cemetery. Vacher de Lapouge, author of L'Aryen. Son rôle social (The Aryan: His Social Role, 1899), believed that the "unfit" must be prevented from reproducing by a process of medical selection.[89] A follower of Galton and Haeckel, he would develop a racial classification between "brachycephalics" (round-headed men with brown hair and eyes) and "dolichocephalics" (men with long, narrow skulls, blond hair, and blue eyes, descendants of the original "Aryans"). The dolichocephalics corresponded to the *Homo Europaeus* who emigrated to northern Germany, Great Britain, and the United States, while the brachycephalics engendered the *Homo Alpinus* who came from Asia Minor and the Balkans to Switzerland and France.

A follower of Herbert Spencer (1820–1903), himself convinced of the biological determination of human destiny, Le Bon believed that the struggle for life would cause inferior people to die out and the best-adapted human races to survive. This racist theory was largely pessimistic, since amelioration of the physical environment did not improve the human race.[90] Like Le Bon, Cazalis also supported Social Darwinism: "Let's educate the majority, which is made up of the common people . . . to avoid destroying our own majority; because as a Darwinian, I repeat that innumerable masses, masters of today's life . . . are always a cause of mediocrity."[91] Cazalis advocated the institution of an authoritarian and elitist government that would erase the historical catastrophe of the French Revolution and rebuild a new democracy: "Hygiene, a branch of aesthetics—because health and cleanliness are necessarily the essential conditions of beauty—hygiene already attempts to give to people's habitations what has for too long been lacking, pure air and the sun that kills pathogenic germs, and light, which is as much necessary for thought and the soul as it is for the body."[92] Cazalis signed his given name to his volume on eugenics, *La Science et le mariage* (Science and Marriage, 1900), dedicating it to nationalist author Maurice Barrès (1862–1923), who wrote a best-selling novel, *Les déracinés* (The Uprooted, 1897), about the eradication of traditions and the unhappy life of uprooted people.[93] While William Morris thought that art should be made *by* the people, Cazalis thought it had to be made *for* the people, as the title of his 1902 book, *L'art pour le peuple* (Art for the People), demonstrated.[94] His hygienic democracy was part of a general eugenics: the doctor wrote books on "scientific" marriage, prenuptial inspection, hereditary diseases, and the protection of health and race.[95] In this period, ethnic cleansing and aesthetic hygiene went side by side.

All of Cazalis's proposals converged in one of his last books, which described "low-cost dwellings and low-cost art" (1903) and was dedicated to Georges Picot, president of the Housing Society of France.[96] Cazalis reminded French authorities that de Foville had published a wondrous study of the types of houses, and maintained: "We must prepare immediately for the workers of the most industrialized parts of the country types of individual houses, such as cottages or chalets, which would be built in the regional style, blending harmoniously with the beauty and appeal of those rural parts."[97] Much more practical than his

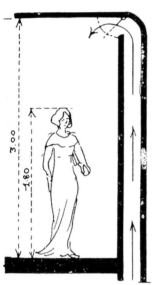

être effectué ce chauffage.

Voici une pièce d'un cube déter- A miné et à une température don- B née dont il s'agit d'élever ou d'a- baisser la tempé- rature. Il serait désirable que l'é- C lévation de tem- pérature en hiver, pût être modifiée en abaissement de température pen D dant les fortes chaleurs de l'été, ce double problè-

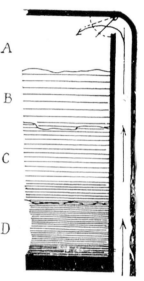

FIGURE 9.

FIGURE 10.

2.11
Room ventilation and accumulation of polluted air; in
Henry Provensal, *L'habitation salubre et à bon marché*
(Paris: C. Schmid, 1908). Courtesy of Princeton
University Library.

previous writings, the book included cooperative single dwellings in Puteaux (named "La Famille") and workers' houses near Beauvais (by Léon Benouville, who had also designed furniture for workers' homes in a restrained Art Nouveau style).[98] The doctor concluded with his Darwinian credo that inequality between men is a universal, natural, and eternal law. Through the elimination of the weakest, the elite in France would win out: "Like true soldiers, they must think only of victory."[99] For humanity the battle was not only political but aesthetic. This aestheticization of politics continued the fight of the Aryans, who inspired

> a religion, or a future philosophy that would help to make life more enticing and exciting for many spirits who are too doomed, too silent . . . while revealing all there is of mystery, all there is of prodigy, all there is that is human and divine, in the lesser animal and in the lesser plant, being able to recognize and to affirm according to the Aryan dogma the kinship that unites all beings.[100]

Another theoretician of *Kulturgeschichte*—Franz Carl Müller-Lyer, whose *History of Social Development* (1912) was read by many in Germany in the 1920s (including Walter Gropius)—put it this way:

> Just as in organic nature a progressive movement exists from the monad to the mammal, so is it in culture. And in both developments the movement goes from small to great, from simple to complex, from homogeneous to heterogeneous, and in these processes of increase, combination and differentiation . . . lies progress—and it lies in nothing else. That is the objective formula of the idea of cultural progress. The happiness of the individual has no place therein. For Nature offers up the individual everywhere with cruel indifference on the altar of—the Type.[101]

Given here as a kind of social program is the Darwinian elimination of the individual on the "altar of the type," a type revealed most clearly in the conscious reproduction of the beauty of organic forms and the renewal of the vitality of an ancient callisthenic culture.

The Altar of the Type

Comments on the suffocating nature of curves in Art Nouveau design were very common, and were echoed by reformers who saw the same constrictions in women's clothing. Many feminist congresses denounced the corset as an instrument of torture, starting, for example, with Catharine E. Beecher's *Letters to the People on Health and Happiness* (1855).[102] Reformers like Beecher sought to replace the corset with an entirely different clothing type. *Fin-de-siècle* clothing reform (*Reformkleid*) was also promoted by Paul Schultze-Naumburg, a painter, architect, and art critic who regularly contributed to the illustrated magazine *Der Kunstwart*, directed by his friend Ferdinand Avenarius. Around 1900, Peter Behrens offered new models of dresses, while Henry van de Velde organized an exhibition on "The Artistic Improvement of Women's Clothing" that united aesthetic and hygienic concerns.[103] Schultze-Naumburg himself organized a similar exhibition dedicated to a new kind of female garment, which he published in his famous *The Culture of the Feminine Body as the Foundation for Women's Dress* (1901).[104] Schultze-Naumburg, who based his model of natural clothing on Greek and Gothic sources, was also a promoter of what was beginning to be called the culture of nudism (*Nacktkultur*). Championing the body in its natural state, he prefigured the fashion in Germany for the practice of nude swimming and sunbathing, which was developed not only as hygienic reform but also as a reaction against moral prudishness. The reform of clothing led to a reform of the body, which became thought of as a natural work of art. Schultze-Naumburg also published books promoting art in the home,[105] and the redesign of modern woman was part of the redefinition of the aesthetics of everyday life and the domestic, based on the notion of organic unity between art and life. The aestheticization and simplification of clothes and modern life would lead to a renewed, reformed environment.[106]

Architects were most likely unaware of all these connections when they began to use the term *typology* in the twentieth century. While this did not diminish in any way the significance of their thinking, it is important to note that, as a consequence, architects did not clearly discuss the profound differences between the classical type, an ur-genesis that repeated the antique form, and modern morphogenesis, which established the abolition of mimesis, the institution of the norm, the repetition of the same, and the prescription of the new. The classical and neo-classical notions of type were based on the embodiment of ideals that referred, through nature and time, to principles and rules that conferred authority to the building, while the modern typology led to disembodiment. The new abstract typology was formed by means of calculation, determined by the laws of evolution, and grafted onto the skin by thousands of inscriptions. Although type no longer informed architecture (except as a revival), the idea of typology reorganized the environment in a thoroughly normative way. In a period such as ours, when architects have often denounced any typological approach while looking for a to-pological definition of the ground of architecture (which should also be analyzed for its methodological fictions), the analysis of how typology has structured social sciences and the arts in the last two centuries, and how normative and prescriptive it was and still is, may help us to better understand the notion of the

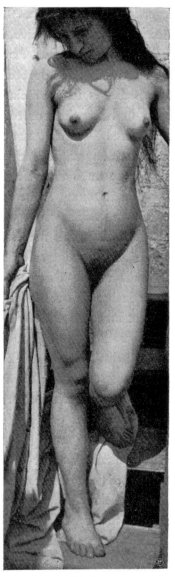

Abb. 73

2.12
Young woman's body before its disfiguration
by a corset; in Paul Schultze-Naumburg,
*Die Kultur des weiblichen Körpers als
Grundlage der Frauenkleidung* (Leipzig: Eugen
Diederichs, 1901), 71, fig. 73. Courtesy
of ETH-Bau Library.

2.13
Reformed female garment; in Paul Schultze-
Naumburg, *Die Kultur des weiblichen
Körpers als Grundlage der Frauenkleidung*,
116, figs. 114–115. Courtesy of ETH-Bau
Library.

Abb. 114   Abb. 115

2.14
Illustration by Peter Behrens for Henry van de Velde's
article on contemporary female dress; in *Deutsche
Kunst und Dekoration* 5, no. 10 (Darmstadt, July 1902),
369. Courtesy of ETH-Bau Library.

2.15
Illustration by Henry van de Velde for his article on
contemporary female dress; in *Deutsche Kunst und
Dekoration* 5, no. 10 (Darmstadt, July 1902), 379.
Courtesy of ETH-Bau Library.

2.16
Nacktkultur dance: solo female dancer from
the Ida Herion Dance School in Stuttgart, operating
since 1912. Photo: Arthur Ohler; in Max Adolphi
and Arno Kettmann, *Tanzkunst und Kunsttanz: aus
der Tanzgruppe Herion, Stuttgart* (Munich: Julius
Püttmann, 1928), n.p. Courtesy of ETH-Bau Library.

2.17
Ecstatic solo female dancer, dressed in veil-like skirt
in an outdoor setting. Photo: Arthur Ohler; in Max
Adolphi and Arno Kettmann, *Tanzkunst und Kunsttanz:
aus der Tanzgruppe Herion, Stuttgart* (Munich: Julius
Püttmann, 1928), n.p. Courtesy of ETH-Bau Library.

body as type—that is, the body as an entity to redesign, which makes it a kind of prosthesis.

For example, a large-scale solidarity of the new Human "type" was to be found in new *Siedlungen* and in the sporting activities of the Weimar period in Germany. According to Count Harry Kessler, an enthusiastic visitor to Ernst May's "New Frankfurt," the architecture of Siedlung Römerstadt could express the new ideals of the German youth: the nude sunbathers "are indicative of only part of a new vitality, a fresh outlook on life, which since the war has successfully come to the fore. People want really to live in the sense of enjoying light, the sun, happiness, and the health of their bodies." And, he adds, the *Siedlungen* "are another expression of this new feeling for life . . . the new domestic way of living." The architecture "is simply an expression of the same new vitality which impels youngsters to practice sport and nudity. . . . This German architecture cannot be understood unless it is visualized as part of an entirely new *Weltanschauung*."[107]

Hans Surén's book *Der Mensch und die Sonne* (Man and the Sun, 1924) was so popular that it ran through sixty-eight reprints (250,000 copies) in its first year of publication. It contained photographs of naked women wading between reeds, muscled masculine bodies throwing a medicine ball, a nude skier practicing the Christiania turn on deserted slopes, group choreography articulating machine-like limbs, javelin throwers, mud bathing melees, archery, and more.[108] "Licht-, Luft- und Sonnenbad" ("light, air and sunbath") was the slogan of another successful Surén book, *German Gymnastics* (1925).[109] After the Nazis took power, Surén, a high-ranking Army officer, quickly adapted to the new situation, publishing a second edition titled *Man and Sun: The Arian Olympic Spirit* (1936).[110] The whole modern suburb seemed ordered by rhythmic gymnastics and geometric mass dancing. The erotic *Nacktkultur* of the Weimar period appears at its best in the productions of the dance school of Ida

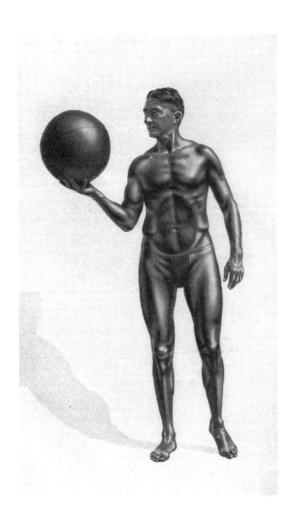

2.18
Man with medicine ball. Photo: P. Isenfels; in Hans
Surén, *Deutsche Gymnastik: Vorbereitende Uebungen
für den Sport—Frottierübungen, Atemgymnastik,
Massage—Körperpflege—Verhalten im Licht-, Luft-
und Sonnenbad* (Oldenburg: Stalling, 1925), 240.
Courtesy of ETH-Bau Library.

Herion, operating in Stuttgart since 1912, and made famous by the book *Tanzkunst und Kunsttanz* (1927), by her students Max Adolphi and Arno Kettmann.[111] Herion linked nudism and ecstatic dance, not to recover a primordial state of freedom, but to acquire a kind of wilderness, a remoteness from the conventional theater stage. In her intensely eroticized images, the body itself creates beauty, elegantly poised and detached from the world.[112] The slogan "Licht, Luft und Sonnenschein" ("light, air and sunshine") celebrated the beginning of an "athletic democracy," as Thomas Mann put it.[113] This was the age of the geometrization of crowds, of "ornamentation of the masses," as Siegfried Kracauer announced,[114] soon to become, as Ernst Jünger prophesied, the era of "Total Mobilization."[115]

Planning and housing were part of the same genealogy, a general policy of building the equipment of the State that allowed individuals to be integrated into the collective channels of sanitary policy, social hygiene, and normative sociology. These disciplines shaped a multiplicity of fluxes channeling the movements of the population and guiding their mutations. The physiology of poverty became eugenics, the science of improving the biological type. Craniometry, and then biometry, the elaboration of a bio-typology, became the knowledge base for the manipulation of the matters of the Social,[116] and society opened its arms to the winners of natural selection. The idea of type was, of course, something German architects found useful during the Nazi period. At the time, Schultze-Naumburg, who had become a National Socialist dignitary, published research on the German *Typen des Wohnhaüser* (Types of Dwelling Houses).[117] In 1929, Paul Schmitthener began assembling a catalogue of the German "framework houses," a return to Semper's *Fachwerk*.[118] For Schmitthener, the traditional framework house was a true ur-house from which one could derive the universal German type of dwelling, thus developing a typology of "built form" (*Gebaute*

2.19
Adaptation of Weimar Republic nudism to the Nazi
regime. Photo: G. Riebicke; in Hans Surén, *Mensch
und Sonne: Arisch-olympischer Geist* (Berlin: Scherl,
1936), 85. Courtesy of ETH-Bau Library.

2.20
Sea wading in an "Aryan-Olympic spirit"; in Hans
Surén, *Mensch und Sonne: Arisch-olympischer
Geist* (Berlin: Scherl, 1936), 137. Courtesy of ETH-
Bau Library.

2.21
Skier practicing nudism. Photo: G. Riebicke; in Hans
Surén, *Mensch und Sonne: Arisch-olympischer
Geist* (Berlin: Scherl, 1936), 223. Courtesy of ETH-
Bau Library.

Form, 1943–1949).[119] The era of "total mobilization" led to the era of the worker, who was understood not as an individual, but as a "type," as explained in Jünger's *The Worker: Domination and Form* (1932).[120] A warrior dandy, Jünger was a decorated World War I officer whose poses recalled attitudes also embraced by writers and artists such as Gabriele D'Annunzio, the futurist Filippo Tommaso Marinetti, or Colonel T. E. Lawrence (of Arabia). In the postwar period, with the bestselling book *Storm of Steel* (1920), Jünger became a successful, though highly controversial, writer, because, as a right-wing nationalist (but never a Nazi), he was part of the conservative revolutionary movement.[121] For him, each war front corresponded to a work front, thus soldiers and workers became equivalent, which generated a new entity, the "worker-warrior." Whether a man in a howitzer crew or a woman joining the industrial workforce, Jünger's universal type tended to become the worker, *der Arbeiter*. In a review of his collected essays *Krieg und Krieger* (War and Warriors, 1930), Walter Benjamin asserted that Jünger was promoting a "mysticism of war,"[122] and remarked, with some irony, that "in the face of this 'landscape of total mobilization,' the German feeling for nature has had an undreamed-of upsurge."[123] Elsewhere he noted: "With D'Annunzio, decadence made its entry into political life, with Marinetti, Futurism."[124] Therefore, Benjamin warned, *"The logical outcome of fascism is an aestheticizing of political life."*[125] As in a chemical reaction, the nineteenth-century crowd of Le Bon disappeared, replaced by working masses able to organize a factory and knowledgeable about the points of control and the new networks. The war, global and civil, created a new uniformity, a suprapartisan and extranational being, whom Jünger called a "type" (*Typus*).[126] The *Typus*, reconciling the organic and the instrumental, will signify the completion of a Darwinian transformation within a new, inherently prosthetic, humanity.

3 DREAM HOUSE

Sofas deep as tombs . . .
  Charles Baudelaire, *The Death of Lovers*[1]

According to Walter Benjamin, an historian's task consists of bringing submerged historical facts to the surface, even though they have lost their original use. In *The Arcades Project* (*Das Passagen-Werk*) he looks at these "historical" relics at the very moment they are falling into disuse, indeed as they aspire to disappear, through annihilation, devastation, or simple negligence.[2] In other words, he focuses on moments of transition, when phenomena seem to vanish like fleeting images fading into oblivion. Taking his inspiration from the Proustian notion of "involuntary memory," Benjamin compares the work of the historian to what happens to consciousness as one emerges from sleep, when it finds itself in a threshold condition:

> *The new, dialectical method of doing history presents itself as the art of experiencing the present as waking world, a world to which that dream we name the past refers in truth. To pass through and carry out* what has been *in remembering the dream!—Therefore: remembering and awakening are most intimately related. Awakening is namely the dialectical, Copernican turn of remembrance.*[3]

For Benjamin, history can thus become a process of remembering (*die Erinnerung*), but only insofar as its mechanism remains similar to that of awakening: "What [Marcel] Proust intends with the experimental rearrangement of furniture in matinal half-slumber . . . is nothing other than what here is to be secured on the level of the historical, and collectively."[4] Essentially, Benjamin is explicitly referring to the distinction, elaborated in 1935 by the Austrian psychoanalyst Theodor Reik, between memory (*das Gedächtnis*) and reminiscence (*die Erinnerung*).[5] Memory, Reik noted, "is to protect our impressions; reminiscence aims at their dissolution. *Essentially memory is conservative; reminiscence, destructive*."[6]

Since it is a passage, the act of awakening from a dream represents both a rupture and a continuity. This transition between the states of dreaming and waking is at the core of Benjamin's thinking: "There is a not-yet-conscious knowledge of what has been (*das Gewesene*): its advancement has the structure of awakening."[7]

Interior Cartography

In many of Benjamin's texts, a nineteenth- or twentieth-century apartment is presented as an *étui*, a lined receptacle forming a kind of protective shell. It is during this period that his idea of "dwelling" was established, with all the variations of meaning encompassed by the notion of habitation (*das Wohnen*):

> The original form of all dwelling is existence not in the house but in the shell. The shell bears the impression of its occupant. In the most extreme instance, the dwelling becomes a shell. The nineteenth century, like no other century, was addicted to dwelling. It conceived the residence as a receptacle for the person, and it encased him

with all his appurtenances so deeply in the dwelling's in-
terior that one might be reminded of the inside of a com-
pass case, where the instrument with all its accessories
lies embedded in deep, usually violet folds of velvet.[8]

Should we preserve these traces, reverently maintain these imprints? Certainly not, for Benjamin, an attentive reader of his friend Bertolt Brecht's *Handbook for City Dwellers*, is mindful of the refrain ringing throughout its verses: "Erase the traces!"[9] This accumulation of marks requires an instrument of salvation, that of the "destructive character": "The destructive character is the enemy of the *étui*-man. The *étui*-man looks for comfort, and the case is its quintessence. The inside of the case is the velvet-lined trace that he has imprinted on the world. The destructive character obliterates even the traces of destruction."[10] As a result, these jewel cases protecting their inhabitants must be considered within the realm of possibility of a topological transformation of the interior into an exterior, where the surface of the sheath becomes an envelope. At first glance, this pure interior (*das Interieur*) seems to be a defensive capsule; yet this very space tends to be put on display, and therefore projected toward the exterior, like goods in a shop window or objects in a museum collection. What was bourgeois interiority, a realm in which calm, security, and privacy reigned, a place asleep or dozing, the drowsiness and the atmosphere of which allude to the various meanings of the notion of comfort (*die Gemütlichkeit*), suddenly awakens and is turned inside out: "The domestic interior moves outside. It is as though the bourgeois were so sure of his prosperity that he is careless of façade, and can exclaim: My house, no matter where you choose to cut into it, is façade."[11] This observation makes it possible to interpret the interior in a situation of mirrors, as if the interior and the exterior were reflecting each other. Such a mirrored duality can be represented by the gaze, for instance the gaze of the "painter of modern life," to use the title of the essay Charles Baudelaire wrote about Constantin Guys, that "kaleidoscope gifted with consciousness,"[12] whose art could render the shimmering of the motley crowd, "as though it were an enormous reservoir of electrical energy."[13] Such a painter, attuned to the vibrations of the big city and capable of capturing the "astonishing harmony of life in the capital cities,"[14] needs "[t]o be away from home, and yet to feel oneself everywhere at home."[15] Nightfall "is that strange, equivocal hour when the curtains of heaven are drawn and cities light up. The gas-light makes a stain upon the crimson of sunset."[16] To Baudelaire, the city is an immense interior, where one can draw the curtains and turn on the lights for the evening.

From that moment, once twilight has faded, there is a definite incursion by metropolitan exteriority, invading interior spaces and generating two concomitant effects: the interior turns into a façade while the passerby becomes a voyeur. Baudelaire writes:

> *Looking from outside into an open window one never sees as much as when one looks through a closed window. There is nothing more profound, more mysterious, more pregnant, more insidious, more dazzling than a window lighted by a single candle. What one can see out in the sunlight is always less interesting than what goes on behind a window pane. In that black or luminous square life lives, life dreams, life suffers.[17]*

To the poet of modernity, on the hunt for "evil's particular beauty,"[18] the glimpsed window must be observed at night, from the outside. With its disturbing exteriority, it frames the anonymous existence of the city dweller and presents a poetic image of his wordless sufferings, an "allegory" of his melancholy solitude.[19]

Threshold Magic

With the phrase "threshold magic" (*der Schwellenzauber*), Benjamin often evokes the magical effect produced by places of transition, such as porches, doorways, and vestibules, sites usually protected by some form of monitoring, such as a guard, a concierge, or a doorman. Influenced by reading ethnologist Arnold van Gennep's 1909 work *The Rites of Passage*, which documented the various ceremonies that mark the successive stages of human life,[20] Benjamin observes that, aside from falling asleep and waking up, performing daily rites has become a rarity: "We have grown very poor in threshold experiences."[21] As a result it is more imperative than ever to precisely identify threshold situations that mark the moments of our life. He notes:

> The threshold must be carefully distinguished from the boundary. A Schwelle (threshold) is a zone. Transformation, passage, wave action are in the word schwellen, swell, and etymology ought not to overlook these senses. On the other hand, it is necessary to keep in mind the immediate tectonic and ceremonial context which has brought the word to its current meaning.[22]

Thus waking up is not a caesura, but the creation of a doorway, a passage to be crossed through a series of rites, leading from the world of dreams to the waking state (*das Erwachen*). It is a zone formed by precise tectonics, an area of knowledge and even of knowability (*die Erkennbarkeit*). Passages and peristyles, porticos and arcades, pronaos and portals, doorways and vestibules, triumphal arches, spaces sacred and profane (from the Latin *pro-fanus*, in front of the temple): these imaginary and tectonic lines create not boundaries, but the space of the intermediate. A figure both in space and in time, the threshold is that which is in the middle, an interval between things. A medium, in a way, that, by allowing entry, opens up the possibility of being in between.[23]

Benjamin's aim in the *Arcades Project* is to illustrate the relationship between the dream world and the waking state, presenting in the process a theory of thresholds that has been rightly seen as the "surreal entanglement of dreams and history."[24] His 1929 article on surrealism had already hinted at this theme: "Life seemed worth living only where the threshold between waking and sleeping was worn away in everyone as by the steps of multitudinous images flooding back and forth; language seemed itself only where sound and image, image and sound, interpenetrated with automatic precision . . . "[25] In the *Arcades Project*, as on an abandoned construction site, it is possible to unearth amid the ruins a "science of thresholds," as illustrated by this observation: "The despotic terror of the hand bell, the terror that reigns throughout the apartment, derives its force no less from the magic of the threshold. Some things shrill as they are about to cross a threshold."[26]

Nevertheless, before Benjamin could claim to be a new kind of historian, capable of interpreting dreams, he had to devise a theory of *Traumdeutung* (interpretation of dreams) that was not directly derived from Sigmund Freud's, too individual (or "bourgeois") to his taste, although the influence of Freud's work is palpable in Benjamin's essay on Baudelaire.[27]

Benjamin seems to have redefined his concepts of memory and forgetting in the course of reading a number of works, including Reik's; he also took inspiration from Dr. Pierre Mabille's essay in the preface to "L'éloge des préjugés populaires" ("In Praise of Popular Prejudices") published in the surrealist journal *Minotaure* in

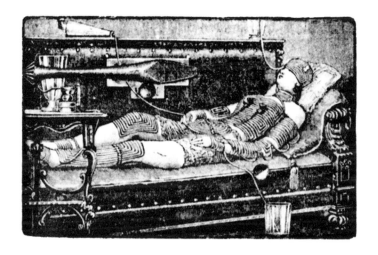

3.1
Max Ernst, *Die Leimbereitung aus Knochen* (The
Production of Glue from Bones), collage-painting;
1921; Dada-meeting in Tarrenz (Tyrol) published
in the magazine *Dada au grand air. Der Sängerkrieg
in Tirol* (Dada in the open air—The War of Singers
in Tyrol) (Paris: Au Sans Pareil, September 1921).
Courtesy Kunsthaus, Zurich.

1935.[28] Here, Mabille, a physician and anthropologist, proposes a confrontation between the "visceral unconscious" of an individual nature, and the "unconscious of oblivion" of a predominantly collective nature. While the unconscious of the individual is doomed to disappear, the collective aspect of the unconscious is made up of "the mass of things learned in the course of the centuries and in the course of a life, things which were conscious once and which, by diffusion, have entered oblivion."[29] The passionate elements of individuals inevitably vanish, and only the elements taken from "the external world [and] more or less transformed and digested" survive.[30] To Mabille, a friend of surrealist author and poet André Breton, this creates the necessary conditions for the emergence of a collective unconscious, composed of things derived from the external world. Like a water table, the elements of social life are transformed into underground materials, ready to resurface from the depths. What emerges is the possibility of a collective interior, an interiority made up of external things, preserved in formless vessels, reappearing after a process of interiorization.

Although Benjamin, having read Carl Gustav Jung's 1932 *Seelenprobleme* (published in English as *Modern Man in Search of a Soul*), rejected Jung's theories of the collective unconscious, he does seem to accept this transposition from the individual to the collective, as represented by the alternating states of waking and sleep: "Of course, much that is external to the [individual] is internal to the [collective]: architecture, fashion—yes, even the weather—are, in the interior of the collective, what the sensoria of organs, the feeling of sickness or health, are inside the individual."[31] Rejecting psychoanalytical procedures that attempt to decipher the symbols of a dream, Benjamin's reading looks in utilitarian edifices, in everyday events, in the most banal of things, for anything that links them to the dream experience—that is to say, the buried, the digested, and the disturbing, and, ultimately, the irrational. Benjamin seeks to abolish the distinction between the dream world and the waking state, whereas, a priori, the surrealists always maintained a difference between the two. The dream becomes the metaphor of the passage, and the passage, as a pure interior, becomes the allegory of the dream. This "transposition"[32] (or transfer) allows Benjamin to generalize the dream experience. Influenced very early by Louis Aragon's 1924 work *Une vague de rêves* (A Wave of Dreams),[33] Benjamin examines his own dreams with the attention of a collector of rare objects; he transcribes them, and these transcripts are published in 1928 by Ignaz Ježower in his dream anthology *Buch der Träume* (Book of Dreams). By transcribing his dreams, Benjamin accords the dream experience the same authenticity as the waking state. Having abrogated the limiting criterion that makes the dream a strictly individual phenomenon, he extends the dream experience to a collective (*das Kollektiv*). In fact, this path had also been breached in the essay by Dr. Mabille, who joined the surrealist group in 1934.

Theodor Adorno condemned this extension from the individual to the collective in his famous letter of August 2, 1935, in which he accused Benjamin of not differentiating himself sufficiently from Jung or Ludwig Klages. Posing the question just "[f]or who is the subject of the dream?"[34] Adorno asks Benjamin to specify what a collective dream is, given that the *Arcades Project* makes so many references to the "dreaming collective" (*das träumende Kollektivum*). After lecturing Benjamin for reducing the dialectical image to the dream and subjecting it to the "spell of bourgeois psychology,"[35] Adorno, in a fit of irrepressible dogmatism, remonstrates with him that "no differences remain between classes in the dreaming collective."[36] This is a denial of everything that gives the *Arcades Project* its power, as the book's major achievement is that it transcends the rigid framework of so-called historical materialism.

Dream City

Benjamin was in no way following in Jung's footsteps, and he seems to have dispelled any confusion in that respect when he challenged the mechanistic idea of a collective dream reduced to the sum total of individual dreams. In fact, he introduces an effective process of analogy between dream and architecture, an idea (more a "trick" than a "method," he writes) he derived from surrealism, and especially from Breton, who "can boast an extraordinary discovery: he was the first to perceive . . . the revolutionary energies that appear in the 'outmoded,'—in the first iron constructions, the first factory buildings, the earliest photos, objects that have begun to be extinct."[37] And later: "They bring the immense forces of 'atmosphere' concealed in these things to the point of explosion."[38] This has rightly been called oneiromancy in reverse, for he takes as his starting point things, objects, fragments, places, locations, and atmospheres, in order to bring out their irrational qualities. Like a collector, Benjamin uncovers these fragments in "that vast intermediate zone in which the aesthetic and the social have not yet assumed distinct forms."[39] As the pieces are put together, fragmentary phenomena become actual structures, and these can be found in the sections of the *Arcades Project* devoted to the "Dream City" (*die Traumstadt*) and the "Dream House" (*das Traumhaus*), which constitute an assortment of obsolete objects collected by Benjamin, who now takes on the guise of a rag-and-bone man. The significance of the following observation is thus made clear: "Fashion, like architecture, inheres in the darkness of the lived moment, belongs to the dream consciousness of the collective. The latter awakes, for example, in advertising."[40] Benjamin reveals that the past, "what-once-was" (*das Gewesene*), is not simply what is covered in the patina of time; this past is always present, still very much of our time.[41]

The dream, which has nothing to do with a collective unconscious teeming with archetypes, is used as an elucidating metaphor and a key to interpretation. The collective dreams solely by living the experience of the world of things that belong to its time: buildings, advertising billboards, images, fashion. This is not a psychological interpretation. The dream vision is treated more like a physical, even physiological, experience—be it that of the man taking a stroll, the woman passing by, the gawking onlooker, the *flâneur*, the laborer, the traveler, but also that of the listener and the spectator—precisely because of the dialectical annihilation to which surrealism leads: "indeed, precisely after such dialectical annihilation—this will still be an image space (*der Bildraum*) and, more concretely, a body space (*der Leibraum*)."[42] For "the collective is a body, too."[43] While the subject endures this profane illumination, the dweller goes through an ecstatic loss of self, allowing him to penetrate a genuine "image-space" (*der Bildraum*), which also has the features of a "body-space" (*der Leibraum*).[44] In developing the implications of this theory, Benjamin establishes the "image-space" as the quintessential locus of metropolitan habitation. As the realm of technology expands, he predicts that "when in technology body and image so interpenetrate . . . all revolutionary tension becomes bodily collective innervation."[45] This is a profound anticipation of a world of technology (and media) whose space is innervated by images and sounds passing right through our bodies.

The history Benjamin writes does not categorize eras, forms and styles, or even types, but rather accumulates a constellation of intermediate zones for which he provides a topography: "Dream houses of the collective: arcades, winter gardens, panoramas, factories, wax museums, casinos, railroad stations."[46] All these edifices, typical of the nineteenth-century notion of "novelty," are characterized by their transparency, achieved through the use of new materials like metal (iron, steel) and glass.[47] Steel, in particular, is used for the construction of buildings housing transport activities or serving "transitory" ends, the unusual qualities of which Benjamin brings to the fore.[48] As a result, he sheds light on the new subjectivity engendered by new construction methods, described, for example, in Alfred G. Meyer's *Eisenbauten* (1907)[49] and Sigfried Giedion's *Bauen in Frankreich* (1928).[50] Benjamin had the latter book sent to him in Berlin, and in the letter of thanks he sent to Giedion on February 15, 1929, he reveals his enthusiasm, noting that he was immediately "electrified," then seized by an irrepressible emotion as he set out to read it: "Your book is one of those rare cases that each of us has probably experienced: before we face something (or someone: a text, a house, a person, etc.), we already know that it is of the highest significance," adding that in general such an expectation is not disappointed.[51] The compliment that follows could be merely a standard expression of courtesy, were it not that Benjamin introduces an interesting distinction among several forms of radicalism, discerning in Giedion's work a "refreshing difference between radical attitude and radical knowledge." Armed with such knowledge, he continues: "You are able to shed light on tradition (*die Tradition*) based on the present (*der Gegenwart*), or rather to discover the former based on the latter." This was exactly the theoretical program Benjamin himself was in the process of elaborating. His letter concludes with praise for the "radicalism" (*der Radikalismus*) emanating from the book.

In *Bauen in Frankreich*, Giedion, a Swiss historian, wrote that "the nineteenth century provided all new creations, in every area of endeavor, with historicizing masks. This was no less true in the field of architecture than in the field of industry or society. . . . This historicizing mask is indissolubly bound to the image of the nineteenth century, and is not to be gainsaid."[52] Later in the text he writes: "The nineteenth century: singular fusion of

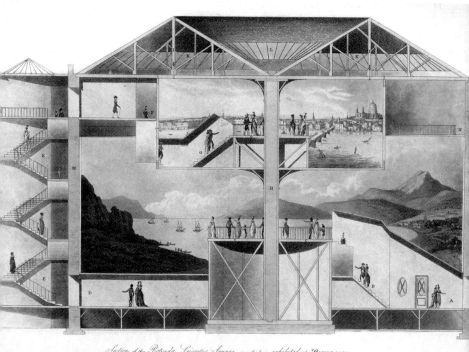

Section of the Rotonda, Leicester Square, in which is exhibited the PANORAMA.
Coupe de la Rotonde, dans laquelle, on l'exhibition du PANORAMA, Leicester Square.

3.2
Panorama, *Section of the Rotonda, Leicester Square,
in Which Is Exhibited the Panorama*, aquatint; in
Robert Mitchell, *Plans, and Views in Perspective, with
Descriptions, of Buildings Erected in England and
Scotland* (London: Wilson, 1801), pl. 14. Courtesy the
British Museum, London.

individualistic and collectivist tendencies. . . . [S]ubterraneanly, in despised everyday domains, it necessarily furnishes, as in a delirium, the elements for a collective formation. . . . With this raw material, we must occupy ourselves—gray buildings, market halls, department stores, exhibitions."[53] In the *Arcades Project* there is again indication of the use Benjamin would make of this book: "Attempt to develop Giedion's thesis."[54] Giedion had asserted that "in the nineteenth century, construction plays the role of the unconscious."[55] Benjamin aims to radicalize a thesis whose radicalism he has already certified. Giedion's framework is simple, not to say simplistic, for it states that, just as the conscious exists on the surface and the unconscious underneath, the edifices of the nineteenth century comprise two strata. Scratch the superficial layer of "artistic" architecture that serves as a mask, and you uncover the substratum of the structure. Such an analysis is hardly surprising from Giedion, as he was a pupil of Switzerland's founder of art history, Heinrich Wölfflin, who had introduced psychology into this new discipline. This interpretation also carries a value judgment, for it states that beneath the falsehood of the "historicizing masks" lurks the truth of the structure, whose (true) essence would become the foundation of twentieth-century architecture.

3.3
Sigfried Giedion, photograph of Marseille's Pont Transbordeur, built by Ferdinand-Joseph Arnodin in 1905; as a reversed negative, this photo will be used by László Moholy-Nagy for the cover of Giedion's volume *Bauen in Frankreich*, 1928; and, in positive, as figure 60 of the same book. Courtesy of gta Archives / ETH Zurich, Sigfried Giedion archive.

Where a specialist like Giedion identifies in built structures of the nineteenth century the forerunners of construction methods in the twentieth, Benjamin, while admitting that he is not particularly learned in architectural matters, sees them "not at all as anticipatory but as distinctly old-fashioned and dreamlike."[56] He goes on to wonder: "Wouldn't it be better to say [that construction plays] 'the role of bodily processes'—around which 'artistic' architectures gather, like dreams around the framework of physiological processes?"[57] As an alternative to Giedion's simple stratification, Benjamin considers construction as a bodily and organic process enveloped by artistic architectures. To Benjamin, it is as though a decorative device had settled like a dreamy mist, swallowing up the armature of the physiological process.[58] This inversion of Giedion's model is fascinating on several levels, particularly in light of the distance that ultimately separates these two thinkers. It was Ernst Bloch, a friend of Benjamin, who first cast into doubt the pretensions of "Giedion's brand of social-democratic 'modernity'."[59] In fact, Benjamin's—now radical—philosophy would veer away from the "modernist" position of the Swiss critic, while Giedion would become the secretary-general of the Congrès Internationaux d'Architecture Moderne (CIAM). In any case, as with Benjamin's similar attempts with Erwin Panofsky, the exchange of letters between the two writers ultimately led to nothing.

As a whole, the edifices of the nineteenth century give Benjamin the opportunity to rehabilitate their "narcotic historicism" and their "passion for masks,"[60] by assigning them a precise historical existence, which the surrealists were the first to recognize.[61] In the course of his mental voyage through Paris, "capital of the nineteenth century," Benjamin contemplates the melancholy of the "dusty fata morgana of the winter garden,"[62] admires the railway stations presenting the "double aspect of a factory in operation and a ministry,"[63] lets his eye explore the department stores whose "floors form a single space,"[64] and, during the 1867 World Exhibition, walks through the "high galleries, kilometers in length," filled "with the noise of machinery."[65] Spanned by metal frames, these outsized structures create vast collective spaces, so large that they seem to lack exterior walls. They are, strictly speaking, interiors, as are the interminable galleries of the arcades illuminated by glass skylights, the cavernous greenhouses with their murky atmospheres in the botanic gardens, the enclosed rooms of the panoramas, the endless perspectives *en enfilade* down the length of the waxworks galleries, the museums and the casinos, the filigreed arches of the covered markets and the exhibition halls, the "glass-roofed sheds" that are railway stations and factories, where one enters a "pestiferous cavern" of smoke and steam.[66]

Industrial cathedrals of a sort, these "transitory" spaces[67] are the receptacle of the crowd, and these new naves cradle its collective dream. This is a paradox, for the public spaces of the collective appear as interiors, albeit interiors of a particular kind: threshold spaces, where the interior and the exterior commingle, and where the public and the private merge to create a new type. Just as there is a Baudelairean city, there is a truly Benjaminian urbanism:

> The city is only apparently homogeneous. . . . Nowhere, unless perhaps in dreams, can the phenomenon of the boundary be experienced in a more originary way than in cities. To know them means to understand those lines that, running alongside railroad crossings and across privately owned lots, within the park and along the riverbank, function as limits. . . . As threshold, the boundary stretches across streets.[68]

3.4
Max Berthelin (1811–1877), *View of the "Palais de l'Industrie" in Paris*, 1855, Musée de la Ville de Paris, Musée Carnavalet, Paris, France. Scala/White Images / Art Resource, NY.

Benjamin demonstrates that the nineteenth century is not simply a prefiguration of modernity, but that its fundamental history, or its prehistory (*die Urgeschichte*), elucidates the advent of the transitory and of transparency as the key motifs of the twentieth century. The nineteenth century is not just a period of transition; it is an era in which insecurity and nomadism, that ensemble of phenomena summed up by Gilles Deleuze and Félix Guattari under the (rather awkward) term "deterritorialization," manifested themselves. Whatever Giedion's more or less direct influence may have been, there was an objective connection between him, who knew that the destiny of architecture had to be an "intoxicated interpenetration" of air and light,[69] and Benjamin with regard to their inspired vision of "modern" man, finding his abode in the ephemeral, the nomadic, and the crystalline. What Benjaminian archaeology added to Giedion's was the dimension of the dream, floating above the city like a primordial phantasmagoria, made accessible through an intoxicated, and even hallucinatory, penetration.

Exteriorized Interior

The famous cutaways of Parisian buildings, published several times during the nineteenth century, illustrate the phenomenon of transparency. From 1845 to 1911, a particular style of iconography was in vogue in Paris in which the building was represented as a dissected body, allowing the eye to penetrate its interior in order to study its life, its functions, and its organs.[70] This theme had already been established in literature, with the 1707 publication of the novel *Le diable boiteux* (The Lame Devil) by Alain-René Lesage (a second edition was published in 1726); not unusually for the time, this work had been freely inspired by that of Luis Vélez de Guevara, published in Spain as *El diablo cojuelo* (1641).[71] In the Spaniard's story, a devil is able to penetrate walls in order to spy on the activities of humans, most likely a metaphor for the prying eye of the Inquisition. Lesage, author of the famed picaresque novel *Gil Blas* (1715–1735), borrowed only the basic idea and the devil character from Guevara; his hero is transported by the devil onto the roof of each house in order to observe the life of its occupants, providing an occasion for subtle depictions of social mores.[72]

In 1845 and 1846, this theme reappeared when Pierre-Jules Hetzel published the two volumes of *Le diable à Paris* (The Devil in Paris), largely illustrated by J. J. Grandville and Paul Gavarni, with texts by Balzac, George Sand, Charles Nodier, and others. These books featured gorgeous cutaway illustrations revealing the social life inside a building, allowing the eye to wander from one floor to the next, from the starched comfort of the bourgeois drawing room to the drunken excesses of the bohemians in the garrets.[73] Where the public spaces of transit take on the form of immense caverns, the Louis-Philippe or Napoleon III interiors exposed by the architect's cutaway drawings, dissected by the scientific gaze and unveiled by the intimist or social literature of writers like Balzac, Eugène Sue, and Émile Zola, become façades. Like a reversible surface, the interior opens out into an exterior. For Benjamin, this is a systematic inversion of interior and exterior: "Arcades are houses or passages [*Häuser oder Gänge*] having no outside—like a dream."[74] Like dreams, the arcades form a pure interior, even as they distill qualities emanating from the exterior. At the same time, the glassed-in interior of the arcades acquires a configuration of pure exterior. For Johann Geist, "In the context of architecture history, the arcade is above all a place of transit [*Durchgang*], a space with a beginning and an end. But this space contains, like an envelope, an edifice that becomes autonomous, and its function is differentiated. It is the passerby who uses it."[75] In their ambiguous capacity, somewhere between building and street, the arcades, simultaneously "houses" (*Häuser*) and "corridors" (*Gänge*), become the envelopes

3.5
Unsigned illustration in the 1759 edition of Alain-
René Lesage's novel, published again in *Le diable
boiteux par monsieur Le Sage*, new ed. (Amsterdam:
Pierre Mortier, 1789), woodcut, p. 112. Private
collection of the author.

of a phantasmagoria and the supports of a semiawake collective dream.

There would be different degrees of intensity in the interiors. Some were normal, banal, and everyday; others, extremely intensified, displaying the hallucinatory qualities described by Proust or by Rainer Maria Rilke in *The Notebooks of Malte Laurids Brigge* (1910).[76] For instance, Benjamin emphasizes that "the inside of the museum appears as an interior magnified on a giant scale."[77] He later observes that "the arcade, too, is a windowless house."[78]

Maison Close

Suddenly, during the nineteenth century, there was an "oneiromantic" incursion of the philosophies of positivism and utilitarianism, those new religions that were supposed to guarantee everyone a home and ensure that industrial society had a stable habitat. During his study of Baudelaire, Benjamin had collected a large number of books, including a biography by Charles Asselineau, a friend of the poet, and Asselineau's *Mélanges tirés d'une petite bibliothèque romantique* (Mixtures Taken from a Small Romantic Library, 1866),[79] a book he asked Gretel Karplus (the future Mrs. Adorno) to send him from Berlin after he had fled to Paris to escape persecution.[80] In a text on Baudelaire entitled

3.6
Section of a Parisian residential building on January 1, 1845, drawing by Bertall, lithography by Lavieille, published in *Le diable à Paris: Paris et les Parisiens* . . . (texts by Balzac, E. Sue, G. Sand, et al.), series of engravings with captions by Gavarni et al. (Paris: J. Hetzel, 1845–1846), 2 vols, vol. 2, facing p. 26. Private collection of the author.

3.7
Philibert Louis Debucourt, *Le passage des Panoramas
à Paris* (The Passage of the "Panoramas" in Paris),
1807, gouache, Musée de la Ville de Paris, Musée
Carnavalet, Paris, France. Photo: Erich Lessing / Art
Resource, NY.

3.8
The "spider web," glazing work, c. 1810–1820, within
the Passage du Caire, Paris, built between 1799 and
1828. Photo by the author.

"Central Park" (1938–1939),[81] Benjamin shows that he knew about a dream Baudelaire had related to Charles Asselineau in a letter dated March 13, 1856. In the course of this dream quest, the poet loses his way inside a brothel arranged in a labyrinth of rooms and corridors that lead him to a gallery full of drawings: "I find myself inside vast, interconnecting galleries—poorly lit— of depressing and faded aspect—like old cafés, ancient reading rooms, or shabby gaming houses. . . . What strikes me is that the walls of these vast galleries are decorated with drawings of all kinds—in frames—not all are obscene—there are even architectural drawings and Egyptian figures."[82] This art gallery, which seems wrought by Grandville's grotesque vision, forms a space that, to Benjamin, is similar to that of the arcades, which are characterized by the frenetic activity of the collector whose hunt for new pieces and their classification and arrangement create a "perpetual flux": indeed Benjamin considers Parisian arcades "as though they were properties in the hand of a collector" who is experiencing an episode of dream life.[83] Penetrating the dreamed space, Baudelaire goes on: "In a remote corner of one of these galleries, I find a very singular series. Among a multitude of tiny frames, I see drawings, miniatures, photographic prints. They represent highly colored birds of very bright plumage, whose eyes are *alive*."[84] What matters to the collector is the order in which each of his objects is arranged, yet these may be "ordered, however, according to a surprising and, for the profane understanding, incomprehensible connection,"[85] thus arranged according to a system that is startling and even incomprehensible to the layman, creating an encyclopedia in which one gets lost. Benjamin goes on to write that, in the process, the true collector "detaches the object from its functional relations,"[86] by liberating, in effect, "things from the drudgery of being useful."[87]

Continuing his tour, the poet is then brought into a kind of curiosity cabinet, which might be a mannerist collection, arranged

3.9
Constantin Guys, *Study for a House of Prostitution*,
circa 1860, ink and watercolor, Paris, Musée
Carnavalet. Courtesy of Musée Carnavalet, Paris.

into *naturalia*, *mirabilia*, and *exotica*. But it could also be an exhibition of anatomical oddities, or even the teratology section in a medical museum:

> *Yet among all these creatures, there is one who has survived. He is a monster born in the house and who remains forever on a pedestal. Although alive, he is thus part of the museum. He is not ugly. . . . He crouches, but in a strange and contorted position. There is also something blackish wrapped several times around him and around his limbs, like a large serpent. I ask him what this is, and he tells me it is a monstrous appendage coming out of his head, something elastic like rubber, and so long, so long that if he were to twist it around his head like a tress of hair, it would be far too heavy and absolutely impossible to bear—that as a result he is forced to wrap it around his limbs, which in any case produces a better effect. I converse at length with the monster.*[88]

As soon as these objects are collected, arranged, and exhibited, they undergo a remarkable mutation, passing from an inorganic state (the drawings) to a state of extreme, almost uncontrollable organicism in which flesh mutates into prosthetic protuberances whose function remains a mystery and whose symbolism defies all facile interpretation. In the section of the *Arcades Project* devoted to Baudelaire, Benjamin reproduces annotations taken from the work on *The Defeat of Baudelaire* (originally published in Paris in 1931), by Dr. René Laforgue, who conjectured that Baudelaire, as a child, might have witnessed his wet nurse or his mother having sexual intercourse: he would have assumed the position of the third party (the outsider), and having fixated on this, would have become a "voyeur." Subsequently, as in the dream analyzed by Laforgue, Baudelaire would have frequented brothels as a mere onlooker, an observer of sylphids and sa-tyresses. This fixation on the gaze would be the root of his infer-nal outlook and his nefarious predilection for the absolute.[89] It would also be the source of his interest in the works of Constan-tin Guys, painter of "macabre nymphs and living dolls,"[90] and of Paul Gavarni, "poet of chlorosis [and] hospital-beauties."[91] In the first lines of "Central Park," a collection of fragments on Baudelaire, Benjamin asserts that Laforgue's hypothesis on the poet's behavior in the brothel strikes him as entirely plausible and corroborated in all points by conventional literary history.[92]

Some years later, in an essay inspired by the same dream, Mi-chel Butor was keen to emphasize: "What a treat for a psychoana-lyst! Ah, let us not interpret in haste," adding that "[Baudelaire] finds himself back in the time of his first visits to brothels. . . . *He* is the little monster," finally deciding that "[t]he school-brothel is a museum."[93] Whatever the interpretation, since we cannot consider a Freudian "penis envy," a very serious "prosthesis envy" might be envisaged. A remark by Benjamin seems to echo the vi-sion of the museum-brothel as re-created in the poet's dream: "The physiological side of collecting [*das Sammeln*] is important. . . . With the nest-building of birds, collecting acquires a clear biological function."[94] In fact, the *maison close* (literally "closed house," and a French term for brothel) in Baudelaire's dream is a covered arcade containing a collection in which the organic and the inorganic cohabit; as such, it evokes a fragmentary body of work whose aesthetic is indeed that of the grotesque.

As if analogous with the dream experience related by Baude-laire, Benjamin's strolls through the covered arcades can take on aspects of fantasy, giving the illusion of passing through walls. "The dread of doors that won't close is something everyone knows from dreams,"[95] he writes. "I learned of this phenomenon in a dream in which, while I was in the company of a friend, a ghost appeared to me in the window of the ground floor of a house to

3.10
Arthur Henry Roberts (1819–1900), *An Interior View of One of the Rooms in Mr. Sauvageot's Apartment Prior to Transferring His Collection to the Louvre*, 1856, oil on canvas, Louvre, Paris. Courtesy of Réunion des Musées Nationaux / Art Resource, NY.

our right. And as we walked on, the ghost accompanied us from inside all the houses. It passed through all the walls and always remained at the same height with us."[96] Benjamin links this experience to the arcade, a genuine *Traumhaus*: "The path we travel through arcades is fundamentally just such a ghost walk, on which doors give way and walls yield."[97]

This evocation can be traced to numerous formulations examining the nature of transparency, be it the transparency of spaces or of materials such as glass, a recurring leitmotiv in Benjamin's work: from his reading of André Breton's *Nadja* (a "'book with a banging door'"),[98] continuing with the illustration of the "well-ventilated utopias of [Paul] Scheerbart,"[99] the twin brother of [Charles] Fourier, and the theme of "objects made of glass [that] have no 'aura.'"[100] This explains his rather peremptory declaration that "to live in a glass house is a revolutionary virtue par excellence,"[101] insofar as it is the fruit of an indispensable "intoxication, a moral exhibitionism, that we badly need."[102] Moreover, the traditional concept of the right to a private life loses most of its meaning "in a society that perpetrates the political radioscopy of sexuality and family, of economic and physical existence, in a society that is in the process of building houses with glass walls, and terraces extending far into the living rooms that are no longer living rooms."[103] Finally, Benjamin's admiration for Scheerbart's *Glasarchitektur* (1914)[104] apparently earned him access to the Maison de Verre in Paris, built by Pierre Chareau and Bernard Bijvoët for Dr. Jean Dalsace between 1928 and 1931, where Benjamin would have given a lecture, had the owner, to his great chagrin, not fallen gravely ill.[105]

Dream Kitsch

One of the lessons Benjamin retained from his reading of Meyer's *Eisenbauten* is that the origin of all iron and glass constructions is the greenhouse, literally a "house for plants," and that

Joseph Paxton, the designer of the Crystal Palace at London's Great Exhibition in 1851, was a gardener and the creator of the greenhouses at Chatsworth.[106] This house for plants is also the subject of the French caricaturist and lithographer Grandville, whose work frightened Baudelaire: "This man . . . spent his life remodeling creation. He would take it in his hands, twist it, rearrange it, explain it, comment on it, and nature would turn into apocalypse."[107] What continued to fascinate Baudelaire was the lithographer's ability to penetrate the labyrinths of analogy and metamorphosis, as revealed in a society undergoing mechanization, at the moment in which, through the systematic reproduction of identity, the enigmatic side of things emerges: "Indeed it is through the mad side of his talent that Grandville is important. Before he died, he applied his always stubborn will to recording in graphic form the series of dreams and nightmares, with the precision of a stenographer taking down an orator's speech."[108] One plate from *Un Autre monde* (Another World, 1844) shows a turtle with a dog's head chasing a lion riding on a beetle, while a serpent-headed pachyderm passes by in the distance, along with other oddities that have come to be called zoological grotesques.[109] The nineteenth century is, emphatically, the century of biology: forcing the hybridization of natural or technological things, or crossing them with human beings, made it possible to visualize the multiple phenomena of mixing, acclimation and (re-) production unique to industrial society. In the lithographer's work, Benjamin is able to trace the apparition of the immutable (*das Immergleiche*) and track down the repetition of identity within the sensation of the new. Another plate shows a procession composed of various figures, each seemingly metamorphosing into the next: a stylized bird, a bow and quiver, a *bilboquet* (a cup-and-ball toy), a candelabra, a flower vase, and a female figure holding a flower.[110] Each form derives from the one that precedes it, through a gradual transformation based on physical resemblance, mimicking the zoomorphism of hybrid beings and the couplings of men and machines. In yet another plate, "Apocalypse of the Ballet,"[111] a rapidly spinning top transforms into a ballet dancer, through an effect similar to one used in the then popular game of "persistence," based on the phenomenon of retinal persistence, the impression of continuity experienced by the human eye when seeing a series of light phenomena flash by in rapid succession.

Grandville manages to present the collective chimeras of his age as truly infernal phantasmagorias. The cycle of "another world" takes us into an alien universe that exposes the grotesque, clownish, and cynical underside of transfigured things—in fetishist fashion. Benjamin notes:

> Grandville's masking of nature with the fashions of mid-century—nature understood as the cosmos, as well as the world of animals and plants—lets history, in the guise of fashion, be derived from the eternal cycle of nature. When Grandville presents a new fan as the "fan of Iris," when the Milky Way appears as an "avenue" illuminated at night by gas lamps, when "the moon (a self-portrait)" reposes on fashionable velvet cushions instead of on clouds, then history is being secularized and drawn into a natural context.[112]

This is the dreamlike transmutation of an unsettling history. The identical is linked to the distant, the disparate, and the extraordinary in the guise of their shared affinities. What Benjamin calls Grandville's "graphic utopia"[113] is the product of the dream's moral indifference, of its absence of values, of its neutrality toward things. This can also be seen as a sort of graphic sadism.[114] The predilection for the comical, the banal, and the affinity for kitsch—"dream kitsch"[115]—all this contributes to the visualization

APOCALYPSE DU BALLET.

3.11
"Apocalypse of the Ballet," a reference to the toy based
on vision's persistence; in J. J. Grandville, *Un Autre
monde* (Paris: H. Fournier, 1844), pl. 53. Courtesy
Werner Nekes Collection, Mülheim/Ruhr, Germany.

of the indifferent forms of the dream and leads to an intoxication of ornamentation, which results in beaux-arts architectural features crystallizing like misty dreams around constructions and buildings.

What Grandville describes are the effects of the dominance of commodity objects, which must be continually renewed, giving it a temporality linked to the rapid flux of fashion and endowing it with a nature in which the organic is paired with the inorganic. Through his images, he extends the realm of fashion to everyday objects as well as to the universe itself: "In taking [fashion] to an extreme, [Grandville] reveals its nature," Benjamin writes,[116] "Fashion stands in opposition to the organic. It couples the living body to the inorganic world. To the living, it defends the rights of the corpse. The fetishism that succumbs to the sex appeal of the inorganic is its vital nerve. The cult of commodity presses such fetishism into its service."[117] Celebrations of the "sex appeal of the inorganic,"[118] these anthropomorphoses are laughable, grotesque and monstrous; they reflect a world in which plants, animals, things, and human beings establish new kinds of relationships.[119] And Grandville endeavored to present images of this world, as though they were a collection in a museum of natural history.

Ultimately, interiors are the receptacles of things, but also the support of affects. These things are not simply the objects that provide material support for memory, as evoked by Proust. They are also commodities on display, on offer in the market. For Benjamin, the Marxist concept of fetishism provides a theory of phantasmagoria, enabling him to chart an interpretation of complex relationships between object and spectator. This theory describes with precision the fantastic relationships engendered by the accumulation of luxury items, antique art objects, collector's pieces, knickknacks no longer in fashion, frivolous trinkets, mismatched fragments, outdated images, and obsolete instruments.

All this forms an environment filled with objects and people, capable of generating a landscape of dreams and agoraphobia, of claustrophilia, obstinately turned inward. Here, the spectator is in search of lost time, and the objects are like alembics distilling its duration. With Benjamin, however, phantasmagoria is not merely an effect of the reification of commodities; it also produces a transmutation. World exhibitions, department stores, arcades, and cities of glass all represent experiences that make it possible to combine technology with a fantastic dream state, creating "thought images" (*Denkbilder*): "Yes, this epoch was wholly adapted to the dream, was furnished in dreams."[120] Subjecting the "dream house" to a radioscopy, Benjamin offers a precise catalogue of the "dream furniture" that haunts its enclosed spaces. When he assuredly added the dimension of the dream to phantasmagoria, he also added a dimension of illumination, even of transfiguration.

4 THE WAVE

[The] French capital . . . a kind of interior in the open air.
—Hannah Arendt, "Walter Benjamin," 1968[1]

The spirit of the interior giving birth to plein air.
—Walter Benjamin, "Schema and Gloss about *Jugendstil*,"
1930–1931[2]

With *The Man with the Broken Nose*, Auguste Rodin gave form to
an animated face "full of motion, full of disquiet and crashing
waves [*Wellenschlag*]," wrote Rainer Maria Rilke in his seminal
book on the sculptor. Rodin's art, he argued, departed from classical canons that favored monumental stillness (*gravitas*) over
movement (*celeritas*), insofar as "there was always motion in nature," and any art that would "present a faithful interpretation of
nature could not idealize a motionlessness that existed nowhere."
For Rilke, even in ancient cults, which preferred hieratic gestures, it was possible to discern this *celeritas*—for example, in
"the restlessness of living surfaces . . . like water within the walls
of a vessel." A similar kind of gesture could also be found in the
effigies of the gods, "like a fountain rising from the stone and
then falling back again, covering it with innumerable waves."[3]

In this lyrical vision of the sculptor's art, it is always a universe in flux that is captured, frozen, and crystallized. However,

whether this is achieved through the lapidary quality of archaic art or by the flowing lines of *Jugendstil*, the wave always seems to be the single point of reference—a symbol of life and death and of a material ebb and flow.[4] For Art Nouveau and *Jugendstil*, the metaphor of the breaking wave also offered a remarkably clear representation of the artistic volition, or *Kunstwollen*, with which authors such as Rilke were so familiar—not least in the case of Rilke, since he had written a critical report in July 1898 on the "new art" in Berlin, in which he commented on Henry van de Velde's furniture: "Everything is in plain wood, everything is light, quiet, healthy. Every movement is a heavy swell, a rhythmic compensation between stress and resistance. . . . The movement swings as if [on] strong hinges. . . . Every line lives its life until the end."[5] Such a balance between stillness and strain seemed to allow the artist to restore a kind of unity, conciliating all the disparate elements of a work of art.

This theme had already appeared in "Notizen zur Melodie der Dinge" (Notes on the Melody of Things), an unpublished essay dated 1898, in which the poet, then searching for the underlying, vital harmony in things and forms, argued that "one must extract the rhythm of the waves from the roaring turmoil of the sea, and free the vital line . . . from the confusion of day-to-day speech."[6] In another text from the same period, Rilke asserted that art, more than any other worldview (religious, scientific, or metaphysical), translates life in the form of an extended line, "part of a circumference adopting the form of a straight line, because its radius is infinite."[7] Titled "Über der Kunst," this essay was published in three parts between November 1898 and May 1899 in *Ver sacrum*, the review founded by Gustav Klimt in Vienna in January 1898. There, Rilke tried to lay the foundations for a new understanding of art. But above all, it was his encounter with Rodin's work in 1902 that led to a refinement of his aesthetic vocabulary, and to his idea that the defining challenge for

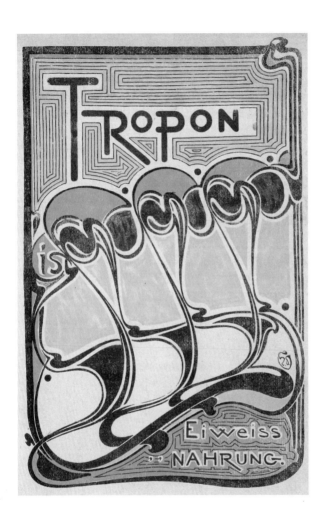

4.1
Henry van de Velde, *Poster for the Food Company
Tropon*, 1898, version published in the magazine
Pan 4, no. 1 (1898), color lithograph. LWL—
Landesmuseum für Kunst und Kulturgeschichte,
Westfälisches Landesmuseum, Münster, Germany.

a sculptor was in modeling a surface in which each contour and vibration bore witness to a life. The sculptor's engagement with concrete materials in modeling tangible things directed Rilke toward completely new paths in his own literary work, revealed most notably in his *Duino Elegies* (1922) and *Sonnets to Orpheus* (1922), where the dynamics of line and surface reappear: "Aspire to transform . . . / that generative spirit, master of earth and all therein, / holds nothing dearer than the pivot point of the evolving line." For many poets, and especially for Rilke, inspiration is equated with respiration—the invisible takes form and transforms itself into a general respiratory process: "Breath, you poem beyond all seeing! . . . / Lone wave, whose gradual sea / am I; . . . / Do you know me, you breeze, so full of spots / hitherto mine?"[8] Thus the poem literally transmutes into breath, while an Orphic breeze wafts around the atmosphere. Through this verse, and at the very outset of the twentieth century, Rilke also inaugurated the rediscovery of the crucial, modern issue of atmosphere, in which the question of air would be dealt with from both qualitative and quantitative points of view, in science as well as in conscience.[9] Rilke, along with Stefan George (the poet and translator of Charles Baudelaire), was part of the literary baggage of the young Walter Benjamin. Rather surprisingly, Benjamin met Rilke during his year-long stay in Munich in 1916, when they both attended university seminars given by Walter Lehmann, a scholar of Aztec mythology.[10] However, neither these encounters between the two writers nor their subsequent brief epistolary relations ultimately mattered so much as their common interest in French literature and art. What established a link between the experiences of the two German writers was that they both chose Paris, chiefly in order to perfect their education, but also to look for (and follow) their vocation—be it Rilke, with his *Notebooks of Malte Laurids Brigge* (1910), or Benjamin, with his major opus, *The Arcades Project*. In choosing Paris as their home and place of study, they made the city a site of alienated modernity, simultaneously uninhabitable, welcoming, and impenetrable, whose secrets and enigma had to be immediately revealed. Even during his first trip in 1913, Benjamin was able to perceive the French capital in a way that anticipated his later vision—as a city lived in "as we would inhabit the confines elsewhere," a kind of inner space "in the open air."[11]

In section S of *The Arcades Project*, dedicated to *Jugendstil*, Benjamin writes: "Perhaps an attempt should be made to extend the scope of this inquiry up to the threshold of the war, by tracing the influence of *Jugendstil* on the youth movement [*Jugendbewegung*]."[12] An indicator of epistemological ambition, this is also an autobiographical note and a hint at Benjamin's own upbringing. At the age of twelve, the young Benjamin was sent to the famous Haubinda School in the Thüringen countryside, where he stayed for two years, between 1904 and 1906, before returning to his old school in Berlin and passing his university entrance examinations in 1912. According to Benjamin, it was at Haubinda that "the grains of his future life were planted."[13] A text fragment from around 1913 describes the Haubinda landscape: Above villages and forests, "on a very gentle hill, there is a manor house . . . what they call a half-timbered house." From there, "handsome teenagers came down wearing red caps. . . . Tomorrow, the young people will go for a walk in the most hidden places of this landscape."[14] For a time, the Haubinda School was run by Gustav Wyneken, an adherent of the *Reformpädagogik* movement, which promoted progressive education.[15] In deliberate contrast to the existing authoritarian Prussian educational model, the goal at Haubinda was to integrate into a conventional education a series of outdoor pursuits, including gardening, walks through the meadows or woods, and naked lake and river swimming, soaking up the virile rural atmosphere.[16] Benjamin felt particularly at ease in this school "in the country," which offered freedom at work, life in the open air, naturalism, and active participation in cultural debates.[17]

Characteristic of Haubinda (and of other reform movements in the same period) was an acknowledged homoerotic atmosphere,[18] and Benjamin was by no means unaware of the ambivalence of the *Jugendbewegung* in which he actively participated until 1915.[19] Moreover, he would also have been familiar with other male-dominated groups at the time, such as the *Wandervögel* (Wandering Birds), an organization for adolescent boys dedicated to group hiking. In associations like these, all typically founded shortly after the turn of the century, young men practiced folkloric rites based around hiking, camping, and an almost religious celebration of nature, expressed through kitsch "medieval" ceremonies, traditional singsongs, and the new rallying cry—"Heil!"—with which they greeted each other. These pursuits and rituals were essentially those of neoromantic anarchism, amplified by a virulent xenophobia and a latent anti-Semitism.[20] Decorating their periodical reviews with engravings in a style similar to *Jugendstil*, and celebrating a mythical *Volkskultur* inspired by Wilhelm Heinrich Riehl's cosmology, the *Wandervögel*, with their general animosity toward cities and industry, exalted the values of an agricultural world and vanishing craft traditions while taking a fierce stand against conventional educational models. Their utopian project was to "defeat capitalism through hiking," as Benjamin noted with a certain wry disdain.[21]

While the ambitions of the *Volkskultur* may have provoked a certain derision, this period was of utmost importance in the development of Benjamin's thinking, with the two youth movements—the *Jugendstil* in the arts and the *Jugendbewegung* in a social and political context—appearing to him as two sides of the same coin.[22] Impelled by the plays of Henrik Ibsen and Frank Wedekind, as much as by the youth-inspired philosophical ideals of Friedrich Nietzsche, the period was also one in which the power

4.2
Rudolf Bosselt, *Bronze Jewelery Dish*, 1901; in
Deutsche Kunst und Dekoration 5, no. 3 (Darmstadt,
December 1901), 97. Courtesy of ETH-Bau Library.

of Eros and Sexus would come to the fore. As a key figure within this cultural milieu, Benjamin produced a text titled "Die singende Blume oder die Geheimnisse des Jugendstils" (The Singing Flower, or the Secrets of *Jugendstil*), of which only fragments dating from around 1930 survive. This essay seems to have been intended as an analysis of a novel titled *Tagebuch einer Verlorenen* (Diary of a Lost Girl), published in 1905 in Berlin by Margarete Böhme, accompanied by a "comprehensive inventory of sexual commerce, from matchmakers to gigolos."[23] Benjamin hoped to draw the secret of this text and its incipient sexuality out of the reform movement: "The *Jugend* in Munich [the review founded by Georg Hirth in 1896] was probably the most important newspaper of this mysterious emancipation movement which inhabits the tone of this verse." Recalling the allegorical figure of the flower (something he borrowed from Stefan George's 1897 book of poems *Das Jahr der Seele*), Benjamin continues: "In the flower, the idea of perversion is linked to that of youth. Only then did we understand the very heart of *Jugendstil* . . . Emancipation is linked to perversion."[24]

On June 6, 1929, in a letter to his friend Gershom Scholem, Benjamin declares that he is working on a study of *Jugendstil*.[25] Of the study itself, the only remaining traces are a series of notes titled "Schemata und Glossen zum Jugendstil" (Schemas and Gloss about *Jugendstil*), dated 1930–1931 and published in *Fragments*, as well as annotations collected in section S of *The Arcades Project* and a brief digression on *Jugendstil* in "Paris, the Capital of the Nineteenth Century," written in May 1935 for the Institute of Social Research.[26] With the help of a little contextual exploration, however, it might be possible to reconstruct Benjamin's lost essay on *Jugendstil*, in which he aimed to theorize the possibility of an "open air architecture," a kind of environment "in the open," where air and water would become controlled and conditioned (a terminology that introduced a characteristically twentieth-century lexicon). As much as anticipating a future condition, Benjamin's study established an archaeology of the experiments explored by the *Jugendstil*, which enabled him to go back in time and deal with nineteenth-century arts from Baudelaire to the caricaturist J. J. Grandville—a century he knew quite well, and one he makes frequent reference to in *Berlin Childhood*: "Like a mollusk in its shell, I had my abode in the nineteenth century, which now lies hollow before me like an empty shell."[27]

What Grandville pioneered (and the surrealists later played upon) was the idea that in a nineteenth-century society that idealized progress and comfort, a general feeling of discomfort seemed to prevail—a sensation of disquiet later famously diagnosed by Freud as *unheimlich* (uncanny). Before then, the traditional bourgeois interior was a place of melancholy, where ennui became crystallized.[28] Grandville's art, which unnerved Baudelaire, led the poet to imagine a domestic space subverted by a series of optical distortions so as to become the place of unease par excellence:

> *When I read Grandville's work, I feel rather uncomfortable, as if I [were] in an apartment where disorder would be organized systematically, where ridiculous cornices would stand on the floor, where paintings would appear distorted by optical manipulations, where objects would hurt themselves on angles, where furniture would hold its feet in the air and where drawers would be pulled in instead of out.[29]*

The metaphor of the inverted table is a recurrent one in nineteenth-century literature—for example, in Honoré de Balzac's novel *The Government Clerks*, which quotes "grotesque furniture" standing on its head during the moving of an office[30]—while in a famous passage in *Das Kapital*, titled "The Fetishism of Commodity and Its Secret," Karl Marx describes the self-transformation of the industrially manufactured object from a commodity into a "phantasmagoria," with a "mystical character": "But as soon as [the table] emerges as a commodity, it changes into a thing which transcends sensuousness. It not only stands with its feet on the ground, but, in relation to all other commodities, it stands on its head, and evolves out of its wooden brain grotesque ideas, far more wonderful than if it were to begin dancing of its own free will."[31] For Benjamin, obsessed as he was by such a *Fetishcharakter* of the commodity and how to interpret its secret, objects are durable goods, exhibited merchandise made available in the general marketplace.[32]

The transfiguration of commodities into "magical objects" in this period can also be observed in the proliferation of world's fairs. At the same time, the discomforts caused by industrial civilization formed the subject of Grandville's book *The Petty Sorrows of Human Life* (1843), which offered a number of cartoonish misadventures prompted by the misuse of various industrial objects and technical gadgets.[33] And just as Grandville influenced Baudelaire, so Benjamin took his cue from the poet, once again taking from Baudelaire's *The Double Bedroom* the theme of *reverie*, which he saw as spreading through the nineteenth-century interior like an atmospheric cloud, animating and metamorphosing furniture so as to transform tables and chairs into endlessly flexible, stretching, yawning, extending limbs: "In a prefiguration of *Jugendstil*, Baudelaire sketches 'a room that is like a dream, a truly *spiritual* room. . . . Every piece of furniture is of an elongated form, languid and prostrate, and seems to be dreaming— endowed, one would say, with a somnambular existence, like minerals and vegetables'."[34] Elsewhere, in a prefiguration of atmospheric architecture, Baudelaire comments on "all these phantasmagorias," these "fluid architectures" built "with the vapors, the marvelous structures of the impalpable," the great majority of which he could contemplate from his open window.[35]

Evoking the "forests of symbols" in Baudelaire's *The Flowers of Evil*, Benjamin later sees the elucidation of a floral motif as central to the "flower-gazes of *Jugendstil*," the art of which, he writes, "wins back symbols."[36]

If at first Benjamin expressed a negative opinion on what he called the *Jugendstil*—which, depending on the country or region, was also called modern style, 1900 style, Art Nouveau, *Modernismo*, Stile Liberty, or even *Wellenstil* (wave style)—it was because he considered such a movement to be a "repression" of technology, for "its recourse to technological motifs arises from the effort to sterilize them ornamentally."[37] Another factor in Benjamin's opposition was that he was following the arguments of Adolf Loos, who questioned the role of ornament in the context of the Wiener Werkstätte,[38] as well as Sigfried Giedion's somewhat simplistic formulations, uniting diametrically opposed approaches (such as Le Corbusier's free plan and Loos's Raumplan). With *Jugendstil*, Benjamin believed, the bourgeois "conceals his alibi . . . in natural history";[39] however, later and elsewhere, he acknowledged that the bourgeoisie would start "to come to terms with the conditions . . . of its dominion over nature"[40] by integrating technical forms in architecture. The way his views on this developed is confirmed by his comment: "The life of flowers in *Jugendstil*: from the flowers of evil extends an arc, over the flower-souls of Odilon Redon," through to Proust's floral eroticism, before coming back again to "the perverse flower-glance" in Redon's phantasmagoric paintings.[41]

Benjamin is looking here for a genealogy that, starting with Grandville's caricatures and continuing with Baudelaire's symbols, would lead not only to the sinuous forms of *Jugendstil*, but to the technical rhetoric of futurism and, further, to the allegories of surrealism.[42] As part of this surrealist absorption of *Jugendstil*, in 1930 Salvador Dalí, motivated by his contempt for Le Corbusier's purism, launched a rehabilitation of Art Nouveau in built form as "realization[s] of [solidified] desires."[43] Similarly, in a 1933 issue of *Minotaure*, André Breton stressed the closeness of drawing, sculpture, and mediumistic painting, and the ability to recognize in each "the same delight in the never-ending curve (whether it be a growing fern or ammonite or embryonic curl)."[44] For Marx, the commodity is an essentially intangible piece of goods, the actual enjoyment of which is unattainable except through accumulation and exchange. The fetishism of the world of commodities converts everything into a "social hieroglyphic," in Marx's terms.[45] Benjamin attempted to decipher such a secretive sign, the mystery of an immaterial thing, a quest that led him to Grandville's visions: "If the commodity was a fetish, then Grandville was the tribal sorcerer."[46] By forcefully causing things, animals, and humans to mate, Grandville's anthropomorphisms offered visual clues, portraying the effects of industrial production of durable goods on society. For Benjamin, the commodity fetish analysis can be applied to "Grandville's fetishistically animated objects."[47] Having also been influenced by the surrealists in this regard, Benjamin could not help but note the analogies between the Marxist commodity fetish and the architecture and furniture produced around 1900, such as van de Velde's desks, Victor Horta's cabinets, or Antoni Gaudí's biomorphic moldings. Writing about the "revolutionary ornamental architecture" of Catalan *Modernismo*, Dalí said: "No collective effort has succeeded in creating a dream world as pure, and as disturbing, as these *Jugendstil* buildings."[48] Moreover, he offers a psychoanalytical interpretation of such concretions, since these buildings present the "excessively violent and cruel automatism . . . [found] in childhood neurosis."[49]

Underpinning this research was Benjamin's intention to write an essay on *Jugendstil*, but this ambition took something of a knock when Dolf Sternberger published a study on the same subject in September 1934—a study that Benjamin quotes in *The*

Arcades Project: "Every house appears . . . to be an organism which expresses its interior through its exterior, and van de Velde unmistakably betrays . . . the model for his vision of the city of characters."[50] Sternberger himself continues with the idea that "if the city is a garden full of freely growing house-organisms, it is not clear where, in such a vision, man would occupy a place, unless it be that he is caught within the interior of this plant life, himself rooted and attached to the soil—land or water."[51] Benjamin, however, opposed such a thesis. The idea that a house was a plantlike organism in which one could take refuge from the devastating power of industry was too simple a negation, because it did not precisely dichotomize the relationship between plantlike art and technology. Sternberger, in contrast, appreciated the decor that modeled itself on the naturalistic mollusk shells or radiolaria illustrated in 1899 by Ernst Haeckel in his book *Kunstformen der Natur* (Art Forms in Nature): "Just as pieces of furniture gravitate toward one another . . . so it seems that walls, floors, and ceilings are possessed of a peculiar power of attraction. Increasingly, furniture is becoming untransportable, immovable; it clings to walls and corners, sticks fast to floors, and, as it were, takes root."[52]

For Sternberger, fixing artwork onto walls to create a *Jugendstil* interior delivers them from the fatigue of being useful only when withdrawn from the commodities circuit: "All permanent contents of the home are absorbed in exchange, while the occupant himself loses the power of moving about freely and becomes attached to ground and property."[53] The artwork therefore occupies a liberated interior, which presents itself as a testing ground on which traditional boundaries—decorative arts, industrial art, sculpture, architecture, etc.—become blurred. As a consequence, "art in everything" is established as the leitmotiv in the quest for a house for the new man (a quest articulated particularly clearly by the "architect" Halvard Solness in Ibsen's 1892 play *The Master*

Builder).[54] Allowing for the hybridization of the different trades, these *arts nouveaux* also allowed pictures to leave their frames. The interior, accordingly, begins to be articulated through the arrangement of various decorative panels: fresco, mosaic, wallpaper, tapestry, printed fabric, enameled stoneware tile, or polychromatic brick. The play of these different planes generates its own specific tectonics, created by the assimilation of the artworks with their flat surface. Another process involved making the frame itself come alive, so that it then becomes loaded with sculptural potential, proliferating and growing like a protuberant vegetable.[55]

For Benjamin, casting a glow over this decorative interplay was Nietzsche's *Thus Spoke Zarathustra*, which "appropriated . . . the tectonic elements of *Jugendstil*, in contrast to its organic motifs," insofar as all of Nietzsche's works are characterized by "the predominance of the hollow form over the filled form."[56] Further attesting to the strength of this connection, the prophet Zarathustra's rhythm of pauses and silences was seen to find an echo in the scansion of voids and intervals in Art Nouveau—an alliance seemingly made binding in 1908 when van de Velde joined with Count Harry Kessler to edit a lavish edition of *Thus Spoke Zarathustra* for Leipzig's Insel-Verlag.[57] Nietzsche's sister, Elisabeth Förster-Nietzsche, also commissioned van de Velde to install the philosopher's archives at a villa in Weimar in 1903.[58] On Kessler's initiative, the architect would later become a member of the committee for the erection of a memorial to Nietzsche (for which van de Velde would make several designs in 1912—most of them rather unattractive).[59] Through episodes like this it seemed as if a Nietzscheanism—or rather, a *Zarathustrastil*—swept through the thinking and ideas of the period.[60] Even van de Velde, in words if not in his monuments, appropriated the philosopher's sensibilities in defining drawing as "a spontaneous manifestation of the gesture which carries away our whole being, merging with it, shaking it . . . like a sail in the wind."[61]

Earlier, in 1898, van de Velde had returned to that other Nietz-schean trope—the alternating play of solids and voids—observing to Count Kessler and the art critic Julius Meier-Graefe that any line should necessarily receive a complement, so as to create "female and male lines penetrating each other."[62] Art Nouveau, in this way, came to be defined as an erotic art par excellence.[63] As emblem to this eroticism, Peter Behrens hung a copy of his 1898 work *Der Kuss* (The Kiss) on the wall of his living room in Darm-stadt. First published as a colored engraving in the review *Pan*, the picture shows the faces of two women facing each other, as if merging in a mirror.[64] To enhance the concentration of narcis-sistic ego, their mouths meet in a kiss, while all around them the picture plane is filled with their rhapsodic, tangled locks (an in-tertwining that quickly became Art Nouveau's dominant motif). During the same period, Behrens—who had the habit of intro-ducing himself as *der Lebenskünstler* (the "artist of life")—created a desk light in the form of a female figure, in which the effigy holds a transparent shell. A source of life, the woman illumi-nates the darkness with naturalistic light.[65] The literature of the time was similarly inundated with visions of universal procre-ation, culminating in those of the ever-renewing cycle of living substances—a recurrent theme taken up in Otto J. Bierbaum's poem "Faunsflötenlied," dedicated to Behrens and illustrated by the painter Heinrich Vogeler: "Sing, flute, your prayer of lust / This is life's sacred sense."[66]

The idea of lust soon spread after 1900, but was transcended (and briefly desexualized) into the concept of "ether" (itself later taken as a synonym for "space"). [67] This singular idea of a charged and enveloping atmosphere helped to figure the imponderables now seen to be lingering in the air (notably, the fascination with

4.3
Peter Behrens, view of the vestibule of the "House
of Power and Beauty," Hamburg's Vestibule of the
German Section of the International Exhibition on
Modern Decorative Art, Turin, 1902; in *Deutsche
Kunst und Dekoration* 5, no. 1 (Darmstadt, October
1902), 15. Courtesy of ETH-Bau Library.

4.4
Peter Behrens, table lamp, Darmstadt, 1902. Courtesy
Hessische Hausstiftung, Museum Schloss Fasanerie,
Kronberg, Germany.

4.5
View of the bathroom in Peter Behrens's house in
Darmstadt, with fixtures by Volk & Wittner (Strasbourg),
1902; in *Deutsche Kunst und Dekoration* 5, no. 4
(Darmstadt, January 1902), 180. Courtesy of ETH-
Bau Library.

magnetic waves). More generally, it was also through the idea of the ether that one could conceptualize that determinedly modern characteristic of transparency, so as to invest the design of the nineteenth-century interior not only through the material questions of how to use iron or glass in building, but how to represent and contain certain energies. In his essay on the line ("Die Linie," 1902), van de Velde claims that "the line is a force" and that lines are able to translate "latent forces which wait impatiently before transforming themselves into action."[68] It was from this linear source that van de Velde felt able to derive the physical manifestation of life's vital forces—in particular those which integrated imperceptible phenomena such as vibrations or X-rays. As a consequence, the interior begins to be read as a permeable space where X-rayed bodies can act within a field of competing energies.[69] Similarly, in *Panoramas of the Nineteenth Century*, published in 1938, Sternberger, alluding to the "life of nerves" in the metropolis Georg Simmel described in 1903, observed that "the *fin-de-siècle* cult of the nerves . . . maintains this telegraphic image,"[70] and dominates interpersonal relationships. As with everything, Benjamin picks up on this nervousness, adding that "in the typical *Jugendstil* line . . . nerve and electrical wire not infrequently meet," as if to "to mediate between the world of organism and the world of technology."[71]

In his celebrated August 2, 1935, letter to Benjamin, Theodor Adorno writes: "In *Jugendstil*, sex fills the place of inwardness . . . only there does the private individual encounter himself or herself not as inward but as corporeal."[72] Whereupon he quotes Ibsen, Maurice Maeterlinck, Gabriele D'Annunzio, and Frank Wedekind, who staged the vitality and satisfaction of carnal desires with his character Lulu (infringing on social and theatrical conventions in the process).[73] By submitting to the primitive and elementary forces of Eros, Wedekind's characters hoped to find relief from their angst, even if it led them toward destruction and death.[74] Trampling on bourgeois moral standards, this dynamic, vital urge incarnates itself as a possible mediation with natural and original forces.[75] Lulu, the most haunting character in Wedekind's plays, is not an individual, but an allegory for desire.[76] And again, as mirror to this cultural context, Benjamin defined *Jugendstil* as a "regression which, from social reality, leads to the biological and natural realm," and whose instrument is woman.[77] But what type of woman does he mean? Claude Quiguer, in his brilliant *Femmes et machines de 1900*, identifies two opposite forms of feminine types, circa 1900: the first is Lulu, a tragic heroine and fatal regenerator of desire; the second, at the other extreme, the pale and fleshless woman who fades almost into nothingness.[78] Sternberger had also underlined this incorporeal aspect in *Jugendstil* art: "The bare body made of bones, flesh, muscle, skin, nails and hair, seems to fade, seems to dilute itself in the desire which energizes everything, before being absorbed by that movement of universal growth. . . . But even these bodies of young girls, these fine, thin, almost emaciated bodies . . . are always directly connected with the image of an astral body; they are all bodies of souls."[79]

Around 1900 all of these youthful, diaphanous creatures exhibited their charms on tapestries and stained-glass windows. In particular, there seemed to be a fondness for fairies dressed in white, dreamlike evocations tiptoeing across floral meadows or clearings, the virginal whiteness of their appearance always in contrast to the darkness of the surrounding forests. Likewise, in Wedekind's story *Mine-Haha* (1903), a copy of which Benjamin owned, the narrator recalls the idealized physical education she received in a girls' finishing school set in the middle of a large park: "We felt ourselves in our legs and feet more than in our eyes and fingers. Of none of the girls do I remember her way of talking. I only remember how they walked."[80] Situated behind a high perimeter wall, the finishing school is a heterotopy with a distinct "eroto-topical" aspect, and in its protected sphere, girls and boys—be they fictive or real—create the conditions for a free education beyond the censoriousness of puritan morality.

The erotic atmosphere emanating from these colleges—utopian and, at the very least, ambiguous—was captured most obviously in the graphic work of Fidus (the pseudonym of Hugo Höppener, 1868–1948), an artist whose symbolist engravings evoke a playful and erotic universe in which naked girls dance round a moonlit garden and boys raise their arms in "prayer to the sun" (*Lichtgebet*).[81] Alluding to this work, Benjamin stresses that "*Jugendstil* forces the auratic. Never has the sun worn a more glorious aureole; never was the eye of man more radiant than with Fidus."[82] Looming large within these somewhat hackneyed Art Nouveau figures was the lily woman, with her exaggerated purity tempered by an eroticized repressed sensuality.[83] Rehashing something of a cliché of his own, Benjamin saw these qualities as a defining characteristic in prostitutes, lesbians, and pale virgins, because they all steer clear of fecundity: "The depraved woman stays clear of fertility, as the priest stays clear of it."[84] For Benjamin, this issue was so important that he repeated it: "The extreme point in the technological organization of the world is the liquidation of fertility. The frigid woman embodies the ideal of beauty in *Jugendstil*."[85] He then describes his own ideas of 1900 womanhood, defining three lines (or schemata) by which female types appear in literature: the "hieratic line" (from Stéphane Mallarmé to Stefan George), the "line of perversion" (from Baudelaire to Oscar Wilde and Aubrey Beardsley), and the "line of emancipation" (from *The Flowers of Evil* via Ibsen to *Zarathustra*).[86] These three schemes can be distinguished in visual art. The hieratic aspect, for instance, reappears in Max Klinger's *Penelope* (1895) and in the faces of various Medusas, such as those by Fernand Khnopff or Franz von Stuck.[87] The perverse trend can be found in paintings by Giovanni Segantini and Ferdinand Hodler,[88] as well as in sculptures by Hermann Obrist and buildings by August Endell; while emancipation manifests itself in the dance performances of Loïe Fuller and Isadora Duncan, true *sculptures vivantes*,[89] and in the artworks of Fidus and Heinrich Vogeler.[90]

Within this taxonomy, and alongside Behrens's own emblematic, intertwined kiss, another figure that came to define *Jugendstil* was the impossible couple, lovers locked in a kind of contiguity but without any actual bodily contact.[91] The juxtaposition of gestures and looks is perhaps best illustrated by the painting *L'amour des âmes* (The Love of Souls, 1900) by the Belgian symbolist Jean Delville. Benjamin found the same symptoms of closeness without consummation in Ibsen: "Motif of infertility: Ibsen's women characters don't sleep with their men; they go 'hand in hand' with them to encounter something terrible."[92] The corresponding geometry of *Jugendstil* is a conjugality only through proximity, also understood through that other Art Nouveau leitmotiv, *Sehnsucht*, variously translated as longing, nostalgia, regret, or aspiration, a category that was simultaneously moral and aesthetic, lyrical and visual. The German verb *sehnen* (to long for somebody or something) describes the tortures of a soul shaken by repressed desires, the violent effects of which generate a powerful source of energy.[93] This energy drew the attention of a number of *Jugendstil* commentators, notably Sternberger, who, in evoking the image of the couple platonically united but living separately, considered *sehnen* as capable of generating abstract vibrations or even "graphic waves" filling empty space.[94] The interior, in this way, becomes a receptacle for a heady atmosphere of humors, affections, and feelings, and the social confusion and awkwardness that generate this atmosphere soon become the subject of a number of artists and writers, including Edith Wharton, whose short story "The Fullness of Life" (1891) evokes an architecture of frustrated aspirations:

4.6
Heinrich Vogeler, "The Fable of Melusine," engraved
from a drawing in pen, c. 1902; in *Deutsche Kunst
und Dekoration* 5, no. 7 (Darmstadt, April 1902), 306.
Courtesy of ETH-Bau Library.

4.7
Heinrich Vogeler, "Dreams," engraved drawing in
pen, c. 1902; in *Deutsche Kunst und Dekoration* 5,
no. 7 (Darmstadt, April 1902), 311. Courtesy of
ETH-Bau Library.

4.8
Carl Max Rebel, "The Victorious," 1901; in *Deutsche Kunst und Dekoration* 5, no. 6 (Darmstadt, March 1902), 273. Courtesy of ETH-Bau Library.

> *But I have sometimes thought that a woman's nature is like a great house full of rooms: there is the hall, through which everyone passes in going in and out; the drawing room, where one receives formal visits; the sitting-room, where the members of the family come and go as they list; but beyond that, far beyond, are other rooms, the handles of whose doors are never turned; no one knows the way to them, no one knows whither they lead; and in the innermost room, the holy of holies, the soul sits alone and waits for a footstep that never comes.* [95]

For Wharton, as for so many other frustrated "bourgeoises," the female body is like a great house in which certain rooms remain unexplored—a resignation to the idea of abandonment. The aristocratic *enfilade* of rooms leads only to hysteria, and that most secret room, the *sancta sanctorum*, always remains symbolically empty. [96] As a consequence, the interiors of middle-class houses were organized like a patient's body, with rooms as metaphors for affects. The domestic space was composed of both erogenic and hysteriogenic zones. The effects of *Sehnsucht* are like a progressive accumulation of potential energy, similar to actual electric and magnetic charges. These energies are of two types, organically emitted and artificially induced. Caught between the natural and the artificial, these vital energies are the root of this eroticization of spaces and can lead to the convulsions of hysteria. [97]

Similarly, what unites the individual and interconnected episodes of symbolism, Art Nouveau, expressionism, and the crystalline works of Paul Scheerbart and Bruno Taut seems to be the physical transformation of diverse energies into tangible forms. [98] For example, Hermann Obrist's biomorphic drawing *Fantastic Blossom* (1896) represents the crystallization of an erotic spasm. [99] In the Elvira photographic studio in Munich, designed by August Endell

4.9
Carl Max Rebel, "While Longing," 1902; in *Deutsche
Kunst und Dekoration* 5, no. 6 (Darmstadt, March
1902), 272. Courtesy of ETH-Bau Library.

4.10
Gustav Klimt, "Aspiration for Joy Finds Its Consolation in Poetry" ["Die Sehnsucht nach Glück findet Stillung in der Poesie"], 1902; in *Deutsche Kunst und Dekoration* 5, no. 10 (Darmstadt, July 1902), 513. Courtesy of ETH-Bau Library.

(1896–1897), a web of fluid ornaments animates the façades and the interior.[100] In Loïe Fuller's pavilion built for the 1900 World Fair in Paris, the sculptor Pierre Roche (together with the architect Henri Sauvage) made walls as wavy as a veil, imitating the movements of the famous dancer's clothes.[101] In the Hôtel Max Hallet in Brussels (1902) designed by Victor Horta, brick, stone, wood, metal, and glass all appear as molten, and the rear façade overlooking the garden swells and dilates into three bulging bay windows to form a tripartite greenhouse.[102] And in *Münchhausen und Clarissa* (1906), the "Berlin novel" by Scheerbart,[103] the idea of remodeling space by means of removable partition walls is brought into play.[104] Integral to each of these *Jugendstil* exemplars is their allegiance to the qualities of mobility and transparency, but underpinning them all is also a kind of synthetic hybridization. This hybridization followed early-twentieth-century experiments in the remodeling of animal morphology and applied it to architecture, so as to create a kind of panplasticity in built forms understood as alive. The new rules governing art and architecture in 1900 were therefore simultaneously natural, abiding by laws of thrust and growth, ebb and flow, and fundamentally committed to a certain artifice in creating monsters—or, as Sternberger put it, "everything here is transforming into anything."[105]

Benjamin eventually tried to come up with an original interpretation of *Jugendstil* as "a first attempt to reckon with the open air. . . . This birth of *plein air* from the spirit of the interior is the sensuous expression of the situation . . . *Jugendstil* is the dream that one has come awake."[106] Taking this proposition literally, the buildings of Art Nouveau should be considered as "open-air architecture," or, as Rilke put it (preoccupied as he was by the *Wellenschlag* motif), the wave should form the only canopy: "That is the longing: to dwell midst the waves / and have no homeland in time."[107] Such an aspiration is precisely illustrated by the

4.11
Victor Horta, bay windows at the Hôtel Max Hallet,
Brussels, 1902. Photo by the author.

4.12
Victor Horta, bay windows at the Hôtel Max Hallet,
Brussels, 1902. Photo by the author.

4.13
Stained-glass window by Raphaël Évaldre, based on a
drawing by Henri Privat-Livemont, in the living room
of the residence of the architect Paul Saintenoy, Hôtel
Paul Saintenoy, 123 rue de l'Arbre Bénit, Brussels,
1900. Photo: Christine Bastin and Jacques Evrard.

stained-glass panel in the Brussels living room of the home of the architect Paul Saintenoy. Designed in 1898 by Raphaël Évaldre and Henri Privat-Livemont, and titled *The Wave*, the window merges the characteristic iconography of breaking surf and a woman's flowing curls to form a kind of arabesque. Here, interior and exterior are connected in a kind of topological twist. Situated in an interior, but glazed, the stained-glass panel represents a seaside situation, which is an exterior. All around this exterior architecture in the interior are integrated radiators, lamps and light switches, pipes and taps, iron ribs and glazed surfaces, lending a plant-and-animal-like plasticity to the whole and introducing a series of mutations capable of transforming partition walls into living membranes. By covering the building with a diaphanous skin, Art Nouveau makes the envelope crystalline, providing the astral bodies with an epithelial veil whose transparency could not but please Scheerbart.

5 THE STORY OF AN IDEA

Make a welcome of each door / and a face of each window.
—Aldo van Eyck[1]

At the end of the 1950s, one of the topics emerging almost obses-
sively among Team 10 members was that of the "threshold," or
"doorstep," also called the "meeting place" or the "shape of the in-
between."[2] The Dutch architect Aldo van Eyck first proposed his
theory of the threshold—a discourse on the need for architecture
to reconcile spatial polarities such as inside-outside—in 1959 at
the Congrès Internationaux d'Architecture Moderne (CIAM) 11
meeting in Otterlo, the Netherlands. Subsequently, in the Dutch
architectural magazine *Forum*, he published photographs of traditional habitation to illustrate keywords and leitmotivs, such
as "das Reich des Zwischen" ("the realm of the in-between"), or
"la plus grande réalité du seuil" ("the greater reality of the doorstep").[3] As an instance, such icons included images of dignified
children sitting on a mud-built step, in front of a dwelling in
some unidentified locale. Van Eyck (and some of his friends) developed the theory of the threshold by borrowing from an array
of heterogeneous literature that included popular Western metaphysics. Van Eyck was also one of the first designers to introduce
work on "primitive" architecture, citing, for instance, the writings of Franz Boas, one of the first ethnolinguists to focus on the

unconscious nature of cultural phenomena and to situate the locus of such structures within the realm of language, which became an inspiration to the French intellectual movement called "structuralism." Van Eyck's architectural school was often ambiguously defined as one of *Strukturalismus*, which appears to have been a reference to the doctrine of linguistic structuralism. To understand how this term came to be associated with van Eyck's work, one must map the context of various trends leading to the "anthropologization" of architectural discourses in the 1960s. Taking into account recent scholarship that has cast new light on van Eyck's work, a more theoretical reflection will help to illustrate the cultural background in which the notion of "threshold" appeared, to show this "ethnologization" of the discourse was construed, and to show the ambiguities that presided over the idea's birth.

The story of how "threshold" entered the vocabulary of architects begins with theologian and philosopher Martin Buber's notion of the "in-between." Since the publication of Buber's best-selling *I and Thou* in 1936, his existentialist philosophy had been well received, even influencing architects and town planners. In his foreword to Erwin Anton Gutkind's *Community and Environment: A Discourse on Social Ecology* (1953), Buber writes: "The architects must be given the task to build for human contact, to build an environment which invites human meetings and centers which give these meetings meaning and render them productive."[4] This humanist plea was immediately absorbed by the organizers of CIAM, such as José Luis Sert, and by Jacqueline Tyrwhitt, a follower and editor of Patrick Geddes and a founder of the discipline of urban planning.[5] Furthermore, at a 1954 meeting to prepare for the next CIAM conference in Dubrovnik, Croatia, in 1956, Sigfried Giedion made a plea for a new humanism, invoking Buber's dialogic theme: "The demand for the re-establishment of the relation between 'you' and 'me' leads

5.1
"The In-between Realm" ("Das Reich des Zwischen"),
photograph by Ernst Haas, *Forum*, no. 8, issue
on "Drempel en ontmoeting—de gestalte van het
tussen" / "Threshold and Meeting—The Shape of the
In-between," ed. Joop Hardy and Herman Hertzberger
(October 1959), 249–284, esp. 251. Courtesy
Jurriaan van Stigt, *Forum* archive.

to radical changes in the structure of the city." Such a summoning would inspire the English title of Giedion's 1958 book: *Architecture, You and Me*.[6] And during the eleventh and last CIAM meeting in 1959 in Otterlo, van Eyck, a core member of Team 10, quoted the Buberian slogan "Das Gestalt Gewordene Zwischen" ("the in-between that has taken shape"),[7] and asked architects to be aware of "defined in-between places, which induce simultaneous awareness of what is significant on either side," thereby providing "the common ground where conflicting polarities can again become twin phenomena."[8]

In recent years, Francis Strauven has demonstrated van Eyck's connection to Buber's work, based on texts published in *Forum*.[9] In various issues, the theme of the "threshold" was theorized by both van Eyck and Joop Hardy, who cited Buber's definition of the realm of the in-between as the "bearer of inter-human events."[10] In his 1951 *Urdistanz und Beziehung*, a book on "original distance" and relationships, Buber defines art as the "witness to the relationship between humans and nature." This relationship would form the basis of van Eyck's notion of a spatial dialectic, which would be achieved by incorporating the reality of "dual phenomena." With objects and commodities having been arbitrarily divided by the emphasis on efficient production in the technological age, the "dual phenomena"[11] offered a basic principle that provided for a twin reality in which things would find a reconciled gestalt: the threshold.[12] Through readings of Kant, Kierkegaard, Nietzsche, Bergson, and Heidegger, Buber outlined what has been labeled a philosophy of the in-between in his various books, from *Ich und Du* (1923), to *Between Man and Man* (1947), to his anthology *Dialogishes Leben* (1947). The English translation of *Ich und Du*, titled *I and Thou*, was reprinted multiple times, even becoming a textbook for architects and planners.[13]

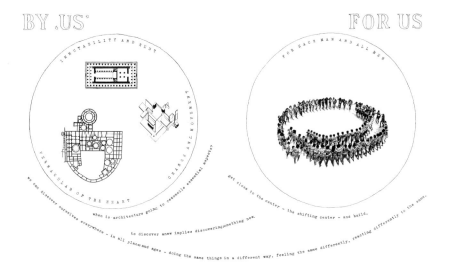

BY .US'   FOR US

5.2
Aldo van Eyck, Otterlo circles, CIAM 11, Otterlo,
1959, detail of a second version, in van Eyck, *The
Child, the City, and the Artist*, manuscript of 1962.
Left: the Parthenon, Pueblo Arroyo in New Mexico
(eleventh century), a contra-construction of van
Doesburg; right: dancing group of Kayapo Indians from
the Orinoco basin in Venezuela. Image © Aldo van
Eyck Archive.

Such an ontology of the interval or "between" is a philosophy of intersubjectivity.[14] Buber's thinking is based on real communication between human beings, hence his emphasis on dialogue, which he characterizes as *Zwiesprache*, the "double speech" of the given and the received. This is a prelude to the double tonality of the soul's "exhalation" and "inhalation"—or its inspiration.[15] In the now famous 1960 issue of *Forum* on the "Door and Window," van Eyck would develop the concept of the in-between as conceived "in the image of man," and propose that, like man himself, the in-between must "breathe both in and out."[16] This respiratory idea is repeated, conjuring "the breathing image" of architecture, when he asks the vital question: "Man still breathes both in and out. When is architecture going to do the same?"[17] This image derives from Buber, inasmuch as the physical act of breathing refers to the response of the *I* to the *Thou*, a pneumatic system that offers not only respiratory metaphors, but also the foundation of a theory of the human spirit, the *pneuma* (breath, spirit). Such is the dialogical force of relation.

For Buber, there are two levels of relations between the subject and the world, the "I-It," and the "I-Thou."[18] In his ontology, the world of objects, defined by the I-It relation, appears as a separate entity, a relation that leads to a world of disconnection. The introduction of the I-Thou dimension, alongside or below that of the I-It, creates a mysterious, quasi-mystical, and subjective force: the double fold (*Zwiefalt*) of the I. The *Zwiefalt* is a bifurcation of the self, established by the dual structure of a totality (I-Thou) together with the multiplicity of separation (I-It). To some, the privileging of the I-Thou duality raised some doubts. Buber's collaborator, Franz Rosenzweig, thought that while Buber's recognition of the role of the "Thou" was groundbreaking, it was at the expense of the "It."[19] Buber's "anthropology" is fundamentally the relation between man and man, a meeting or happening, an occurrence that defines the sphere of the between, of the interhuman (*das Zwischenmenschliche*), which unfolds as the "dialogical."[20] Buber calls the interval between I and Thou the *Zwischen* (in-between), which he sees as the locus where being is realized.[21] Because it is always novel and newly experienced, this meeting takes the form of a constantly renewed occurrence. It is distinguished from the silent dialogue of the mind, and, unlike the mind, does not happen in abstract space.

In Buber's pure spiritualism of dialogue, one might ask if the interval, or the in-between, is not revealed by the consciousness of the *relation*, which he calls either the *Beziehung* (relationship) or *Umfassung* (enclosure, totality). The philosopher does not offer a clear indication of how a state of relation differs from a state of consciousness; moreover, in Buber's work it is difficult to distinguish a relationship from an idealistic, pure conscience. Because man deals with the real world, one must define not only the terms of a spiritual dialogue but also the possibility of a *separation* between the individual and the whole. As Emmanuel Levinas writes: "[Buber] has not taken separation seriously enough."[22]

Even if Buber's idea of betweenness functions philosophically as a category of being, "Man" is still its locus. Having distanced himself from the anonymous world of things, Man is put at the center of being. Thus, Buber's philosophy can be read as anthropology, which is probably why it so easily permeated the readings of architects like Giedion and van Eyck in the 1950s and 1960s. As Michel Foucault would later make clear, anthropology does not refer to the study of various, exterior world cultures, but to the problematic objects of the human condition and its finitude in Western philosophy. "Anthropology," which puts Man at its center, was not an invention of a sixteenth-century scholar during the Renaissance, but a biased manipulation of French and German historians during the late nineteenth century.[23]

How was this ontology of betweenness translated into an aesthetic or architectural theory? To begin to formulate an answer, one has to return to van Eyck's essay in the "Door and Window" issue of *Forum*: "Whatever space and time mean, place and occasion mean more. / For space in the image of man is place, and time in the image of man is occasion."[24] This operation is a "similarity," which is to be understood in a "structural" way: for van Eyck, a building should present a structural analog to the human being, and include anthropomorphic pairings, such as (breathing) in and out, front and back, spirit and body.[25] The source for this theory is again in Buber's thinking; he referred to the theory of imitation—mimesis—in the arts. For Buber, as for van Eyck, while man is made in the image of God, space is made in the image of man. Accordingly, architecture functions in a system of imitation, with each level of similarity, or analogy, "imitating" the next, from the scale of the theological to the anthropological. Since the Greek canon and the work of Vitruvius, an intrinsic aspect of the Western tradition has been to embed human proportions in buildings. Buber's source seems to be located in the many references to architecture made by Saint Thomas Aquinas: what the architect is to the building he erects, God is to the world he creates. Aquinas called the comparison between the realms of the divine and created worlds an "analogy." An analogy enables an appeal to the community between the divine and the created worlds, displaying what they have in common, while preserving their incomparable difference. For Aquinas, the analogy of "God/architecture" shows that the architect is actually an *analogon* of the created world, not so much in terms of harmony and proportions, but inasmuch as architecture bases itself on causes and principles that are imposed and felt throughout the whole of creation.[26]

Many twentieth-century architects, including van Eyck, based their "theory" on a modern version of Aristotle's *mimesis* and Aquinas's *analogy*. Through Buber's popularized theology, van Eyck appropriated the language of traditional Western metaphysics and its particular theoretical vocabulary and terminology, or conceptual array. An example of this "metaphysics" is van Eyck's belief that the work of art, whether concrete or abstract, is to be considered through its representative capacity—that is, it consists of an appearance, which refers to a reality that serves as a model. Van Eyck's theory stands by the Buberian aesthetic regime, which in turn is aligned with Aristotle's "poetic" representation: the oeuvre is both *mimêsis praxeôs* (imitation of an action) and *mimêsis physeôs* (imitation of nature), and is thus caught in the long chain of resemblance and similarity that would be repeatedly taught by the scholastic tradition.[27] (While there were "structural" analyses and critiques of *mimêsis* in rhetoric, literature, and the visual arts in France during the 1960s—by Roland Barthes, Gérard Genette, and Louis Marin, to name a few—van Eyck and his contemporary critics seem to have known nothing of them.)[28]

Van Eyck's metaphors for space are based on such a metaphysical onto-theology. Space, as it were, becomes the receptacle and fundamental meeting place for all humans. Instead of pointing toward brutal spatial contrasts, such as the harsh forms of postwar modernist urban developments, architecture should develop itself as a double entity—that is, as a dual or "twin phenomenon"—that brings the dialogic sides into contact, and reconciles their opposing forces. It is an architecture of reconciliation. *Space* and *time*, created "in the image of man," become *place* and *event*. There is an affinity between the notion of place and the notion of the in-between, both occurring between the polarities of inside and outside, here and there, small and large, part and whole, house and city, form and structure, and so forth.[29] Indeed, van Eyck's entire oeuvre, from the Municipal Orphanage (Amsterdam, 1955–1960) to the Pastor van Ars Roman Catholic Church in Loosduinen (The Hague, 1964–1969), is embedded in anthropomorphic references and shaped by a poetry of betweenness.[30] It is possible to view the nave of the Via Sacra, cutting through the two main parts of the van Ars Church, as a precise illustration of Buberian in-between theory.[31] For van Eyck, space in the image of man signifies that modern architecture must interiorize through its very form(s) the "perceiving, moving and relating subjects."[32] In this way, buildings are "brought to life by their inhabitants."[33] Such an assertion is a strong statement, but one is left with a series of questions about the in-between. If an interval occurs in space, creating a place and offering an event, is such a hiatus to be defined by "things" (inside/outside, large-scale/small-scale, house/city), by "subjects" (humans, divinities), or by both? With van Eyck, as with Buber, one has a sense of dissatisfaction with the definition of the in-between, as it fluctuates from the physical realm of things to the subjective domain of meeting places for people.

Some answers can be found in early-twentieth-century ethnology, specifically in the work of Arnold van Gennep, whose *Rites of Passage* (1908) describes the different phases of initiations in various societies. In chapter six, he focuses on natural features that mark a territory, such as a stake, a portal, or an upright rock (a milestone or landmark).[34] He describes types of thresholds in a village, house, and temple: "The door is a boundary between the foreign and domestic worlds in the case of an ordinary dwelling, between the profane and sacred worlds in the case of a temple."[35] To cross a threshold, van Gennep adds, means uniting oneself with a new world. It is thus an important act in marriage, adoption, ordination, and funeral ceremonies. More generally, van Gennep calls the rites of separation from a previous world *pre-liminal* rites (from the Latin, *prae*, before, and *limen*, threshold or limit), those performed during the transitional stage *liminal* rites, and the ceremonies of incorporation into the new world *post-liminal* rites. He cites, for example, the isolated portal in the fortified city that gave rise to monuments

5.3
View of Aldo van Eyck's Municipal Orphanage
(Burgerweeshuis), Amsterdam, 1955–1960, "a house
like a tiny city," the plan of which was presented at
Otterlo in 1959, and the building of which would win
worldwide admiration. Photo by the author.

5.4
Aldo van Eyck, Pastor van Ars Roman Catholic Church,
Loosduinen, 1968–1969, Via Sacra, detail of skylight.
Photo by the author.

such as the Roman triumphal arch. In another example, he related how orthodox Jews touch a mezuzah with two fingers when passing through a doorway. Van Gennep's *Rites* became especially well known after its 1960 English translation. Joseph Rykwert, a Polish-born British scholar, was familiar with van Gennep and was also an acquaintance of van Eyck. In the magazine *Forum*, which he now directed, van Eyck became the first editor to publish Rykwert's study on "The Idea of a Town" in 1963.[36]

In his analysis of foundation rites of antiquity, Rykwert quoted van Gennep regarding standing stones, the protection of houses and property, and in reference to the double, apotropaic function of the labyrinth and the *templum* as both regenerative and protective, excluding and containing all sorts of menaces.[37] While recounting the history of city foundations during the Etruscan and early Roman periods, Rykwert attempted to show that the original urban design was a reflection of the inhabitants' cosmic conception, and that the foundation (*inauguratio*) was a ritual reenactment of the world's creation (or inauguration). Furthermore, the rites enacted during the establishment of cities and temples, as well as the division of land into four parts, the ceremonial plowing, and so forth, were aimed at reaffirming a state of equilibrium, at balancing cosmic opposites, the reconciliation of which was to be inscribed on the land and commemorated by the rituals of recurrent festivals.

Rykwert's "The Idea of a Town" also relied on a whole set of dissimilar sources, published between the 1930s and 1940s, which give a divergent meaning to his essay: namely, the mythologies of Carl Jung; the Indo-European mythography of the French philologist Georges Dumézil; the mystical symbolism of the cupola as described by the French academic Louis Hautecœur; and the history of religions by the Romanian Mircea Eliade. Jung, the famous founder of so-called depth psychology, developed the theory of archetypes by studying the Pueblo Indians of New Mexico

The idea of a town

By Joseph Rykwert

FORUM VOOR ARCHITECTUUR EN DAARMEE VERBONDEN KUNSTEN · Nr. 3 · 1963

5.5
Cover of *Forum*, no. 3 (1963), showing a curved
labyrinth reproduced from a coin of Knossos (fifth
century BC), the issue including Joseph Rykwert's text
"The Idea of a Town." Courtesy Jurriaan van Stigt,
Forum archive.

and Arizona from 1924 to 1925, while also attempting to determine their nature in Gnosticism, folklore, and the literature of alchemy.[38] In 1941, Jung would publish his *Introduction to a Science of Mythology*, together with Karl Kerényi, a professor of classical philology. Interestingly, the young van Eyck attended Jung's lectures at the Federal Institute of Technology (ETH) in Zurich when Jung was a professor on the Faculty of Philosophy and Political Sciences (1933–1942).[39]

In a conversation about van Eyck, Rykwert confirmed his interest in the theory of archetypes, saying that both of them "always agreed . . . that [architecture] has to do with what you believe about life and death, the way you see society cohere, the way institutions fix certain social notions, the way these notions are represented . . . to the outside world. This approach finally aims at the reconstitution of the architectural object . . . , a connecting with, incorporating, assuming certain archetypical forms."[40] Here Jung's "collective (or impersonal) unconscious" appears; this was constitutive of the human psyche as a congenital condition of intuition, or archetypes.[41] In "The Idea of a Town" Rykwert also mentions Dumézil's renowned theory of the division of the three functions (sovereignty and religion, warfare, and production) that one could supposedly discover in the language, social hierarchy, and mythology of every Indo-European population.[42] Dumézil was a close friend of Mircea Eliade, one of the founders of religious studies in academia.[43] Rykwert would use Eliade's history of religions to propel his underlying thesis that religious experience is a universal and autonomous phenomenon: "I may not have made sufficiently clear that I am touching on one of the great commonplaces of religious experience."[44] Writing about the foundational rite of plowing as a hierogamy, a sacred marriage between earth and sky, Rykwert insists: "The earth is the great mother whose fertility is increased by tilling and ploughing," with a reference to Eliade, and a further insistence on the universality of religious phenomenology: "This is true for many cultures, maybe for most."[45] Today, it is just such a belief in the universality of religions' facts that would be put into question.

It must be noted that a common feature unifies all the aforementioned authors: a connection to conservative thinking. As is well known, Jung accepted the co-presidency of the General Medical Society for Psychotherapy (Allgemeine Ärztliche Gesellschaft für Psychotherapie), a German-based professional association, from 1933 to 1939, and concealed his religion of an Aryan-only cult of redemption and rebirth.[46] Hautecœur was a high functionary in the Vichy regime,[47] and Eliade's extreme-right involvement is now well documented.[48] Finally, while the prewar monarchist engagement of Dumézil has been revealed, he has also been accused—arguably without much justification—of past sympathies for Nazi ideas.[49] Like many, Rykwert probably came to know of all those unsavory associations only in a later period, and he himself had no apparent reason to sympathize with extreme right politics. However, what hovers in "The Idea of a Town," like incense's persistent odor in a sacristy, is a general "mystical" tone, together with an ahistorical belief in the universality of symbolism and a pervasive conviction that religion is a *sui generis* phenomenon, an inclination reinforced by the comparison of Roman foundation rites with the Indian mandala.[50] Perhaps Rykwert was already perceiving the entrapment that so-called "religious sciences" had created around his thesis; this would explain why he opens up the last part of his scholarly essay to ethnology, a field introduced in his discussion of African foundation rites described by the German anthropologist Leo Frobenius,[51] and the analysis of the diagram of a Bororo settlement in Amazonia, borrowed from Claude Lévi-Strauss's bestseller *Tristes tropiques*.[52] This shift certainly would have appealed to van Eyck more than any adherence to a Jungian creed.[53]

Rykwert's expanded study would become a book of the same name in 1976.[54] In this later version, the author adds comparisons with the Dogon's art and rituals in West Africa, the mythic model of the city in archaic China, and other examples. However, in the "analogical" chapters Rykwert persists in focusing on the permanence of the "cosmological structure" throughout the history of humanity. He submits the hypothesis of "irreducible elements" as a fundamental pattern of human essence, appearing to be so recurrent in the most varied of circumstances that these elements must reside in the biological structure of mankind. Quite abruptly, mythography, ethnology, psychology—and now biology—are introduced, as if to uphold and give credibility to the "anthropological" project. In fact, sciences are introduced to give force to a project that is not far from what anthropological linguistics, under the label of "structuralism," had attempted to accomplish in the 1950s and 1960s. The whole book is organized in a double, or even triple, schema: first, "classical" or Greco-Roman archaeology; second, readings in religious symbolism, the pervasive "sacred sciences" and (extremely reactionary) exoteric knowledge; and, finally, a set of sources that, broadly speaking, belongs to the realm of structuralism. But was *The Idea of a Town* a "structuralist" project? In mixing disparate sources and approaches, Rykwert's endeavor risks losing its coherence along the way. Nevertheless, in that last section, one is reassured to find what a scholar of the 1960s and 1970s would be expected to have read: pioneers in linguistics such as Ferdinand de Saussure and Roman Jakobson; Émile Benveniste's volumes on linguistics and Indo-European institutions; Jean-Pierre Vernant's "structural" research on Greek mythology; André Leroi-Gourhan's volumes on the paleography of technology, and so forth. In addition to extensive considerations of the "sacred" dimension in human cultures, there is a discourse, which—very discreetly—hooks up to the structuralist paradigm in almost a shy way, and subsequently sets this mass of information in motion. However, by the time Rykwert's book was published, structuralism was a thing of the past. This brings us to the vexing question of terminology. Van Eyck's school in the Netherlands was often characterized as "structuralism in architecture," referring to the work of John Habraken, Herman Hertzberger, Joop van Stigt, and Piet Blom, who formed the so-called "configurative" movement.[55] Arnulf Lüchinger, their spokesman, opens his 1981 book *Structuralism in Architecture and Urban Planning* with a chapter on "structural" thinking, which begins with a reference to the work of Lévi-Strauss.[56] However, the work of the anthropologist is not actually taken up seriously, and structuralism becomes just an easy label, a new brand promoted by these architects. Comically, the formula of structuralism is opposed to existentialism, poles that are translated into the notions of constraint (structure) versus freedom (existence). To buttress this theoretical gem, van Eyck's 1959 Otterlo lectures are cited, including the idea of dual or twin phenomena, as a prop that could reconcile the epic struggle of "constraint" versus "freedom." Already, around 1960 and until 1968, structuralism had left the desks of academia and become a media phenomenon, part of the *doxa* and fodder for fashion and journalism.

As Jean-Claude Milner has argued, the structuralist paradigm's achievement consisted in integrating objects belonging to culture into the realm of "hard," exact, and Galilean sciences, which were originally developed in connection to nature. Starting with linguistics, the "mother" of all human sciences, the paradigm will subsequently be applied to many domains of knowledge, and, as a result, will displace both ancient oppositions and modern ones, such as nature/history, or nature/culture. It was the Greeks who opposed *phusis* (that which refers to nature) to the *thesis* (which broadly denotes all that is human: mores, usages, customs, laws, society, history, and culture). To

5.6
Piet Blom, "The Kasbah" (1966–1974), housing
project, Hengelo, The Netherlands. Photo by the author.

phusis belonged that which did not depend on the collective human will, but pertained to the regular order of the world. To *thesis* belonged that which was dependent on humanity's collective will.[57] During the twentieth century, there seemed to be some difficulty created by the great polarity that developed between the sciences of nature (hard sciences) and the sciences of man (humanities and social sciences). For structuralism, there was no dilemma. Everything that had belonged to the field of *thesis* could be made the object of science, without reducing the field of *thesis* to that of *phusis*, which would have introduced a naturalization of culture.

Starting in the 1950s and inspired by political economy, ethnology, and sociology, the scientific program of Lévi-Strauss was derived in particular from nineteenth-century comparative grammars of Indo-European languages, and the linguistics of Saussure, Troubetzkoy, Jakobson, and Benveniste. Those disciplines enabled him to assert a theory of *différence* (as opposed to similarity and analogy), demonstrated through the privileged subject matter of language, kinship and parenthood, marriage, myth, tales, eating manners, costumes, ornaments, tools and instruments, and so on.[58] For the "structural" anthropologist, segments of reality, which could be grasped by *différence*, belonged to realms of exchange and communication.[59] To consider the field of culture as the domain of exchange (and/or communication) will bear significant consequences at the level of later theory.[60] The relation between nature and culture will be altered; a theory of knowledge will appear through applying empirical methods to data analysis and processing; and ultimately, a new ontology of being and identity will spread, reshuffling the correlation between the One, the Same, and the Other.

It should be clear that in no way did van Eyck's thought ever pertain to a "structuralist" methodology; and the reconciled dialectics of the Buberian I-Thou does not belong to the binary

UNE MAISON

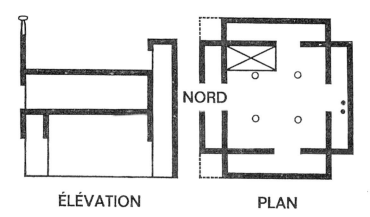

ÉLÉVATION   PLAN

5.7

Plan and elevation (*sic*) of a house, Dogon land,
Mali; in Marcel Griaule (1898–1956), *Dieu d'eau,
entretiens avec Ogotemmêli* (Paris: Éditions du
Chêne, 1948); Griaule, *Dieu d'eau: entretiens avec
Ogotemmêli* (Paris: Fayard, 1966), 103. Courtesy
Fayard.

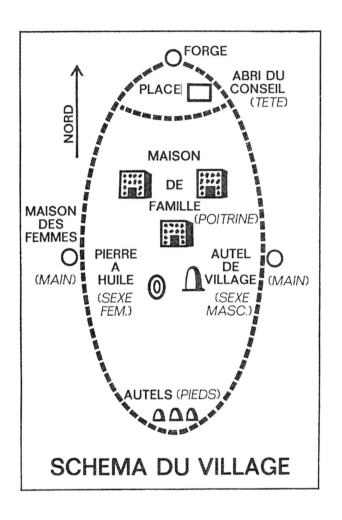

FORGE

ABRI DU
CONSEIL
(TETE)

PLACE

NORD

MAISON

DE

FAMILLE

(POITRINE)

MAISON
DES
FEMMES

(MAIN)

PIERRE
A
HUILE
*(SEXE
FEM.)*

AUTEL
DE
VILLAGE
*(SEXE
MASC.)*

(MAIN)

AUTELS *(PIEDS)*

SCHEMA DU VILLAGE

5.8
Schematic plan of a village, Dogon land, Mali; in
Marcel Griaule, *Dieu d'eau, entretiens avec Ogotemmêli*
(Paris: Éditions du Chêne, 1948); Griaule, *Dieu d'eau:
entretiens avec Ogotemmêli* (Paris: Fayard, 1966),
103. Courtesy Fayard.

operators that linguistics and structural anthropology were practicing. In his reference to the Other, van Eyck's genial intuition consisted in the introduction of exterior cultures studied through various volumes of ethnography, including Marcel Griaule's report on the Dogon of Western Africa, published in *Minotaure* (1933), the surrealist magazine van Eyck read during the war,[61] and Ruth Benedict's study of the Pueblos of the Amerindians of New Mexico.[62] During the winter of 1961, van Eyck visited Taos pueblo in New Mexico, subsequently writing an article on "The Pueblos," published in *Forum* in 1962.[63]

Like Lévi-Strauss, van Eyck's sources are Griaule and the French school of ethnology, but van Eyck does not go on to interpret them in a structuralist manner. Instead, in a startling way, these readings, and his trips to West Africa in 1960 and to the Zuñi pueblos in 1961, confirmed for van Eyck the Buberian dialogical theory.[64] Van Eyck's discourse and knowledge had nothing to with "structuralism" proper (Lévi-Strauss's "structural anthropology"); van Eyck was using the French school of ethnology's studies of the Dogon before the advent of structuralism to confirm Buberian metaphysics, which he in turn interpreted as an anthropological philosophy. This work has been the source of much historical confusion about van Eyck and his relationship to anthropology.

Together with the architect Herman Haan (1914–1996),[65] van Eyck and his wife traveled to observe the Dogon; they were familiar with Montserrat Palau Marti's book *Les Dogon*,[66] but presumably had not read Griaule's seminal work *Dieu d'eau* (1948).[67] When they reached the land of the Dogon, they met Paul Parin, his wife Goldy Parin-Matthey, and Fritz Morgenthaler, three psychoanalysts from Zurich who were attempting to psychoanalyze the Dogon in their search for the universal existence of Freud's Oedipus complex. The three ethno-psychoanalysts, fully aware of Griaule's studies, acted as intermediaries for the

5.9
Herman Haan, "The Pyramids" (1970–1972), student
accommodation, Technical University, Twente campus,
Drienerlo, The Netherlands. Photo by the author.

van Eycks, explaining what Griaule and his school had discovered, but, presumably, without fully revealing their sources. In 1963, they published their book in German with the alluring title *Whites Think Too Much*, a volume translated into French in 1966 and read both by specialists and by many eager students circa May 1968.[68] In 1963, van Eyck began another issue of *Forum* (which would not be published until 1967), for which Parin and Morgenthaler contributed two essays.[69] Subsequently, both essays were translated and published under a new English heading, "A Miracle of Moderation," in the periodical *Via* at the University of Pennsylvania in 1968; and, in 1969, in *Meaning in Architecture*, edited by Charles Jencks and George Baird.[70] The ideas and sources of Griaule and his school are not mentioned in the *Via* articles, or in the book by Jencks and Baird. Was omitting the mention of Griaule's school a simple blunder by the editors, or was the absence of the footnotes significant?

In the study of the Dogon civilization, ethnographers had seen that each village was perceived as "an organ of the landscape body," and that "each house in turn was thought as an organ of the village."[71] Furthermore, it appeared that since man was himself an organ of the house, there was a permanent interaction between body and organ. The cosmology of the Dogon seemed to ratify and substantiate the particular analogy of landscape/body/organ, while reasserting an organic continuity between nature and culture. For architects like van Eyck, the Dogon's world image was an amazing ratification of the Western system of analogies, which van Eyck had enunciated at Otterlo with the reiteration of his classical credo: "A house must be like a small city if it's to be a real house; a city like a large house if it's to be a real city."[72] Such an isomorphism at the base of his conception received an unexpected confirmation in ethnography.[73] The previous analogy of the city/house was further expanded under another form and in a different guise—the analogy of the city with a tree. At Team 10's meeting at the Abbaye de Royaumont in September 1962, van Eyck said: "Tree is leaf and leaf is tree—House is city and city is house."[74] The first analogy of city/house is strengthened with a second metaphor (or "image," to use the architect's terminology). There is a redoubling of the metaphor, which produces a poetic effect. Far from having a purely rhetorical effect, van Eyck's metaphor is not only illustrative of an idea, but also has the power to create a series of new meanings, becoming what Paul Ricœur has defined as a "living metaphor."[75] Here, the metaphor does not proceed only by resemblance or similarity, but also works at a nonrhetorical level, which can be defined by the poetical, or *poïesis*, meaning production. In this case, the metaphor becomes an image that creates a model via its own dynamic.

For both van Eyck and Rykwert, ethnology came to the rescue of a Western metaphysical discourse. While this discourse was initially met with skepticism by Team 10 members, it eventually became one of the dominant theories in the 1960s and 1970s.[76] Such a new orthodoxy, soon to become part of the *doxa*, would spread through numerous publications, beginning with the final edition of the *Team 10 Primer*, edited by Alison Smithson, and its "Doorstep" section.[77] Afterward, the anthology *Meaning in Architecture*,[78] which includes a text by Rykwert, would become a universal textbook in schools of architecture, leading to the anthropologization of architectural discourse and paving the way for postmodernist thinking.

There is a double coda to this story of an idea. Geneviève Calame-Griaule, daughter of Griaule and herself a specialist on the Dogon, published a critical review in 1969 of Parin, Parin-Matthey, and Morgenthaler's book, reaffirming the principle that one should avoid identifying collective processes with individual ones.[79] Moreover, she observed all sorts of irregularities: that the request for an analysis came from the investigators, not from

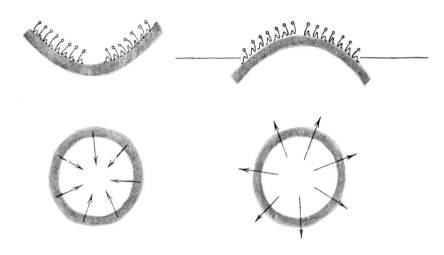

5.10
Aldo van Eyck, "Two kinds of centrality," diagram
illustrating the twin phenomena, a presentation of
"The Wheels of Heaven," van Eyck's unbuilt ecumenical
church project for Driebergen (1963), published in
Domus, May 1965; and in Alison Smithson, ed., *Team
10 Primer* (Cambridge, MA: MIT Press, 1968), 104.
Image © Aldo van Eyck Archive.

tree is
leaf and leaf
is tree - house is
city and city is house
- a tree is a tree but it
is also a huge leaf - a
leaf is a leaf, but it is
also a tiny tree - a city
is not a city unless it
is also a huge house -
a house is a house
only if it is also
a tiny city

say leaf - say tree
say a few leaves still and
many leaves soon - say leafless tree
- say heap of leaves - say this tree
when I grow up and that tree when
I was a child - say one tree, lots of
trees, all sorts of trees, trees in the
forest - say forest (hear: dark, lost,
nest, fire, fairy, owl's hoot, toadstool,
tiger, timber) - say orchard, apples,
apple pie - say fig tree - say fig leaf
- say NUTS! - say house - say
city - say anything - but
say PEOPLE!

5.11
Aldo van Eyck, "Identification of Leaf with Tree,"
original text of 1961, presented at the Team 10
meeting (Abbaye de Royaumont, September 1962);
the handwritten diagram was prepared for *Domus*, May
1965, and published in Alison Smithson, ed., *Team
10 Primer* (Cambridge, MA: MIT Press, 1968), 99.
Image © Aldo van Eyck Archive.

the subjects; that the "patients" were paid, thus assimilated to regular ethnographic informers; and that the interviews were conducted in French with translators, creating a linguistic gap incompatible with orthodox psychoanalysis. And ultimately—some will appreciate the irony—in their *Anti-Oedipus* (1972), Gilles Deleuze and Félix Guattari would use both Parin's and Griaule's oeuvres to demonstrate the nonexistence of an African Oedipus.[80]

6 TOWARD A CYBORG ARCHITECTURE

*Hence, there is coalescence and division, or rather oscillation, a
perpetual exchange between the actual object and its virtual image:
the virtual image never stops becoming actual. . . . This perpetual
exchange between the virtual and the actual is what defines a
crystal; and it is on the plane of immanence that crystals appear. The
actual and the virtual coexist, and enter into a tight circuit which
we are continually retracing from one to the other. This is no longer a
singularization, but an individuation as process, the actual and its
virtual: no longer an actualization but a crystallization.*
—Gilles Deleuze, "The Actual and the Virtual," posthumous,
circa 1985[1]

In 1955, in his celebrated article "The New Brutalism," Reyner
Banham set up a distinction between Platonic geometry and topological design: "As a discipline of architecture topology has
always been present in a subordinate and unrecognized way— . . .
in the Smithsons' Sheffield project [for the 1953 Sheffield University competition] the roles are reversed, topology becomes
the dominant and geometry becomes the subordinate discipline."[2] In fact, in the classifications of topology, "a brick is the
same 'shape' as a billiard ball (unpenetrated solid) and a teacup is
the same 'shape' as a gramophone record (continuous surface with
one hole)."[3] Banham continues: "Such a dominance accorded to

topology . . . is clearly analogous to the displacement of Thomistic [Neoplatonic] 'beauty' by Brutalist 'Image,' and Sheffield remains the most consistent and extreme point reached by any Brutalist in their search for *Une Architecture Autre*."[4] To Banham, the only people in 1960 who seem able to bridge the gap between science and art—that is, between structural engineering and architecture—are "a few liberated spirits . . . notably Lou Kahn with his 'topological' science blocks for the Richards Medical Research Building at the University of Pennsylvania [1957–1962], or Marco Zanuso with his integrated structure-and-air-conditioning schemes."[5] To the extent that Banham defended the notion of an architecture designed to serve—"service architecture"—he valued the approach Zanuso took in his Olivetti factory in Argentina (1956–1964).[6]

One might wonder what exactly the English critic meant by the concept of topology, but a close look at so-called "visionary" architecture might give us some idea.[7] In the 1960s, such topological architecture would in turn be called "fantastic,"[8] "futuristic,"[9] or simply "experimental."[10] During this period, the egg and the crystal formed the two aspects of a process of morphogenesis. In order to support such a hypothesis, one needs to balance considerations of spheres and spheroids (an epigenesis) with those of polygonal forms (a crystallography). The topology in question, then, is what brings together, in space, at membrane level, epigenetic and crystallographic processes. It is noteworthy that Albert Dalcq's book on embryology was the primary source on epigenesis, as much for the designers behind the exhibition "On Growth and Form," held at the Institute of Contemporary Arts in London in 1951,[11] as for Gilles Deleuze.

In fact, Dalcq's epigenesis offered a model for the differentiation/differenciation modus operandi, which was at the heart of Deleuze's thesis. In *Difference and Repetition* (1968), following Gilbert Simondon's theory of individuation, Deleuze attempted to draw a theory of difference, based on biological differentiation, giving a new meaning to the ancient mythologies of the world egg, beginning with Anaximander's cosmic egg: "In order to plumb the intensive depths or the spatium of an egg . . . the potentials and potentialities must be multiplied. The world is an egg. . . . We think that difference of intensity, as this is implicated in the egg, expresses first the differential relations or virtual matter to be organized."[12] The egg metaphor rearticulated the connection between the symbolical and the vital. Among others, Dalcq's morphogenetic embryology[13] and Simondon's theory of individuation helped Deleuze to identify the egg as a vast metaphor of the world

Deleuze will often use the embryo's model to expose the inorganic vitality of tissues, not yet stabilized in the shape of an organ, and capable of multiple transformations: "The body without organs does not lack organs, it simply lacks the organism, that is, the particular organization of organs. The body without organs is thus defined by an indeterminate organ, whereas the organism is defined by determinate organs."[14] In Deleuze's *The Logic of Sense* (1969), everything collapses around the paradigm of Antonin Artaud, whose poetical, schizoid delirium calls for a body beyond its organic determination.[15] For Artaud, the completed organism felt like a form that imprisons the body.[16] During the 1970s, in response to criticism, Deleuze and Guattari explain that they never ask anybody to deprive him-/herself of their organs, but to replace the notion of a full-grown organ by the metamorphic and polymorphic conception of an immature organ while it differentiates. Deleuze's bio-philosophy illustrates the virtuality of intensive forces, while they operate before the organic form is achieved and constituted. What Deleuze and Guattari suggest is a consideration of the virtual axes of informal forces.[17]

From Erwin Schrödinger to Henri Atlan, biological theories have shown that topology and chronology come together in the individuation of the living being.[18] For Simondon, for instance, forms are not given a priori, but embody the very dimensionality of the living being, as the latter is busy individuating.[19] And so the conditions that allow us to theorize about morphogenesis come together. From now on, the genetic processes analyzed by Simondon—those of membranes, or of crystals in their milieu, for example—allow us to rethink the meaning of spatial notions such as inside and outside in an entirely new way. Suddenly, what formed the basis of the traditional categories of space sees its meaning transformed, by transmutation, into a topological contact surface. A (vast) branch of mathematics, topology studies the characteristics of figures, or topological surfaces, such as the Klein bottle, the Möbius strip, or the torus, and, more generally, analyzes the property of objects that are preserved through continuous deformation—whether bending, twisting, or stretching—and can be used to study the abstract, inherent connectivity of objects in any dimensional space while ignoring their detailed form.[20] Of course, several "topological" approaches to architecture and to the city developed

The egg is a primal archetype in Max Bill's sculpture *Continuité* (1946–1947).[21] Three meters high, the concretion takes the form of an endless ribbon, as though an ovoid surface had exploded, launching its membrane into space and then falling back to earth in the form of a Möbius strip.[22] This looped form was later repeated by the architect Luciano Baldessari in his Breda Company Pavilion for the Milan Fair of 1951.[23] As Frederick Kiesler's Endless Theater of 1926 shows, the ovoid form can be thought of as an alternative to the parallelepipedal architecture typical of early modern functionalism. In his 1947 "Manifesto of Correalism," published in *Architecture d'Aujourd'hui* in June 1949, Kiesler, who had by then emigrated to the United States, renewed his attack on "the prison-cube, universal panacea."[24] In relation to the Space House of 1933, Kiesler asserted: "The eggshell is the most remarkable example we know of maximum resistance to external and internal assaults obtained by minimal expenditure of energy."[25] The ovoid is a more solid form than the sphere or the half-sphere (dome). As the French-American industrial designer Raymond Loewy writes in his 1951 autobiography *Never Leave Well Enough Alone*, the egg is "the perfect functional shape. Illustrating the skin tension theory of structural engineering, it is a marvel of design. In spite of its thin shell (7/1000 of an inch), it can support a gradually applied pressure of about twenty pounds without breaking. It is so formed as to create a minimum of friction while progressing through the beast; a good example of streamlining adapted to a slow-moving object. Any other shape—a square, for instance—would make the hen's life intolerable."[26]

The "form follows function" formula has become commonplace for designers. Yet, one might do well to hold on to the notion of a "slow-moving object" adapted to its environment. What is a human being, after all, if not a slow-moving body? This explains the passion for shapes that range between an egg and a sphere: for instance, Nicolas Schöffer's spatiodynamic theater,[27] the plastic experiments of Claude Parent and René Sarger,[28] or the theater referred to as "The Egg," built by Wallace K. Harrison and Max Abramovitz in Albany, New York (1965–1978).[29]

The engineer and architect René Sarger, who created the French Pavilion at the 1958 world's fair in Brussels, stressed the advantages of the ovoid, noting the dynamics of the forces at work in the egg: "The latter is not just a rigid shell enveloping some nondescript contents. It is the whole combination of container and contents that gives the egg a resistance it would not have if it were simply empty. On top of its outer shell, the egg has a membrane or a sort of very fine-textured 'fabric' that is just as flexible as its shell is rigid. Lastly, forms of inner tension maintain the balance of the whole combination of substances that make up the egg."[30]

Contemporary epigenesis provides us with a precise model for a construction built using a thin-shell, flexible-web material and cable latticework capable of generating a membrane architecture. This is precisely what Frei Otto designed with his tents, "stretched membranes offering storm protection," and his houses, "whose four walls are hung with a fine transparent membrane maintained by air pressure."[31] This does not mean that a house should look like an egg. Kiesler writes that "the ideal house configuration with the highest resistance to external and internal assault is not the ovoid model, but the spheroid: a flattened sphere."[32] Like a pebble polished smooth by the movement of water, such a geometry offers a "monolithic shell," designed by and for the movement of the body through space. No longer the result of an abstract play of volumes assembled in the light, form derives directly from the proprioceptive capacities of the inhabitant, whose moving body is inscribed in space following a "proprio-spatial dynamic."[33]

Kiesler's remarkable biologism should not obscure the fact that it was a trend already being followed by numerous architects: Le Corbusier, before and after the war, and the Finnish architect Alvar Aalto, for example. In 1947, Aalto noted in his essay "The Trout and the Mountain Stream" that

> Architecture is . . . connected in a way to biology. [It is] perhaps like large salmon or trout. . . . They are born many hundreds of miles from their proper living environments. . . . As the fish egg's development into a mature organism requires time, so it also requires time for all that develops and crystallizes in our world of thoughts. Architecture needs this time to an even greater degree than any other creative work.[34]

Such a metaphor, associating eggs (a form of epigenesis) with crystallization, recalls the architect-engineer Auguste Perret's habit of exclaiming about the ostrich egg he had kept in his rue Franklin studio in Paris: "Now, that's perfection for you."[35] Perret also said: "Composition is the art of getting the most complicated services to fit into the simplest volume: an egg."[36]

In his 1954 book *Survival through Design*, Richard Neutra tried to define what he called "biological realism," or "biorealism," as an organic mode of thinking influenced by biology and psychology.[37] A keen reader of Erwin Schrödinger and Norbert Wiener, Neutra was very familiar with the biological theories of the day: "That entire concept of the *environment versus the organism* now seems to experts an abstraction . . . often impractical to operate with. Indeed every cell is the environment of the other cells."[38] Relying by turns on the criminal psychiatry of Cesare Lombroso, the physiological psychology of Wilhelm Wundt, and the theory of conditioned reflexes developed by Ivan Petrovich Pavlov,[39] Neutra inaugurated an organic theory of housing based on the satisfaction of "senses called proprioceptor"[40] and on "what is called stereognosis" (coordination of the senses),[41] capable of satisfying the needs of the human neuro-mental system.[42] Neutra writes: "If architecture is an affair of many senses, the stage assigned to it, space itself, is in fact also a multisensorial product which begins to evolve for us while we are still in the uterus. The *prenatal experiment of shelter*, floating in the evenly warm liquid medium of the mother's womb, is a primary factor molding our later relations to an outer world, and to the architectural compartments that we construct for our later life."[43]

For Neutra, the house's occupant has a somato-aesthetic experience of space, coupled with a sense of direction and of distance acquired after birth with apprehension of the visual and auditory faculties. The archetype of the embryo or the fetus leads the architect to define the physiological and psychological characteristics of space that ultimately should hold sway. Like a soul doctor, or a neurologist, the architect has to design an environment that is good for the nerves, able to attain and maintain a "neural balance."[44] This conviction would lead Neutra to build "glass houses" on the arid ground of southern California, but the many references to a primal form could well have led him to an architecture that was, if not ovoid, then at least matricial and crystalline.[45]

Such primal forms often take the shape of bubbles. The American designer Eliot Noyes, famous for overseeing IBM's image, realized his famous Bubble House at Hobe Sound, Florida, in 1954, by covering a balloon used as formwork in cement.[46] Noyes designed the bubble house using techniques perfected by Wallace Neff in California between 1941 and 1946. Both a wealthy heir and an "architect to the stars," Neff developed the Airform House to meet the urgent demand for housing for ex-soldiers returning from the Second World War. Neff tied a Goodyear rubber balloon to a concrete slab and inflated it, then sprayed the entire surface of the balloon with concrete—the Gunite system. When the operation was finished, the balloon was deflated.[47] (Coincidentally, Neutra's Lovell House had been built out of metal and then covered in a layer of Gunite in 1927–1929.) For Noyes's Bubble House, the sprayed-on concrete was covered with layers of insulation, which were then protected by another layer of sprayed-on concrete.

The "All-Plastic" House, built by the French architect Ionel Schein in 1955, seemed to fulfill the hopes for a biorealist architecture. Schein met with the French Coal Board (Charbonnages de France) and the architect René Coulon through Marguerite Duval, editor in chief of *Elle*, to further his idea.[48] In collaboration with Coulon and the engineer Yves Magnant, Schein then

6.1
Wallace Neff, Neff Residence (Airform),
construction, 1941. Courtesy of Huntington Library,
San Marino, California.

6.2
Wallace Neff, Goodyear (tire and rubber company)
Balloon House (Airform), exterior, no date. Courtesy of
Huntington Library, San Marino, California.

designed an entirely plastic house, from the structure to the furniture. In April 1955, the Architecture Department at the Massachusetts Institute of Technology invited Schein to participate in
their summer program, "Plastics in the Design of Building Products." Shortly after, the World Plastics Fair in Los Angeles asked
him for a prototype for their next exhibition. The house was finally realized and exhibited at the 1956 Salon des Arts Ménagers
(Domestic Housewares and Appliances Show) in Paris, financed
by the French Coal Board and Northern Coalmines (Houillères
du Nord), who used the opportunity to publicize the potential of
plastic materials extracted from coal. Formed around a single,
molded circular core containing the toilet and kitchen units, the
house spirals outward "following the natural form of a shell."[49] All
of the constructional elements—floors, framework, and facings—
constitute a single, monolithic block. Its appendages, containing
the three bedrooms, were designed like an automotive body.

In September 1956, Schein and Coulon drew up plans for a
mobile hotel cabin, the prototype of a plastic housing unit that
was to go on show in December that year. This capsule contained
a double bed that could be folded up during the day, transforming into a sofa and accompanying breakfast table, and a skylit
shower-toilet unit. Accommodating two people, the mini-abode
was fully serviced and could be transported by truck to hotels
needing extra rooms during peak season. The next year, Schein
put forward his project for a mobile library. Banham wrote about
the transportable cells in the *Architectural Review* in early 1960:
"Some of the products envisaged by the French group around
Coulon and Schein call for the off-site fabrication of complete
functional volumes such as bathrooms and kitchens, a procedure which both has structural advantages and makes it possible
to complete most of the fabricating work under controlled, labo-
ratory conditions. The result seems likely to be a house put together from large non-repeating units."[50]

6.3
Ionel Schein (with René Coulon and Yves Magnant),
model of the Plastic-made House, exhibited at the
Salon des Arts Ménagers, Paris, 1956. FRAC Centre
collection, Orléans, France.

In the mad rush to embrace the "all-plastic," British architects Alison and Peter Smithson realized their House of the Future, a life-size model of a plastic house, with definite surrealist overtones, shown in London at the 1956 Ideal Home Exhibition.[51] In 1957, the Americans Richard W. Hamilton and Marvin E. Goody built a House of the Future financed by the Monsanto Company. This house would be exhibited for more than ten years at Disneyland, where it was visited by upward of twenty million people.[52] Meanwhile, the American Sanford Hohauser made a model of a concrete, ovoid seaside house in 1956, while also designing a crystalline ribbed Memorial to the Victims of the Hungarian Uprising.[53] Here, too, epigenesis and crystallography defined the paths morphogenesis would take. In 1959, John M. Johansen drew up his Sprayform House n. 2 in Weston, Connecticut, which, though never built, was to be made from shotcrete using a process derived from Neff's Airform.[54] Johansen was a student of Walter Gropius and Marcel Breuer, and the husband of the Gropiuses' adopted daughter Ati. Banham, of course, did not let slip the opportunity to comment on the radical nature of such a proposition: "Certainly John Johansen's *Airform* [sic] House has the appearance of a radical reversal of attitude."[55] In 1961, the Englishman Arthur Quarmby realized plastic shelters to protect British Railways' electrical relay stations.[56] In 1962, Victor Lundy completed a transportable pavilion for the South American part of the touring exhibition "Atom For Peace," commissioned by the United States Atomic Energy Commission. This was an inflatable architecture, built by Birdaire Structures and comprising two domes with double membranes joined together.[57]

In 1958 a different plastic appeared in *The Blob*, an American movie directed by Irwin S. Yeaworth Jr. It would become a classic example of "camp" aesthetics.[58] Would the hero succeed in ridding the small town of the shapeless monster, an amorphous mass of sticky plastic, a sort of tentacled intestine with amazingly efficient powers of digestion? This creature, in the form of a "blob," perfectly illustrated the spirit of the times, which was translated into architecture by new trends such as the one that produced buildings that "show their guts," or expose their bowels (a trend described as *bowelism*). In the same spirit, the English architect Mike Webb designed offices for the Furniture Manufacturers' Association Building (1957–1958), producing a building that exposed its innards to the eyes of all.[59]

During this period, Charles Vernon Boys's book on the properties of soap bubbles was never out of print.[60] In the United States, Eduardo Catalano published his studies on the geometry of warped surfaces at the Raleigh School of Design in 1958.[61] In Israel, Alfred Neumann, together with his students Zvi Hecker and Eldar Sharon, developed a polyhedral architecture, implemented in the Dubliner Apartments at Ramat Gan in Tel Aviv from 1960 to 1963, followed by his masterpiece, Bat-Yam City Hall, between 1963 and 1969.[62] In the age of space frames and other three-dimensional structures, Neumann, Hecker, and Sharon turned to naturally occurring crystal geometry.[63] Neumann would try to invent a system of harmonious proportion in the arts, which he would then apply in his projects. Known as "the m phi system," it aimed at "humanizing space."[64] It was published by André Bloc in 1956 in one volume in the *Architecture d'Aujourd'hui* series, with a preface by Walter Gropius.[65] On the basis of these models, Neumann would attempt to formulate a theory of "morphological architecture," which he presented at a conference in Canada in 1963: "The morphology of design is analogous to biological morphology. It is also a science in its infancy. But if it agrees to follow scientific methods, we can hope for it to evolve normally. Similarly, in architecture we could follow the transformation in shape and size that each element undergoes from one cell to the next (on aggregate), with the laws of symmetry determining combinative forms."[66]

Seeking a morphological process whose genesis would evoke biological and crystallographic processes, Neumann imagined space via sets of Platonic and Archimedean solids:

> *Architecture is the projection of spatial images in an embodied form. In the development of architectural space, the well-known parallelism between ontogenesis and phylogenesis is equally present. We have acquired profound knowledge about children's perception of space. A topological stage is reached after passing through a projective stage right up to the Euclidean space perceived by adults. Humanity's activity of building throughout the world follows this evolving pattern. This is not only true of the single building but also for the whole environment that man has created for himself and particularly for all his envelopes.*[67]

For Neumann, the "grammar of space" should gradually develop toward a new "topological discipline." One might wonder whether Neumann was aware of the paper presented to the Royal Institute of British Architects in April 1937 by John Desmond Bernal, the celebrated crystallographer who made a number of discoveries in X-ray diffractography. In that paper Bernal announced that architecture thereafter needed to take inspiration from science in order to progress in new ways. In particular, two branches of mathematics could be applied to architecture: symmetry and topology. Bernal also provided a succinct space-group definition of a crystal system, before recalling that Evgraf S. Fedorov and Arthur M. Schönflies had (independently) demonstrated the existence of 230 such groups, representing all possible combinations of symmetry operations.[68]

It is likely that Neumann was aware of this conference paper, especially because it was republished in Bernal's book *The Freedom*

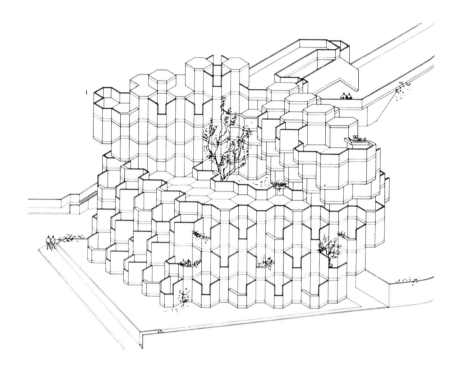

6.4
Alfred Neumann (with Zvi Hecker), Dubliner Apartment
Block, Ramat Gan, Tel Aviv, 1960, axonometric view.
Courtesy Aaron Sprecher, McGill University.

of Necessity (1949). Whatever the case, during the 1950s and 1960s Neumann developed a theory of architecture based on group theory and symmetry in crystal structures. He then unveiled his theory of "Architecture as Ornament" in an article of the same name, published in *Zodiac* in 1969. Like Bernal, Neumann starts with the acknowledged fact that crystallography is concerned with the regular division of space according to the laws of symmetry, a feature that the science shares with ornament and architecture: "The possibility of 230 crystal types was independently proved by three crystallographers, E. S. Fedorov, Schönflies and [William] Barlow, and later confirmed by [Max] von Laue with X-ray diffraction patterns by crystals."[69] In three-dimensional space, therefore, "there are 230 crystal groups." At the same time, "there are 17 possibilities for area-covering ornament and 7 possibilities for all strip symmetries." Ornament, then, "is one manifestation of the general category of symmetry." Neumann writes:

> *Today the term of symmetry varies from a vague use in matters of art to mathematical precision. . . . Symmetry . . . is the property of geometric figures to repeat their parts. . . . It is a play of rotations, translations, reflections and inversions. The combinations of these symmetry operations impose certain restrictions. . . . This property [helps define] the crystallinity of the solid [state]. In ornament we meet with similar structures in its evolutionary process. The shape of separately developed signs has a sort of topological equivalence. . . . Only after these elements appear in a denser packing do they enter into a symmetry induced pattern. The form of the elements is dependent upon the density of the motives constituting the ornament. The packing system can deform these elements until they are no more recognizable. . . . The formation of an ornament presupposes equal constituting elements.*[70]

For example, these mathematical processes are indeed what fashion the ideal design of ceramic tiles, whose motifs can be repeated according to natural laws and multiplied by precise rules. As a result, for Neumann, "architectural space is discontinuous, non-homogeneous and interpenetrated by anti-space"—that is, formed by nonspatial intervals. This being so, "ornament is a crystallographic inorganic structure. [But] the artist always strives to insinuate organic life into this structure."[71] Neumann rightly stresses that examples abound in the history of art. In the final analysis, he thinks that such a notion of ornament can be applied to architecture: "If it is admissible to consider ornament as two-dimensional crystallography, it is equally justified to call crystallography three-dimensional ornament. For architecture is related to crystallography from the space packing point of view."[72] Such an amazing statement both connects architecture to topology and anticipates contemporary packing techniques of geometric forms through all kinds of algorithms.[73] Neumann owned a complete set of books on topology and group theory (Paul Alexandroff, Jerome H. Manheim, Edward M'William Patterson), as well as on morphogenesis (Ernst Haeckel, D'Arcy Thompson, John Tyler Bonner), soap bubbles (C. V. Boys), symmetry (Jay Hambridge), and crystallography (Alan Holden).[74] Neumann's theories also come within the province of analogous research, such as Anne Tyng's work "Geometric Extensions of Consciousness."[75]

Among the abundant, similar research one might cite that of Günter Günschel, a member of the Paris-based Groupe d'Études d'Architecture Mobile (GEAM), founded by Yona Friedman in 1958, which explored crystalline concretions.[76] Such a neoexpressionist investigation evokes Bruno Taut's and Wenzel Hablik's crystal-like shapes,[77] and recalls the crystalline, massive concrete body for the Pilgrims' Church in Neviges (1963–1973) by the German Pritzker Prize recipient Gottfried Böhm.[78] David

Georges Emmerich, another member of GEAM, was one of the first to experiment with tensegrity prisms. He generated self-tensioning spatial structures with the aid of mathematical topology based on crystallography,[79] and claimed: "Since Pasteur's fundamental discoveries in molecular dissymmetry in 1860, it has become well known that all manifestations of mineral or organic life stem from some kind of defect in symmetry. In the realm of nuclear physics, Pierre Curie has observed that certain elements of symmetry do not necessarily exist. Dissymmetry is what creates the phenomenon."[80]

At the same time, Yona Friedman designed the structured nappes that formed the "Spatial City" project of 1958–1964,[81] which was similar to what Eckhard Schulze-Fielitz designed in his "Space City" (*Raumstadt*, 1959) with its complex polyhedral structure.[82] Schulze-Fielitz writes: "Interchangeability of spatially co-ordinated quanta offers flexibility and adaptation in dynamic developments. Serial building will be influenced by geometry, topology, group theory and the principles of combination. . . . The Space City accompanies the profile of the landscape as a crystalline layer; it is itself a landscape."[83]

Nicolas Schöffer, the creator of interactive art who designed a spatiodynamic tower in Liège in 1961, also came up with a project for a cybernetic city that was to be organized according to five topologies revealed in a kind of manifesto, published in 1964:

1. *Time: the topology of rhythms, in reference to the density of visual events;*

2. *Light: the topology of light, in relation to diurnal and nocturnal installations;*

3. *Sound: the topology of the audible, with natural and artificial sounds;*

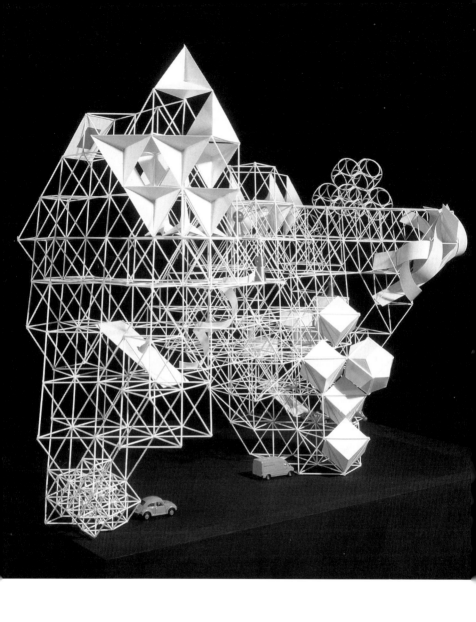

6.5
Eckhard Schulze-Fielitz, *Raumstadt* (Space City),
model, 1959, soldered metal. FRAC Centre collection,
Orléans, France.

*4. Climate: the topology of natural and artificial
climatic currents, playing on temperature, humidity,
wind;*

*5. Space: the topology of space where circulation is
organized horizontally and vertically, but also obliquely,
ensuring space therapy through space.* [84]

The cyber-artist concluded by prefiguring a new kind of territory: "The structure will be crowned . . . by large cybernetic centers. That way a true homeostatic social system will be able to be created ensuring that collective life is harmoniously flexible."[85]

Lastly, one should not forget the observations on the labyrinth made by Abraham A. Moles, a professor at the Ulm Hochschule für Gestaltung and at Strasbourg University who was behind the aesthetics of information theory in France,[86] and a colleague of Max Bense in Germany. Moles developed a psychosociological theory of space: "A labyrinth is above all a way of partitioning space according to rules of connection or prohibition, the whole set of which constitute what is known in mathematics as topology."[87] Moles suggested that toposociology was "an endless dialectical game" where concentration and dispersal, in space as well as in time, constituted *"a theory of holes in space-time,"* adapting this "according to the laws of perception proper to a being's *shells*."[88]

Blobs and bowels, bubbles and balloons, shells and membranes, capsules and cells, warped surfaces, crystals and nappes, cables and webs, labyrinths and topological surfaces: these indeed defined the *Zeitgeist* of the era.

Between 1958 and 1959, the Swiss architect Pascal Häusermann realized a weekender at Grilly, in the Ain district of France, that consisted of a concrete shell construction without any formwork. The ovoid shape produced a few simple constraints (compression or traction) that allowed the thickness of the concrete to be reduced to five centimeters. Steel reinforcement, covered in chicken wire netting, served as support for the concrete.[89] Starting in 1960, Häusermann and his collaborators began to realize numerous projects, including two houses at Pougny, also in the Ain district, which appeared in *Elle* magazine in 1966. Along with Jean-Louis Chanéac and Antti Lovag, Häusermann defended the idea of an "organic" architecture and a "cellular" abode, and with Patrick Le Merdy invented evolving "domobiles,"[90] or mobile domestic capsules.

The "futuristic" architects of the early 1960s tried to connect their plastic cells to "house-bearing" structures. There was Chanéac and his "multipurpose cells" of 1960, his cell stacks of 1961, his "crater cities" of 1963,[91] and his "multipurpose cell" prototype of 1964;[92] similarly, there was Häusermann and his project for an agglomeration of plastic cells of 1960–1961. Arthur Quarmby invented a "bee-hive village" in 1962, developed his "cell with garden" in 1964, and later, between 1962 and 1964, perfected "Corn on the Cob," his masts, or columns, designed for cells to be hooked onto them. If an owner decided to move to a different neighborhood, the cells could be slipped off the support and transported elsewhere, or even converted into individual houses. Quarmby's column-shafts, Kisho Kurokawa's helicoidal high-rise blocks, Kiyonori Kikutake's "trees," and Häusermann's "scaffolding" all offered the possibility of accommodating cells in a collective (mega-) structure.[93] Whether used in Kikutake's Marine City of 1958–1960, or his Box-type of 1962, which plugged prefabricated cells into structures designed by Kurokawa, the trees designed by the Japanese Metabolist group were supports for transitory accommodation, cells that grew and fell like "leaves" according to the seasons, each attuned to the time of its own "metabolism," thereby setting up a self-sufficient system and ensuring homeostatic equilibrium.[94] Hooking

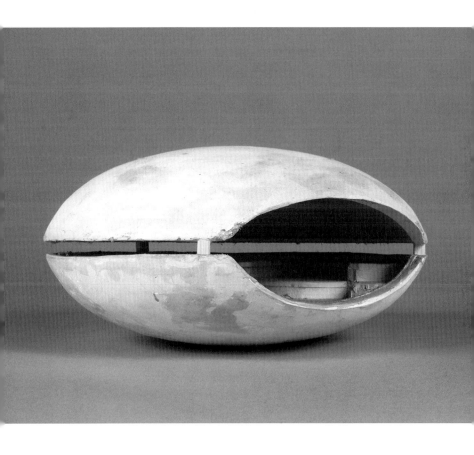

6.6
Pascal Häusermann, cellule, model, 1960, polyester
resin. FRAC Centre collection, Orléans, France.

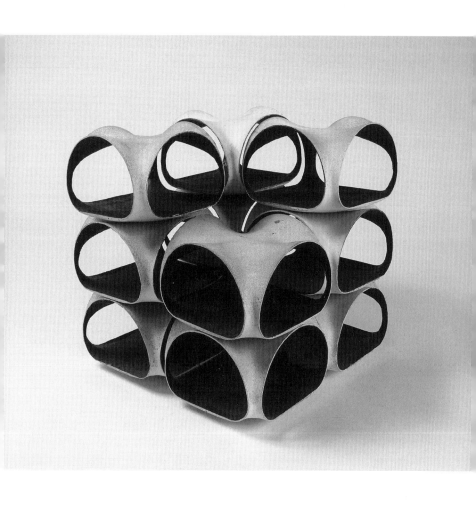

6.7
Chanéac (Jean-Louis Rey), plastic polyvalent cellules,
1960, model. FRAC Centre collection, Orléans, France.

cells onto these new "megastructures" was supposed to lead to the complete destruction of urban agglomerations, followed by their reconstruction.

Behind these "prospective" explorations hid the dream of even more extensive industrialization leading to assembly-line production of cells, just like automotive bodies. So why not hook backpacks onto trees, or caravans onto vertical pylons? Later, Michael Webb would propose just that with his Cushicle prototype of 1966: "The Cushicle is an invention that enables a man to carry a complete environment on his back. It inflates-out when needed. It is a complete nomadic unit—and it is fully serviced."[95] This nomadic kit came in the form of three avatars: the folded abode, the intermediate abode, and the unfolded and fully functioning abode.[96]

In defense of the curve, Häusermann took aim at the right angle. "Independently of the economic value of the forms of housing described," he remarks, soft shapes "are better adapted to man's life. In fact, the curve makes a volume more luminous, less sharp, and fosters a more intimate ambiance."[97] That is precisely what David Greene claimed, apropos his Spray Plastic House, which appeared in the first issue of *Archigram* in May 1961: "Why don't rabbits dig rectangular burrows? Why didn't early man make rectangular caves?"[98] In a way, Häusermann's intentions foreshadowed those of Peter Cook and Dennis Crompton, published in the form of the sexier (and better-drawn) concept of Plug-in Dwellings in *Archigram* in 1965, where a fixed metallic structure accommodated an array of services to be plugged in or attached.[99] An apex is reached with the beautifully crafted Ragnitz (1965–1969), a "spatial" megastructure designed by Austrians Günter Domenig and Eilfried Huth, in which the colossal frame hosts the supply network, giving the plumbing a colorful visibility as a result.

Here one should mention the Un-house (Transportable Standard-of-Living Package/The Environment Bubble) designed by

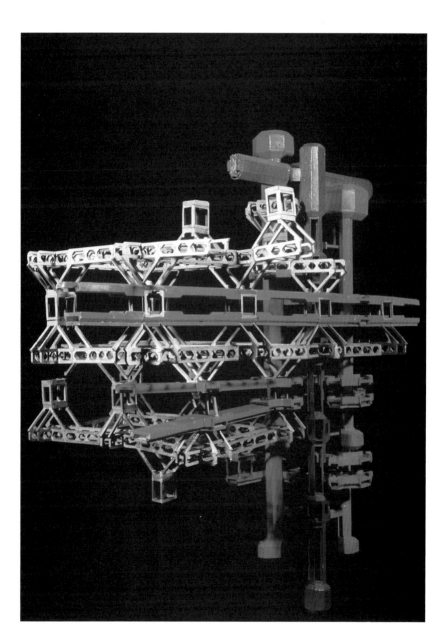

6.8
Eilfried Huth and Günther Domenig, Ragnitz, Austria,
model of the megastructure (fragment), wood and
plastics, 1965–1969, original color photograph. FRAC
Centre collection, Orléans, France.

6.9
Eilfried Huth and Günther Domenig, the megastructure
Ragnitz (Austria, 1969), colored 1966 drawing
showing ground-floor plan with the scheme of
functions. FRAC Centre collection, Orléans, France.

François Dallegret in 1965. Dallegret was behind the brilliant drawings illustrating Banham's article "A Home Is Not a House," published in *Art in America* in 1965, in which one sees a cell reduced to its fittings alone and enveloped in a protective membrane. For Banham, the hearth makes the home, four walls make a prison, and wall openings don't allow ventilation when there is no wind, which is when ventilation is most urgently needed. Windows don't let in light when it is most needed—at night. A habitable building functions by combining the structure with plugged-in fittings—the structure being an inflated polyethylene membrane and the fit-out a "standard-of-living package" according to Buckminster Fuller's formula, offering the minimum necessary for comfortable living.[100]

"With very little exaggeration," writes Banham, "this baroque ensemble of domestic gadgetry epitomizes the intestinal complexity of gracious living—in other words, this is the junk that keeps the pad swinging. The house itself has been omitted from the drawing, but if mechanical services continue to accumulate at this rate it may be possible to omit the house in fact."[101]

All the "functions" are provided by a technological tool kit, rendering obsolete the use of walls, windows, and furniture—components replaced by the inner, "biological" functions of an organism, such as skin, epithelial bodies, transmitters and receivers, circuits, cables, and antennae.

The American architect Charles Deaton, whose Sculptured House[102] was a huge shell form built west of Denver in 1963, said: "People aren't angular. So why should they live in rectangles?"[103] This desire for a biomorphic form was fulfilled when the architects Pascal and Claude Häusermann were given the opportunity to design the restaurant Le Balcon de Belledone, at Sainte-Marie-du-Mont, in the Isère district of France, in 1966.[104] Its shell-like cantilever was similar to the "organic" masterpieces of the 1960s, such as John Lautner's belvedere Chemosphere (Hollywood,

The Environment-Bubble
Transparent plastic bubble dome inflated by air-conditioning output

6.10
François Dallegret, "Transparent Bubble (Transparent plastic dome inflated by air-conditioning output)," drawing for Reyner Banham, "A Home Is Not a House," *Art in America* 53, no. 2 (April 1965): 70–79. Courtesy of François Dallegret, Westmount, Quebec, Canada.

1960);[105] the concrete shell Science Museum, Evoluon, built by the engineer-architect Louis Christiaan Kalff for Philips at Eindhoven in 1966; and prototype 001 of the capsule-like, plastic Futuro house by the Matti Suuronen, a mobile contrivance built in many locations starting from 1968.

Certain experimental inventions in particular—in France, England, Germany, Japan, Italy, and especially Austria—continue to raise interest today because of their vast theoretical potential, including the "space" machines created by Coop Himmelb(l)au.[106] To those one must add the wild and wacky visions of Haus-Rucker-Co with their Gelbes Herz (Yellow Heart) of 1968, an inflatable organ palpitating with life.[107] These are indeed spaces designed for cyborgs. Kisho Kurokawa said in his "Capsule Declaration" of 1969, which focused on the livable, detachable capsule as a movable home: "Article 1: The capsule is cyborg architecture. Man, machine and space build a new organic body which transcends man and equipment. . . . Article 2: A capsule is a dwelling of *Homo movens*."[108] In this work the architectural body is no longer the one imagined by Vitruvius, or even the one taken into account by Le Corbusier. It is the body of a technological organism, improved and connected, and fitted out with prosthetics. As Banham underlined in 1968:

> *All architecture has to mediate between an outer and an inner environment in some way. . . . An inflatable . . . in its state of active homeostasis, trimming, adjusting and taking up strains, is malfunctioning if it* doesn't *squirm and creak. As an adjustable and largely self-regulating membrane it is more truly like the skin of a living creature than the metaphorical "skin" of, say, a glass-walled office block. . . . A blow directed at the enclosing skin would produce a flurry of reproachful quivering and creaking, quickly dying away as the even tenor of its normal breathing ways was resumed. I like that.*[109]

The building creaks, squeaks, and groans; the membrane gets excited and moves, stretching and adapting; the dermis reacts and interacts while the epidermis blushes with shame, blanches with rage, or pales with apprehension. This topology is indeed one that filters substances and elements passing through membranes: endosmosis and exosmosis, effort and movement, humor and information, percept and affect.[110]

The point of departure for these theoretical projects, which examine the mutant body of architecture, is linked not only to interrogations of design or fashion, but also to the latent eroticism of clothing, the at once essential and superficial nature of covering, the secret language of the skin, the outfit, the mask, the screen, the natural and/or artificial habitat. Like the shell of an egg, or the cell's membrane, isn't the epithelial organ paradoxically the deepest? As the boundary between inside and outside, a protective barrier, an envelope of flesh, the skin divides and isolates. As the interface between pleasure and pain, the skin is at once both arm and armor. Breathing, blushing, blanching; sweating, shivering, quivering: our skin, like our eyes and mouth, is also a medium, a communication tool. So, in the architecture of Walter Pichler, Hans Hollein, and Archigram,[111] the house is like a body: it has membranes, presents its openings and its orifices, and shamelessly offers its erogenous zones. But these are improved, prosthetic bodies, technological organisms. These parts, carved up and reinforced, then mechanized, are thereby "fetishized" and rendered inaccessible.

The models of houses in the form of space capsules, by Haus-Rucker-Co and Coop Himmelb(l)au, or the 1967 Dyodon designed by Jean-Paul Jungmann from the group Utopie,[112] are parodies of orthopedic instruments that participate in a techno-medical aesthetic. These cruel defense mechanisms condition the onlooker's "gaze," while ruling out any approach. What is being played out again on this stage is the tragicomedy of the bride

6.11
Jean-Paul Jungmann (born 1935), *Dyodon—Pneumatic
Experimental Housing*, 1967, pencil and ink drawing.
Courtesy of Collection MNAM, Centre Pompidou, Paris,
France. Agence Photographique (RMN) / Art Resource,
NY / ARS (Artists Rights Society, New York).

stripped bare that bachelors can attain only by suffering tortures that they bring on themselves. It all simulates a communication breakdown, even though that communication seemed guaranteed by the transparency of the plastic membrane. This is because, instead of putting on display as though through the "window" of perspective, of the peep show or of the voyeur, the capsules shatter common references and suspend everyday meanings. As Michel de Certeau writes, "Among desiring subjects, there remains only the possibility of loving the language that substitutes itself for their communication. And that is indeed a model of language furnished by the machine, which is made of the differentiated and combined parts (like every enunciation) and develops, through the interplay of its mechanisms, the logic of a celibate narcisism."[113] Based on these languages that mime their own death, on these orthopedic machines that guide torture, and on these prophylactic devices that eliminate contact, a new engineering, a new "architecture," is born, one built around such prosthetic supplements. Such a form of engineering allows us to make nonstop transfers and to multiply transformations which, from that moment on, are no longer articulated like the words of a language but lead to a disarticulation.

At the end of the day, three films best illustrate the atmosphere of the "sixties." The 1968 film *The Touchables*, directed by Robert Freeman, had a set for which the architect Arthur Quarmby built an inflatable sphere (Banham had introduced the architect to the film's producers). The key moment in the film is the introduction of an inflatable sphere twenty-four meters across, made of transparent PVC and reinforced by a net of nylon cables. The subject of the film is eminently risqué: four women living in a lakeside pleasure dome capture a handsome young man and compete to obtain his favors. Second, the set of the 1968 film *Barbarella*, directed by Roger Vadim, was designed by Mario Garbuglia. Inspired by Jean-Claude Forest's comic strip, the film depicts a range of environments in the form of membranes, as well as a space shuttle lined with fur. In a famous scene, the actress Jane Fonda is manhandled by a mechanical blow-up resembling an organ of pleasure. As a totally prosthetic subject, she is delivered up to an electronic dildo. Lastly, Woody Allen's 1973 film *Sleeper* was filmed partly on the work site of architect Charles Deaton's Sculptured House. Waking up some time in the future, the film's hero explores the best of all possible worlds, which reveals incredible progress such as the "Orgasmatron," a machine that replaces sex, an ironic reference to the psychoanalyst Wilhelm Reich's orgone box, a wacky device invented to elevate one's orgiastic potential.

During the 1960s, the egg and the crystal offer two powerful paradigms for architecture and design. They inform two aspects of morphogenesis, in which topology coalesces in space epigenetic and crystallographic processes. It is not coincidental that Deleuze stressed the necessity of recognizing the predominance of multiple forces active on form. In *Difference and Repetition*, he determines the link between forces and forms as the two vectors of difference.[114] The crystal's individuation is the formation obtained physically by a difference of potential. Such a difference is the entropic arrow between tension and matter.[115] Deleuze translates this differentiation in terms of oscillation, a quasi-simultaneous vibration between the actual and the virtual, which are coexistent. Both statuses are real, but the actual characterizes the completed individual, such as the materialized crystal, while the virtual refers to the problematic field of the pre-individual, when the intensive differentiation is not yet actualized.

Through Simondon, Deleuze defines interiority as topological in nature, relative and differential. Simondon defines the living as what lives by the polarized membrane, the limit between two different milieus: the interior and the exterior. As expected, there is a difference: while the living lives at the limit, on its borders, inasmuch as membranes repolarize themselves continuously, the crystal polarizes once for all. In a living being, interiority and exteriority are everywhere.[116] In the *Logic of Sense* (1969), Deleuze uses Simondon's analysis of crystal formation to redefine time and events: "Events are like crystals, they become and grow out of the edges, or on the edge."[117] Everything happens at the border, and, as in a mirror, everything is reduced to the opposite side of the surface.[118] As in a Möbius strip, the outer surface is continuous with the inner surface. It envelops the entire world and makes that which is inside be the outside, and vice versa.[119] The event's border is a demarcation, a line or surface, between the virtual and the actual.

Topology and chronology coincide in the individuation of the living: they are not a priori forms, but the dimensionality of living while it is individualizing. For Simondon, thus are met the conditions to think morphogenesis.[120] As a result, the genetic processes of membranes or crystals allow us to rethink spatial categories, such as inside and outside, depth and height, transparent and opaque, top and bottom, front and rear, light and heavy, mobile and immobile, fast and slow, nomadic and sedentary, smooth and striated. Suddenly, the primary elements of architecture (basement and attic, wall and partition, floor and ceiling, passage and disruption, ground and roof) enter into a baroque metamorphose and transmute into topological surfaces of contact.

7 PROSTHETICS AND PARASITES

Hyper-spaces /
Approach the gaseous waters of infinity /
To be crossed with the arch /
Built against every malady.
—Antonin Artaud, untitled text (1948)[1]

The Greco-Roman concept of isomorphism was based on the representation of a canonical body that was constituted prior to the production of the work of art. But following the dismissal of this classical theory that called upon architecture to imitate or "reflect" the proportions of the human body, how is it possible to rethink the relation between body and built environment? It henceforth seems urgent to interrogate the dynamic relations between the terms of the body and the world. Does a body exist? Is it a possession or a tool? Do we *have* body? What is *a* body? Is this body "inhabited"? How do body and brain interact with the world? A brief examination of theories of the body should help us assess the effects produced on our conception of the environment—constructed or not—as well as on the project of architecture.

Body without Organs
In *The Logic of Sense* (1969), Gilles Deleuze alluded to the rather dramatic interjection that Antonin Artaud uttered on leaving the

psychiatric hospital in Rodez, where he had been a patient: "No mouth No tongue No teeth No larynx No esophagus No stomach No intestine No anus I shall reconstruct the man that I am."[2] This statement invoked a continuous, fluid body of blood and bone, one not reduced to each of its organs. Later, in *Anti-Oedipus* (1972), Deleuze and Félix Guattari hypothesized a body conceived as a libidinal machine, a "desiring machine" that points to the theoretical possibility of a "body without organs." This body was again based on texts by Artaud, such as "To have done with the Judgement of God" (1947): "For you can tie me up if you wish, but there is nothing more useless than an organ."[3] Or another text, from 1948: "The body is the body / it is all by itself / and has no need of organs / the body is never an organism / organisms are the enemies of the body."[4]

Today, we are confronted by two hypotheses that seem almost mutually exclusive: on the one hand, there is a "body-without-organs"—that is, a notion of the body based not on the singularity and autonomy of each organ, but on organs that are allegedly indeterminate. On the other hand, there is a notion based on the organic organization of organs, called "organism," which corresponds to the conventional idea of the body as functioning according to the internal logic and hierarchies that have long dominated physiology and clinical discourse. These two explanations of corporeality seem diametrically opposed, yet one does not exclude the other. One approach favors a "body-without-organs," the (fertile) dream of schizophrenics, which considers the body purely in its *exteriority*, in relation to other bodies, perceived through relationships of surface, difference, affect, and desire, and functioning "as a virtual and smooth space, connected with the fluxes and flows that run through and across it."[5] The other version stresses the reality, or normality, of the organism, conceiving the body exclusively in terms of its interiority, its regime of internal distribution, in which autonomous organs fragment the whole into multiple parts, breaking up its integrity. This logic is reflected in the arrangement of a hospital complex into various nosological specializations. This kind of functionalism also subtends all so-called "modern" architecture, which, in fact, is nothing other than an application of organicism.

Deleuze and Guattari's analysis of the body adopted a critical stance with regard to certain trends in psychoanalysis that were influenced by linguistic structuralism. They notably criticized psychoanalysts' conception of the body as a tabula rasa, a kind of blank slate on which events traced by language may inscribe themselves, and on which power and authority could write the text of the law. This conception of the body—Lacanian, broadly speaking—seemed to involve a punctuation of the void desire by the Signifier, creating a phallic order, namely, that of the family and, consequently, that of the State.[6] Contrary to traditional gloss from Plato to Lacan, desire is always full. It is always a positive affirmation that creates machinic entity—that is, body-without-organs. At all times it is something constructive. In the Nietzschean meaning of a "gay science," it characterizes a joyous, free person. The worst misinterpretation of desire would be to think of it as something wanting, which would open the door to a transcendental Oedipus, governing every mind and body, together with our institutions. Deleuze and Guattari stressed that desire lacks nothing, that it does not miss its object, that desire and its object are one and the same—that desire is a machine, and the object of desire is just another machine connected to the first.[7] In *A Thousand Plateaus* (1980), Deleuze and Guattari view the body as a multifarious surface with skinlike folds:

> *It is also the skin as envelope or ring, and the sock as reversible surface. It can be a house or part of a house, any number of things, anything. . . . A body without organs is not an empty body stripped of organs, but a body upon*

> which that which serves as organs . . . is distributed ac-
> cording to crowd phenomena, in Brownian motion, in
> the form of molecular multiplicities. . . . The body with-
> out organs is not a dead body but a living body all the
> more alive and teeming once it has blown apart the or-
> ganism and its organization. . . . The full body without
> organs is a body populated by multiplicities.[8]

Within this topology, dwellings come across as something reversible, like the skin of a dead animal or the form of a sock. Forging a new kind of organicism, the interior becomes exterior, while, vice versa, the exterior folds itself into surfaces that may be folded and unfolding, invaginated or exogastrular.

Organs without a Body

Today, the very idea of a prosthesis is drawn toward applications that are basically divided between restoration of infirmities of perception, tests with tissue cultures, and organ transplants, which, with varying results, are increasingly attempted today. A graft or transplant is the subtlest form of prosthesis: it links a separation of substance to functional reparation through an exchange of mutual otherness. Nowadays, the "body-without-organs" is confronted with the disturbing prospect of organs without a body—namely, transplants stored in aptly named organ banks. An almost freakish hybrid, the graft is a new species made of flesh and apparatus. Removed from the "donor" organism, a transplant becomes a "free" organ—available on the open market like any commodity, as amply illustrated in Michael Crichton's 1978 film *Coma*, where demand for organs triggers worldwide contraband. A transplant organ is thus *bodiless*—orphaned and celibate, trapped between life and death. It comes from "the interval created *between* relational and functional death."[9] Transplant surgery also introduces a caesura between organ and body, the organ remaining "other" in its new body, in which, in order to forestall rejection by its new host, it must undergo intensive regulatory medication (cyclosporine, for example).

The replacement, transplanted organ then becomes "another" within the "host" organism, simultaneously correcting a pathological discrepancy and "triggering a new regulatory system, defining a different normality"[10] that leads to different pathologies, as witnessed by transplant survivors. In *The Intruder* (*L'intrus*, 2000), philosopher Jean-Luc Nancy—himself the recipient of a heart transplant—adopts as an epigraph a lament by Artaud: "There is in fact nothing so ignobly useless and superfluous as the organ called the heart, the filthiest invention that beings could have invented for pumping me with life."[11] After years of medical "treatment," Nancy admits, in passages worthy of Michel Foucault, that he "wind[s] up being no more than a fragile thread, from pain to pain and from strangeness to strangeness."[12] He can no longer escape "the general feeling of now being indissociable from a web of measurements and observations, of chemical, institutional, and symbolic connections . . . which . . . deliberately keep life constantly aware of their presence and surveillance."[13] Having become an object of mutation, Nancy ironically commented that he was becoming a sci-fi android.[14] To Jacques Derrida, mockingly, he said: "At the end of the day, I am the best of all Derridians. I took your concept of graft, literally."[15] Deleuze and Guattari's description of the libidinal machinery also evokes fragmentation, as revealed in *Anti-Oedipus*: "[E]verything functions at the same time, but amid hiatuses and ruptures, breakdowns and failures, stalling and short circuits, distances and fragmentations, within a sum that never succeeds in bringing its various parts together so as to form a whole. . . . We live today in the age of partial objects. . . . We no longer believe in the myth of the existence of fragments . . . or in a final totality that awaits us at some future date."[16] Fragments no longer imply a whole, whether past or future. For Deleuze and Guattari's desiring machines, cuts are productive and are themselves joinings. Unable to reassemble the parts of the "body in pieces" through reflection or representation, the Lacanian mirror can no longer assemble the fragmented phantasms of the prenarcissistic body. For Deleuze and Guattari, the mirror stage becomes the repression of fragmentation, which merely results in a fetishization of the lost object of desire.

Moreover, in opposition to a Kleinian interpretation of the split object, now the fragmentation of the object is the result of a body-without-organs. In the desiring machine of Deleuze and Guattari, the body-without-organs founds the means to be productive. Contrary to the pulsional machinery constituted by split objects, the body-without-organs establishes in the machine a relational mode to the object. In the desiring machine, there are cuts or splits, which authorize desire. Connections and couplings are everywhere: "An organ machine is plugged into an energy source machine: the one produces a flow that the other interrupts."[17] Here, the essence of the machine, whether a social machine, a desiring machine, or a technological machine, is based on ruptures: "This process is what we call a flow. But, again, flow is an everyday, unqualified notion that we needed. It can be a flow of words, a flow of ideas, a flow of shit, a flow of money. It can be a financial mechanism or a schizophrenic machine. . . . We define the machine as any system that interrupts flows."[18] The system functions either through power breaks, outages in the transmission of meaning, interferences or impediments in communication, line interference in a signal within telecom circuits, or is acted upon by the schizophrenic as a universal producer. As an outcome, *Anti-Oedipus* is a celebration of divisions, splices, cuts, partial objects, conjunctions and disjunctions, connections and recordings.

What emerge are two distinct, yet interrelated, hypotheses on the fragmentation of the body. The first is defined by the formulation *organ-without-body*. Such an organ, released from the body, may be sold as a commodity, as well as "grafted onto" another body, another organism, be it biological, mechanical, or computational. Insofar as the term *graft* derives etymologically from *graphein*, the Greek verb "to write," every graft becomes a script or a code, and every writing, every graph, becomes a graft.

The second hypothesis defines the *body-without-organs*. The body becomes liberated, libidinal, and desiring: a body of pure surface. Constantly intersected by grafts, connections, and codes, it can be incessantly traversed by ephemeral experiences that give rise to artificially induced vital effects: tact and contact, sensation and vibration, brush and touch, caress and rubbing, fleeting pleasures and momentary satisfactions, flux and outflow.

Embodiment and Incorporation

Beginning in the 1960s, the visual arts reintroduced the human body through performances in which the artist would engage his or her own body. As early as 1961 Robert Morris exhibited himself in a "box for standing" (*Untitled [Box for Standing]*). He also presented his self-portrait in the form of monochrome bottles arranged within a frame (*Portrait*, 1963); in fact, these vessels contained his bodily fluids (blood, sweat, sperm, saliva, phlegm, tears, urine, feces). In 1964, Morris made an untitled piece composed of imprints of feet and rulers (*Untitled [Footprints and Rulers]*), confirming an engagement between body and space.[19]

In *From Hand to Mouth* (1967), artist Bruce Nauman made a wax cast of a woman's mouth, shoulder, and arm;[20] in a way, this cast conveyed the path from mouth to hand, located outside of any organological logic. In 1968 and 1969, Nauman carried out numerous filmic experiments, exploring various parts of the body (hands, arms, testicles, thighs, knees, feet), which led to a series of performances based on twisting his lips, as seen projected on glass in *First Hologram Series: Making Faces* (1968).[21] Like Morris, Nauman was concerned with measuring, metering, with making prints, casts, and holograms, all of which recorded marks made by the body. In *Drifts* (1970), Vito Acconci photographed bodily traces left on sand. Other works are situated halfway between photography and cinema, such as *Trademark* (1970), a twenty-minute film that features the marks made by his teeth after biting his own flesh. In a three-minute filmed performance titled *Lick* (1970), Acconci unleashed his masochistic drive by licking the gallery's floor. Finally, in a series of *Conversions* (1971), Acconci stood before the camera naked, hiding his genitals between his legs, effecting a change in attribute that sought to re-create a hermaphroditic body. Once his body became a smooth surface, inscriptions could be added, engraved or erased.[22]

As disturbing as they are poignant, Rebecca Horn's early work sketched a cartography of the subjective and physiological functions of the human body. Her "body sculptures" were made from fragments of biomedical equipment (tubes, ligatures, membranes, pumps), as seen in *Overflowing-blood-machine* (1970), in which eight transparent tubes were vertically strapped to the body of a nude model to reveal the flow and rhythmic throb of circulating blood outside the skin.[23] Like surgical operations and technological "embodiments" (X-rays, ECGs, EEGs, PET scans, MRIs), Horn's work presents the functioning of the viscera and isolated parts of the vegetative systems (circulatory, respiratory) to our "gaze"—a gaze hitherto forbidden, dangerous, or even fatal.

At the heart of body art we discover a fragmented, destroyed, decentered body. One of the best examples was Chris Burden's performance *Shoot*, staged at the F Space in Santa Ana, California, on November 19, 1971. That Burden received a bullet in his arm was, ultimately, an accidental and anecdotal side of the story. What was really being played and replayed was the body as the ultimate field of experimentation. Charles Ray, in a work titled *Shelf* (1984), exhibited himself nude, with his back to the wall of the gallery; a horizontal shelf placed at neck level made his head, painted gray, just another one of the objects, also painted gray, sitting on that shelf.[24] Starting in 1985, French artist Orlan underwent a series of seven surgical operations culminating in *Omnipresence* (1993), the spectacle of her lipo-suctions—broadcast live to several galleries across the planet—becoming unbearable for some viewers.[25] The transformations Cindy Sherman performs on her own body—her own "figure"—are documented and recorded on huge cibachrome prints, of-ten sparking uncomfortable feelings in the beholder. In her *Untitled* series (1989–1990), Sherman donned various masks or bulbous breasts and other protuberances that turned her into an archetypical *Madonna Lactans* (*Untitled 216*). Such art can make reality more real—sometimes too real—producing a disturbing hyperrealism that perturbs our perception of real-ity and our image of the body, scrambling logical or semiotic connections.[26]

A less spectacular, if equally convincing, fragmentation of the body was explored by Gary Hill, whose installation *Inasmuch as It Is Always Already Taking Place* (1990) displayed, in real time, partial images of his body on sixteen video screens of varying sizes.[27] In what might suggest a strange inversion of the "mir-ror stage," the body was first decomposed in partial objects, then "recomposed" technologically as the image of the "body in pieces" in which revealed and cut-out body parts are simultane-ously "fetishized" and rendered inaccessible. Again, in Matthew Barney's video *Cremaster 4* (1994), bodies and machines undergo uncontrollable genetic and morphological mutations through the sudden appearance of excrescences as ephemeral as they are inexplicable. Here again, the sleek bodies of magnificent her-maphrodites display their pectorals.[28]

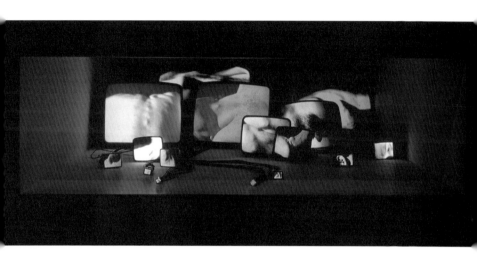

7.1
Gary Hill (born 1951), *Inasmuch as It Is Always
Already Taking Place*, 1990. Installation: sixteen
videos (black-and-white, sound), sixteen black-and-
white TV tubes and wires, recessed in a wall 42
inches from the floor, overall 16 × 53¾ × 68 inches.
Courtesy of The Museum of Modern Art / Licensed
by SCALA / Art Resource, NY / © ARS (Artists
Rights Society, New York).

Through this work and that of a number of artists, the body has become not only the site of criticism of the disciplinary apparatuses of society, but also the site of a process of incorporation, or embodiment, which, at least in theory, can be tested to the extreme limits of disembodiment. Those limits engage the vulnerability of the body itself.

Cyborgs

In the twentieth century, the development of biomechanical equipment was marked by two stages that attained the status of "theoretical fiction" or paradigm. First was the inception of the term *robot*, which arose as a figure of the industrial worker. Coined by Karel Čapek (1890–1938) in his 1921 play *R.U.R.* (an acronym for *Rossum's Universal Robots*),[29] *robot* comes from the Czech *robota*, meaning "boredom" or "monotony," and alludes to slavery, forced labor, or the repetitive tasks demanded by factory assembly lines. In the play, the robots attempt to revolt, like slaves seeking freedom. Because men were becoming like machines or motors, the robot machines had to resemble men.

Later came the term *cyborg*. An abbreviation of "cybernetic organism," *cyborg* designated a hybrid, almost freakish being that embodied the daunting, but exhilarating idea of an automaton, something simultaneously human and alien. Such was the terminology proposed by Manfred E. Clynes (a musician and engineer who studied physics, mathematics, and neuropsychology) and Nathan S. Kline (a psychiatrist), who were working in the Dynamic Simulation Lab at Rockland State Hospital in Orangeburg, New York, on a biocybernetic study on living conditions in outer space.[30] It may well appear that robots and cyborgs are not just two stages in our technological evolution, but rather two alternatives, two developmental paradigms. For it is significant that the former emerged from an industrial factory while the latter were born in a hospital—that is, an environment governed by biology and *fin-de-siècle* electronics.[31] The theory of homeostatic systems had been developed in the context of World War II, and the study of the man/machine interface led to the generalization of cybernetics. From control of machines via self-regulating systems to generalizations about the configuration of the body as an information system (as conceived by the fathers of cybernetics: Norbert Wiener, Claude Shannon, Léon Brillouin, and Warren McCulloch), we have moved into sensorially stimulated environments able to re-create the world (such as virtual reality, which should henceforth be understood as a fairly ordinary form of cyborgism).[32] Between 1960 and the present, the robot and the cyborg have been merging, even if some authors try to maintain the distinction between them. Pop-sociological analyses such as Vance Packard's *The People Shapers* (1977), and vulgarizations such as David Rorvik's *As Man Becomes Machine* (1978), predicted the coming domination of intelligent machines over the human body, which would be subjected to multiple mutations via prosthetic implants, cloning, and biological feedback devices.

It seems today that cyborg culture is questioning not only the classic distinction between organism and machine, but also the dividing lines between notions of intelligence and sensitivity, animal and human, nature and culture, male and female, primitive and civilized, virtual and real. In 1985, Donna Haraway, an American biologist, published her "Cyborg Manifesto," arguing for a reconception of the conventional boundaries delimiting the world:

> *High-tech culture challenges these dualisms in intriguing ways. It is not clear who makes and who is made in the relation between human and machine. It is not clear what is mind and what body in machines that resolve into coding practices. In so far as we know ourselves in both formal discourse (for example, biology) and in daily*

practice (for example, the homework economy in the in-
tegrated circuit), we find ourselves to be cyborgs, hybrids,
mosaics, chimeras. Biological organisms have become
biotic systems, communications devices like others.
There is no fundamental, ontological separation in our
formal knowledge of machine and organism, of techni-
cal and organic.[33]

This link between *techne* and *organon* is not new; it was raised
by the ancient Greek philosophers and, in the seventeenth century, by René Descartes. But the cyborg has shifted the boundary between organism and machine by coupling biological
organisms with cybernetic devices, blurring the animal and the
human by replacing cognition with neuronal feedback and rendering obsolete the distinctions between animate and inanimate
through a theory of the behavior of homeostatic systems.

The bizarre novelty of cyborgs produces the conditions for a
redesigned and improved identity and (perhaps) an unfamiliar
and enhanced sexuality, which leads to an eroticism describable
only in fiction—Philip K. Dick, obviously—and film. For Haraway,
"The replicant Rachel in the Ridley Scott film *Blade Runner* (1982)
stands as the image of a cyborg culture's fear, love, and confusion."[34] In the 1980s, Haraway's work made it possible go beyond
the myths of the Greek Chimera and classical "monster" (from
a Golem to Frankenstein), to define a new hybrid produced by
information technology: the hybrid (and gender-conscious)
cyborg. This cybernetic version of the Chimera yields original
mutational possibilities that call for a revision of the notion of
evolution, because in cyborg culture, bodies are no longer born,
but manufactured. Cyborgs are products of an analytical process
that combines human elements with organic and living "generative processes" belonging to the high-tech environment, such
as "information systems, texts, and ergonomically controlled

laboring, desiring, and reproducing systems," as Haraway writes.[35] These new species of machine become "cyborgs," even if only partially, in that they are communication and processing systems. Such ergonomic apparatuses are governed by the principles of autopoiesis, and capable of storing memory and making decisions. Losing its traditional walls, the "house" acquires a biocybernetic power. Haraway's cybernetician approach redefines the rigid opposition between human and animal, and between human and machine. Finally, Haraway's cyborg theory resists the idea of an Oedipal control on the organic family, suggesting that a new social dyad should be thought of, through the blurring of the family's boundaries.[36]

Ecotechnics

Our being cannot be defined by our organs, for we are able to transform some of them and even replace others (although it is not always so simple). However, reasoning on a part is not the same as arguing for the whole, and it is this theoretical disjunction between the body and each of its organs that raises the possibility of subtle ontological distinctions between *having* and *being* a body. A subject is not a mind inhabiting a body; far from *having* a body, we *are* a body—indeed, a body whose parts all "think." Jean-Luc Nancy goes even further when he asserts, in an almost Deleuzian passage, that "there is no such thing as *the* body. There is no body. Instead, there are patient and fervent recitations of numerous corpuses. Ribs, skulls, pelvises, irritations, shells."[37] In "Corpus" (2000), a brief essay on bodily technology, Nancy pursues this thinking to argue that every body is "multiplied, multi-sexed, multi-figured, multi-zoned . . . organized, inorganic."[38] Bodies are created, and this "creation" leads to a technology of the body that determines, almost exclusively, the truth of the world. Nancy writes: "Our world is the world of the 'technical,' a world whose cosmos, nature, gods, entire system is, in its inner joints, exposed as 'technical': the world of the *ecotechnical*."[39] This technological *oikos* acts as a machine, yet also as an organ. Ecotechnics derive their power from technical devices to which every organ is connected—through and through. "What it *makes* are our bodies, which it brings into the world and links to the system, thereby creating our bodies as more visible, more proliferating, more polymorphic, more compressed, more 'amassed' and 'zoned' than ever before."[40] Like a cyborg, but without the excitement of science fiction, first the body is created, then it is wired everywhere, and at last it is reconfigured.

In his cyberpunk novel *Neuromancer* (1984), William Gibson coined the phrase "jacking into cyberspace," defined as a "consensual hallucination" shared by everyone hooked up to a computer. Gibson's inspired fiction evokes the incestuous mating between organs and machines, with all the sexual connotations of total embodiment in desiring machines and couplings in continuous flux. Envisioning an imaginary branching of neuronal systems and digital networks, users could travel through a new landscape, one that was the "graphic representation of data abstracted from the banks of every computer in the human system. Unthinkable complexity. Lines of light ranged in the non-space of the mind, clusters and constellations of data. Like city lights, receding."[41] Gibson's novel evoked a nonmaterial space of representation whose immediate data were those of digital simulation, enabling the reader to explore the caesura between physical presence and a consciousness—a "spirit"—able to navigate in cyberspace—and this, just as Jean-François Lyotard was preparing his Paris exhibition on "Les immatériaux" (1985).

The original idea for the exhibition was proposed to Lyotard by the Centre Pompidou's Centre de Création Industrielle (CCI) on the basis that innovative materials (like Kevlar) were actually "immaterial," because they were engendered by information technology and computers.[42] Matter was no longer a given, ready to be used and transformed; rather, it was the message that generated materials, which became "immaterial," because its essence was based on digital codes. Later Lyotard suggested that the exhibition should be organized and articulated on the basis of the etymological derivations of the Sanskrit word *mât-*, which is at the root of terms such as material, matrix, matter, maternity. To interpret the new conditions of human activities, a framework of five problematic fields was drawn up: Maternity (as an addresser, or sender of messages), Matrix (the code), Matter (Fr., *matière*, as a reference), Material(s) as a substantive (Fr., *matériau*, the support of the message), and Materiel as an adjective (Fr., *matériel*, as a recipient or addressee). The fields created a labyrinth of routes through the show. Paradigmatic examples from art were introduced in the maze, including work by Marcel Duchamp, László Moholy-Nagy, Joseph Kosuth, and Dan Graham, together with Peter Eisenman's series of houses, which exempli fied the generative reversal of an architecture of mere syntax and pure code.[43]

Since then however, architecture has, for better or for worse, entered the era of digital codes. Recalling a landscape in which statistical data banks give shape to the forms of a new city was precisely what Dutch architects MVRDV attempted to do in their 1998 video installation *METACITY/DATATOWN*.[44] Conceiving an architecture that, through graphs and grafts, would transform itself into perpetual mutation is also what architects such as Toyo Ito, NOX (Lars Spuybroek), and Mark Goulthorpe (dECOI), among others, envisaged. After years of splines and parametrics, Form*Z-aided forms and X-treme formalizations, it seems that designers like Jürgen Mayer H., Didier Fiuza Faustino, and Hernan Diaz Alonso are finding innovative ways to coalesce spaces imagined on the screen with structural realization.[45]

7.2
Didier Fiuza Faustino, Bureau des Mésarchitectures
(Office of Mis-architectures), *Stairway to Heaven*,
2001, Castelo Branco, Portugal. Courtesy Didier Fiuza
Faustino / Bureau des Mésarchitectures.

7.3
Didier Fiuza Faustino, Bureau des Mésarchitectures
(Office of Mis-architectures), *Opus incertum*, Biennale
of Venice, 2008, mixed media. Courtesy Didier Fiuza
Faustino / Bureau des Mesarchitectures.

7.4
JÜRGEN MAYER H. office (Berlin), Metropol Parasol,
Plaza de la Encarnación, Seville, 2004–2011. Photo:
David Franck. Courtesy the architect.

Spheres

The "radical" architecture of the 1960s and 1970s exposed the inherent, zoological weaknesses of humanity: the fragility of the human species in the face of technological and industrial developments, the solitude of individuals in the abyss of digital landscapes, the vertiginous obliteration of differences between animate and inanimate beings, and the disquieting mutations of the human body at the immunological level. Indeed, to cite just one example, the Austrian neo-avant-garde drew inspiration from the imagery of space research, as seen in the Pneumo-City (1966), and in the Mobile Hotel project (1972) of Gernot and Johanne Nalbach: a tower block rising from a base set on a tractor-trailer, onto which twenty-four rooms could be grafted.[46] Gernot Nalbach designed the Pneumatic Furnishing Carpet, called also Pneumatic Armchair (1967), which, through inflation or deflation, became a mobile, evolving environment.[47] In Vienna, where the influence of the *Aktionismus* movement was felt directly, the practice of alternative architecture by the counterculture seemed to converge with the approach associated with happenings and performance.

Prosthetic tendencies can be clearly detected in the lunar pods inspired by the Haus-Rucker-Co group, such as their famous Pneumacosm (1967) and Gelbes Herz (1968), as well as their multisensorial helmets, Mind Expander (1967), Fly Head (1968), and Mind Expander II (1968–1969), which evoked huge insect heads and pointed the way toward an exploration of intermediality.[48] In Haus-Rucker-Co's Ballon für Zwei (1967), and Oasis No. 7 (1972), a couple was exhibited in a glass house that took the form of a transparent bubble. This device was parasitically attached to the façade of a building so that its inhabitants were thrust into the street. Privacy was yanked from its preserve, taken out of doors, placed on view, made into a spectacle. With the projection of the inhabitants onto the exterior, the project also rejected the idea of the private subject. Such a provocation seemed to imply the destruction of intimacy and the devastation of private spaces. In this experiment, however, the "baring" was deliberate—the bodies were self-exhibited, exhibiting skin in a playful, joyous manner: albeit an exhibitionism that might lead to a veritable apocalypse of being. Prosthesis can also be perceived in the organic associations of work by Coop Himmelb(l)au, notably the inflatable Villa Rosa (1967), the breathing, lunglike Cloud (1968), and the Astro Balloon (1969), which emitted sounds and light to convey the beating of a heart.[49] Here, extreme architecture exposes and experiments with the body's state of extreme defenselessness.

It is fair to ask whether everything tested in these multiple architectural projects had not already been anticipated by Marshall McLuhan, who, first in the prologue to *The Gutenberg Galaxy* (1962), second in *Understanding Media* (1964), and then in *The Medium Is the Massage* (1967), repeatedly argued that media are extensions of our human senses, bodies, and minds.[50] In calling media extensions of the human nervous system, McLuhan believed he was offering an elegant image; however, he was not aware that such concepts had been fully explored by nineteenth-century physiologists, such as Étienne-Jules Marey and Hermann von Helmholtz; or by Wilhelm Braune's and Otto Fischer's physiology of the human's walk. Nevertheless, like skin, tools, and the media, architecture was allegedly becoming an extension of the human being. Consequently, the environment was being conceived and designed in terms of the superimposition of various spheres: skin and epithelial envelopes; objects, tools, utensils, equipment, and machines; earth, air, fire, and water; light, clouds, stars, climate, weather; and media interfaces. Such architecture would indeed be "atmo-spheric," a condition exemplified by Diller + Scofidio's Blur Building (2002), which evoked Peter Sloterdijk's opus on spherology, *Bubbles* (1998).[51]

7.5
Coop Himmelb(l)au, *Villa Rosa*, Vienna, 1966–1970
(model 1967), plastic, wood, and mixed media. FRAC
Centre collection, Orléans, France.

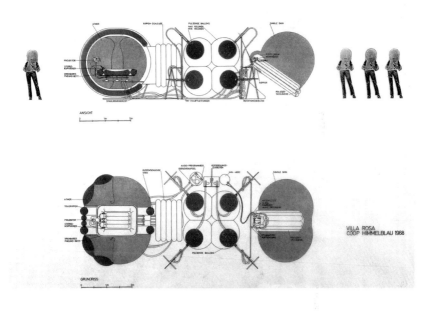

7.6
Coop Himmelb(l)au (Wolf D. Prix, Helmut Swiczinsky,
Michael Holzer), *Villa Rosa*, Vienna, 1968, ink
drawing. FRAC Centre collection, Orléans, France.

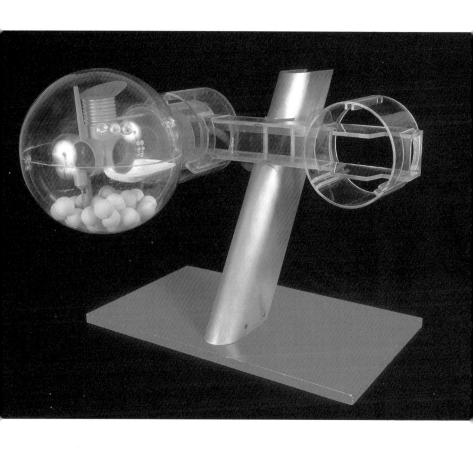

7.7
Haus-Rucker-Co (Laurids Ortner, Günther Zamp Kelp,
and Klaus Pinter), *Pneumacosm*, 1967–1971, model
1968, plastics and Plexiglas. FRAC Centre collection,
Orléans, France.

As Sloterdijk showed in *The Domestication of Being* (2000), the idea of habitation is above all linked to the occupation of the ground, and especially to the clearing of a space that must be equipped.[52] The notion of "clearing" is derived from *Lichtung* as used by Martin Heidegger in his "Letter on Humanism" (1947).[53] This idea also derives, as Jacques Derrida demonstrated in 1993, from the Platonist *khôra*, conceived as the matrix of all dimensions and the receptacle of all Becoming.[54] It is in this sense that the notion of sphere relates to the primal, "womblike" receptacle of dimensions and directions. Independent of all metaphor, this sphere may be seen as a glass house or bubble, insofar as it establishes special climatic conditions. The environment—that guarantee of organic life, that region or land enveloping us—is first of all a cage, a bubble, a ring. It takes the form of a median world located between the organic projection of animal life and the projection of hominids—via a clearing—into the world.[55] The sphere is topologically intermediate. On one side there is an (animal) being surrounded by a ring or coil, an enclosure, a border; on the other side, a (human) being capable of an *ek-static* act of exceeding oneself by opening up—making a clearing—to an indeterminate world. The sphere, as intermediary, also plays the role of intermediality.

Defining the conditions of domestication, spheres are envelopes, ontological membranes between interior and exterior. Spheres determine (and are determined by) the interval between here and there.[56] Placed between proximity and distance, the finite and the infinite, the limited and the limitless, and the symbolic and the diabolical, spheres are defined precisely by an *inter*-betweenness, from the Latin root *inter*, which is also part of *inter*ior, *inter*mediary, and even *inter*mediality. Indeed, explains Sloterdijk, spheres are media, ones that preceded contemporary media.[57] In their intermediate role between encirclement (corporeal and animal) and symbol (corporeal and human), spheres

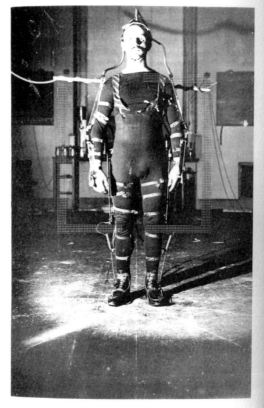

Das Versuchsindividuum in voller Ausrüstung.

7.8
The Human's Walk; in Wilhelm Braune and Otto
Fischer, *Der Gang des Menschen*, Abhandlungen
der Königlich Sächsischen Gesellschaft der
Wissenschaften; mathematisch-physische Klasse
(Leipzig: Hirzel, 1895–1904), Part 6th, pl. 2. Courtesy
Werner Nekes Collection, Mülheim/Ruhr, Germany.

create a state of intermediality. By providing a shelter where physical contact, metabolic processes, and reproduction and incubation are all possible, spheres provide a medium for organic needs, thereby insuring a habitat in the biological sense of the term. The habitat is both an abode and a "house" in the Heideggerian sense of "house of being," the site of humanity's Becoming and Destiny. This conception views the house as that which allows for acclimatization on an ontological level. Spheres offer an opportunity to stop somewhere, to domesticate, to interiorize; at the same time, through an *ek-static* process (from Greek, *ek-stasis*, stepping forth), spheres offer an opening toward symbolism and language, in the direction of the external world, allowing access to objects beyond reach, such as the horizon and the stars. However, as Nancy reminds us, "circles, spheres and their imbricated harmonies" are all forms of "the *annulment* of space," because neither our bodies nor the world are circular or spherical.[58] Ecotechnical creations must not hide the fact that things are not "well-rounded."

Parasite

At the heart of this problematic of the sphere is the urgent question of the interaction between framework and prosthesis: frame as extension and projection of instrumentality, prosthesis as a new form of hospitality. From there, we must work on concepts of hostility, unusualness, discomfort, alienation, and the uncanny. Indeed, a prosthesis, like a graft or transplant, can be simultaneously hospitable and hostile. It vacillates between those two poles—*hospes* and *hostis*, guest and enemy[59]—as is already recognized on the surgical level. Arborists, for instance, know how to graft a scion from one tree to another. In a gastronomical context, the *hospes/hostis* divide challenges the usual meaning of *table d'hôte* (a common dining table frequented by an indiscreet, parasitical guest). On a political level, the ambivalence between the terms hospitality and hostility is contradictory only at first sight. The Latin proverb "Hospes hostis!" implied that "every foreigner [is] an enemy." It stemmed from the fact that the establishment of any state (a commonwealth, the *polis*, an organism) is ultimately determined by the identification of an enemy (foreigner, invader, colonizer, virus, parasite) whom the "state" must resist.[60] This leads to an examination of other categories, like the graft and parasite. In a context of lack or absence—a gap or a specific need—a transplant indeed acts as a replacement. The realm of replacement then opens onto possibilities of placement, displacement, and replacement, a new definition of the term *place*, and the logic of substitution in the architectural sphere.

The position defended here is that environments for cyborgs do not need to be depicted (or "designed") because they already constitute their own surroundings. This does not mean that one should argue about the pointlessness of virtual architecture or, to be more precise, reject the use of digital tools in architecture. However, it is urgent to conceive the (human) body in relation to these new means—these new media: digital, virtual—which have become unavoidable. Perhaps one should conceptualize them as a new means of transforming our manner of seeing and conceiving the world, just as perspective was developed in the Middle Ages and the Renaissance. One should also be wary of certain shortcuts. The opposition is not between the real and the virtual, but between the actual (the given, existing reality) and the virtual (Latin *virtus*, force). The virtual is not currently present, but posits itself as a potential force.[61] This means several things: first, the virtual has long existed, prior to the arrival of the digital. The virtual has been with us at least since the Renaissance—artificial perspective is virtual; Descartes's dioptrics were virtual, as were Athanasius Kircher's mirror devices and the eighteenth-century camera obscura. Furthermore, it is useful to stress that the actual and the virtual are equally real. The actual and the virtual are

7.9
Klaus Pinter (born 1940, one of the founders of Haus-Rucker-Co), *The Cocoon*, 1971, collage and photomontage (photography). Collection Centre Pompidou, Dist. RMN / Photo Georges Meguerditchian / Agence Photographique (RMN) / Art Resource, NY / ARS (Artists Rights Society, New York).

not opposing or mutually exclusive terms, but express a differentiation that could be conceptually articulated, as Deleuze has shown, through the configuration of the fold.[62]

The cyborg environment is configured like a hybrid organism: a kind of organless body, pervaded by information (messages) and noise (parasites). Information theory, for that matter, teaches that message and noise are simultaneously contradictory and necessary to one another. "We are surrounded by noise,"[63] remarks Michel Serres in *The Parasite* (1980). And he grimly insists: "we are buried with ourselves; we send out signals, gestures, and sounds indefinitely and uselessly. No one listens to anyone else. Everyone speaks; no one hears."[64] Work means bringing order and sending an audible message: "What is work? Undoubtedly, it is a struggle against noise."[65] If this predicament appears alarming, it is because it carries the burden of negative entropy, which, since Claude Shannon and Warren Weaver, rules the telecom environment.[66] However, some hope remains, since, like static in communication systems, "the noise is a joker. It has at least two values . . . a value of destruction and a value of construction."[67] According to Serres, the right question to ask is: "Where am I now?"[68] The beginning of an answer would be: "I have found a spot where, give or take one vibration, [something] causes the noise to become messages and the messages, noises."[69] During the seventeenth century, Gottfried Wilhelm Leibniz was probably right to think that "monads [were] closed; they neither hear one another nor listen to one another. And yet sometimes there is agreement. The most amazing thing in the world is that agreement, understanding, harmony, sometimes exist."[70] Otherwise there would be no music. Computer science revisited the same problem. Norbert Wiener's models of communication suggested that "the probability of harmony is weak in the multiple distributions of senders and the qualitative weakness of reception,"[71] plunging in a "habitual cacophony."[72] Sadly, according to Wiener, "the collective is a black box. The set makes noise. . . . The collective is white noise itself."[73] The outcome is that "noise separates us, individualizes us. . . . The thick wall that exists between us is built of noises and cacophony."[74] Nevertheless, amid this noisy milieu, within such chaos, it is possible to recognize patterns, to visualize shapes, to perceive forms. "In the beginning is the noise; the noise never stops. It is our apperception of chaos, our apprehension of disorder, our only link to the scattered distribution of things."[75] For Serres, "Noise destroys and horrifies,"[76] but, at the same time, "noise nourishes a new order. Organization, life, and intelligent thought live between order and noise, between disorder and perfect harmony."[77] In some unexpected ways, when such a miracle happens, order emerges from chaos.

Technology may not be integrated by "imagining" a new environment, but perhaps by reconfiguring the body itself, pushing outward to where its artificial extremities encounter the "world." It is not so much a case of devising new dwellings for cyborgs. Those semihuman, semisynthesized, constantly mutating entities are already environments, milieus, surfaces where relationships between self and world come into play. The cyborg thus entails a reconsideration of the body, literally (re)crafting it as an improved organism equipped with instruments, so that it can "inhabit" the world and negotiate transactions with the multiple spheres of physical and mental comfort, media, and information. Through technologies of implantation, autoplasty, and amplification, the categories of well-being, media, and information can henceforth become multiple—a multiplicity that leads to a multiplication of registers.

The interior of the dwelling, finally, might be redefined as the movement of the body toward the exterior, in a state of *ekstasis*, through the various filters—thresholds, frontiers, wireless networks—that delimit our surroundings. It would be possible to turn inside-out the multiple surfaces that frame our "place-of-being." Like a Klein bottle—or an ordinary sock—the interior will conceivably be able to turn itself logically, and topologically, into an exterior. Architecture is thus transformed into a device that participates in this staging of an "ecstasy." Given this novel situation, an architectural design no longer simply leads to something to look at (such as an object or building), but rather becomes an apparatus that allows the viewer—that is, the user—to behold something other than the thing itself.

8 WINDOWS AND SCREENS

Whoever leads a solitary life and yet now and then wants to attach himself somewhere, whoever, according to changes in the time of day, the weather, the state of his business, and the like, suddenly wishes to see any arm at all to which he might cling—he will not be able to manage for long without a window looking on to the street.
—Franz Kafka, "The Street Window" (c. 1904)[1]

Instead of being a painter, I would have liked, on this occasion, to be thought of as a fenêtrier.[2]
—Marcel Duchamp

Once the current loss of traditional public spaces is acknowledged, the border between the public and the private realm will need to be redrawn. The question today is whether one can imagine a public space founded in plurality—that is, a public space conceived not as a unique place, but within a multiplicity. Perhaps what needs to be explored are the shifting limits between the intimacy and publicity opened up by new media, offering the rise of a digital *flâneur* and leading to a worldwide *dérive*. These novel confines are outlining original zones where one can dwell, singularly as well as collectively. At present, issues that are urgent to address include the topic of the "gaze," concerns about the rise and fall of privacy, and the concept of the "in-between." Moreover, one might ask how the notions of window, door, frame, and screen have unfolded in time, and how, under new guises, they contribute to the emergence of a virtual terrain or digital topographies.

Scopic Regimes

Human beings could be characterized as "animals with windows," inasmuch as between world and subject there is always something that mediates—not so much a medium per se, but something that connects all outside things and us. In his seminal book *Fenêtre* (Window, 2004), the psychoanalyst Gérard Wajcman recalls that a "window" is not only a literary trope or metaphor, but also an actual mechanism, referring to the real window—an actual window built with a set of frames and glass panes, often protected on the outside by shutters and on the inside by curtains.[3] However, if one were to rip off the frame and mullions holding the glass panes, one would be left with just an aperture, bay, or gap in the wall that lets one look through. Such an opening would function as an apparatus of vision—as an eye. And if the window can be an "eye," then the eye can be a window. In human history many things have been our windows: spectacles, paintings, cameras, videos—instruments that help us connect to the world in which we are constantly immersed.

Like any other instrument (including language), the window is an apparatus that separates and unites. The English word *window* derives from *wind* and *eye*; this etymology helps define the window aperture as a complex instrument that both admits light and ventilation to an interior and enables the eye—that is, one's vision.[4] Since Leon Battista Alberti's famous treatise on painting, the metaphor for painting has been an "open window (*aperta finestra*) through which the subject (*historia*) to be painted is seen."[5] This comparison established the Western way of seeing the

8.1
Albrecht Dürer, *St. Jerome in His Cell*, engraving,
1514. Victoria and Albert Museum, London.

world as a picture; it also transformed the actual window, which at the time of Alberti was neither squared nor perfectly glazed or transparent. Beginning with the Renaissance, the window presents, on the one hand, its utility as a means for lighting, ventilation, insulation, and the like; on the other hand, it is thought of as something to look through. The window is an "architectural" feature that serves both as a useful, hygienic device connected to the body's needs, and as an "optical" apparatus, a kind of magnifying glass or pair of spectacles. In the latter instance, it is as if the window were equipped with an "artificial eye," and it appears as such in some of the engraved plates of Athanasius Kircher's treatise on optics, *Ars magna lucis et umbrae* (Art of Light and Shadows, 1646). A polymath Jesuit, Kircher founded and directed the Museum Kircherianum in the Collegio Romano in Rome, where he exhibited a collection of antiquities along with devices of his own creation. In his description of the museum (*Romani collegii Societatus Jesu musaeum celeberrimum*, Amsterdam, 1678), he wrote one of the earliest explanations of how to build and use a magic lantern.[6] As a musician, Kircher was also interested in the propagation of sound. In his *Phonurgia nova* (New Soundcraft, 1673), he showed interest in wind harps and echo chambers, explained how to test the power of horns, and gave many details on how to build various noisemaking devices, including megaphones with the practical purpose of amplifying the voice through a building, but also useful for spying.[7] In his *Musurgia universalis* (Rome, 1650), the first universal history and compendium of world music, one illustration depicts a listening device plugged into a piazza: voices in the piazza are taken in by the horn up through the mouth of a statue in a room on the *piano nobile* above, allowing for both espionage and the appearance of a miraculous event.[8] Inspired by Vitruvius's notes on devices found in Roman theaters, Kircher designed resonance chambers to enhance the voices of the actors.[9] In a volume published by another Jesuit, Mario Bettini's encyclopedic *Apiaria universae philosophiae mathematicae* (Collection of Mathematical Curiosities, 1642), an entire room is made a camera obscura: light is brought through small apertures in a covered window to project images on the surface of the opposing wall, which becomes a "screen." The window has been essentially blinded, which allows a counterfeit, "virtual" spectacle to appear.[10]

Alberti's painting-as-window creates the conditions for the modern spectator. One can stare through a window at the view or at the passersby without being seen. The rise of the modern spectator parallels that of an onlooker armed with his "gaze" (here, one can refer to all that has been written on the concept of *le regard*, "the gaze"). The world seen through the window as painting shows no continuity with the space where the observer stands—instead of a continuum there is only distance, which is underlined by the frame. The onlooker's gaze is asymmetrical, because he sees without being seen. This lack of symmetry, which appears during the Renaissance with the so-called "invention" of perspective, will become a more and more powerful phenomenon, bolstered by new devices such as Jeremy Bentham's Panopticon (1791).[11] Yet, the Albertian window is not merely an aperture toward an exterior. It also defines many opposite sets of spaces: the exterior and the interior; the illuminated and the adumbrated; the visible and the invisible; the manifest and the hidden. As Wajcman points out, the idea of painting-as-window frees man from a tyrannical, divine gaze, "thus becoming the Viewer of the World, of a world that has become image."[12] With the hidden comes the possibility for the intimate, a term derived from the Latin *intimus*, the superlative of *interior*, which describes what is hidden from the Other's gaze. Intimate is a stronger notion than private. Privacy was (and still is) mainly ruled and circumscribed by law. It is founded on prohibition and advice: "It is forbidden to look or to peep, and, please, be discreet."

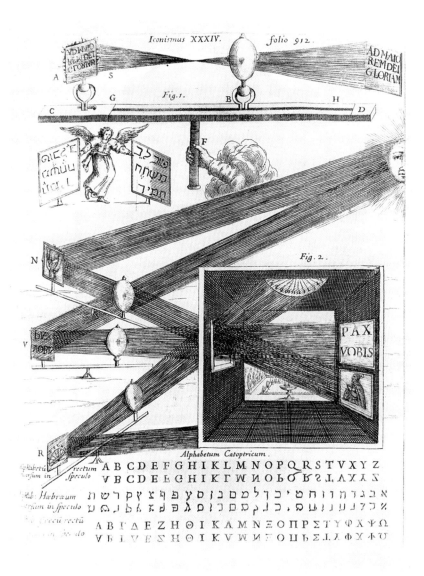

Iconismus XXXIV.   folio 912.

Fig. 1.

Fig. 2.

PAX
VOBIS

Alphabetum Catoptricum.

A B C D E F G H I K L M N O P Q R S T V X Y Z

Hæb. Hebraeum

A B Γ Δ E Z H Θ I K Λ M N Ξ O Π P Σ T Y Φ X Ψ Ω

8.2
Projecting inscriptions through a set of lenses; in
Athanasius Kircher, *Ars magna lucis et umbrae* (Rome:
H. Scheus, 1646), 912, pl. 34. Courtesy Werner
Nekes Collection, Mülheim/Ruhr, Germany.

8.3
Camera obscura; in Mario Bettini, *Apiaria universae
philosophiae mathematicae* (Bologna: typis J. B.
Ferronii, 1642), VI, 38. Courtesy Werner Nekes
Collection, Mülheim/Ruhr, Germany.

Indiscretion determines a highly mutable territory, one that is difficult to map.

Every gaze is potentially indiscreet, but when it penetrates domestic interiors it becomes intrusive, a violation, even a rape. For a Christian, to let the gaze enter a house is correspondent to an act of violence.[13] To stare is like opening up the house as if it were a body, letting corruption cross the threshold and threaten the soul inside, to which only a divine power has access. The dangers of indiscretion are illustrated in an engraving by Cornelius Galle, published in Jean David's *Veridicus Christianus* (1601), in which a house appears in the shape of a human head.[14] The harmful gaze might infiltrate this "house" through the mouth (the door), the nostrils (a ventilation porthole), or the ears and eyes (windows). As is customary in baroque emblems, on top of the engraved image, a lemma, or maxim, is inscribed, warning the reader: "Adspectus Incauti Dispendium" (Looking does harm to the careless person).[15] With the body of the house threatened by indiscreet, sinful gazes, priests and moralists of all confessions are called in to protect the domestic space with all its gaping orifices—including the feminine sex. Beneath the same image by Galle, an epigram is inscribed in Latin, Old Dutch, and archaic French, once more advising the reader that the indiscreet, prying gaze can lead to eternal death.[16] Religious authorities' repeated condemnation of the flesh will help draw a new geography of the hidden, which gives a renewed importance to the image of naked bodies and leads to a new eroticism, of which voyeurism will be a consistent and active part. As Wajcman writes, "If one speaks of voyeurism . . . it is because the body itself is conceived as a house. To look inside through the window amounts to entering a forbidden body, thus performing a highly prohibited act that by all means every authority was attempting to prevent."[17] While the gaze penetrates inside, a new *jouissance* is born: to look. The prohibition always contains its opposite—its violation.

Public and Private

Next to the progression of privacy, it seems necessary to investigate the origin and rationale underlying the delimitation between public and private spheres. Without referring to the lengthy history of its delimitations in philosophical and legal sources, one can perhaps rely on the economist and historian Albert Hirschman's book *Shifting Involvements: Private Interests and Public Action* (1982), in which he explains that the term *private* was born as a negative concept, derived from the Latin *privare*—that is, to deprive someone of something, to dispossess someone of what he has. Thus private was a (negative) notion of subtraction, in relation to the positive one of public affairs, the commonwealth. From an historical point of view, privatization has been a less-than-evident process. According to Hirschman, the innovative opinion that emerged between the sixteenth and nineteenth centuries was that the pursuit of private interests was most likely to ensure a harmonious social order. The English philosopher Bernard Mandeville argued this point in his *Fable of the Bees, or, Private Vices, Publick Benefits* (1714), writing: "Fraud, Luxury and Pride must live / While we the Benefits receive."[18] Even during the eighteenth century, a term like *happiness* still implied a public dimension. In that period, the translation of the collective imperatives of society into the practice of architecture was made through the theory of urban beautification or improvement (*embellissement*). In reality, this notion was a mask that dissembled the changes taking place in the city. "Public" architecture—that is, buildings commissioned by the monarchy—was part of what historians have termed the "system of luxury."

Quid, qui emiſſitios nuſquam non iactat ocellos?
Hoc agit, vt pandas mors inuolet atra feneſtras.

Wat doet hy, die ſyn vogh' int ſien niet en beswaert?
Hy heft die vensters hoogh, al waer de doot inbaert.

Qui laiſſe s'eſbatre / Sa veue folatre / Quel malheur l'attend?
La mort æternelle / Par ces trous eſchelle / L'ame, et la ſurprend.

8.4
Original lemma in Latin: "Adspectus Incauti
Dispendium"; English translation: "Looking does harm
to the careless person"; a maxim inscribed on top
of an engraving by Cornelius Galle in Jean David,
Veridicus Christianus (Antwerp: ex officina Plantiniana,
1601). Courtesy Werner Nekes Collection, Mülheim/
Ruhr, Germany.

8.5
Window in a Renaissance house, Moenchgasse,
Goslar, Lower Saxony, Germany, 1562, detail; in Karl
Schaefer, *Die Holzarchitektur Deutschlands vom XIV.
bis XVIII. Jahrhundert* (Berlin: Wasmuth, 1883–1888),
pl. 21. Courtesy of ETH-Bau Library.

Luxury marked out an area in which the expenditure of the king or prince was to be displayed, thereby demarcating a social area in the city. The ostentation of wealth, which defined the very space of its action, constituted what could be called a network of monuments. In the eighteenth century, luxury was thought to be the most effective means of establishing order in society.[19]

Within cities of this period, one might observe the contiguity of two heterogeneous and opposing spaces: orderly luxury and the world of indistinct chaos. Until the 1760s, architecture linked its field of application to what was known as the "luxury of decorum."[20] Chaos, by contrast, characterized the space of the private. The private was regarded as a negative space in relation to luxury, which was the space of public affairs—what was publicly displayed as spectacle. Luxury and chaos established two opposing systems in the city. This was precisely stated in the urban theory of the day,[21] which set out to formulate a political program for the "improvement" of the city. The monument presented a spectacle, regulated by its own logic, which could, moreover, be dictated by architecture, as described in Jacques-François Blondel's *Cours d'architecture* (1771–1777): "To the eyes of strangers and citizens alike, each of these buildings ought to offer, through their diversity, the image of the various orders of a policed state."[22] The private was not administered by these theories of luxury. Rather, theories about the private were based on a system described in treatises published by the police, including the *Traité de la police* (1705–1738) by Nicolas de La Mare. Edifices known as private buildings formed the indistinct background of a town.[23] The term *particulier* was used in eighteenth-century France to define private space. "Private buildings" were thought to be uncontrollable and thus had to be governed not by architectural, artistic, or aesthetic rules, but by police regulations. The caesura between the two regimes was clear: public buildings need few regulations, because liberal arts already rule them;

private houses, which do not belong to the realm of architecture, require intensive surveillance by the police.

The term *police* derives from *polis*, the Greek word for city. However, between the *polis* idealized in all discussions of architecture and city planning, and the suspicious and cautious "police" who organized control and scrutiny through the imposition of minute regulations, some singular relations were created. City planning, like sanitation, was invented to bring order to the disordered. The distinction between the concepts of *monumental* and *particular* constituted a sort of archaeology of the division of the *polis* into public and private spaces, a division that would be forcefully established during the nineteenth century.

Framing the Gaze

While the window always performs through a double nature, the architectural aspect of the window is based on need for light and air, although it does not exclude optical use. It seems, however, that except for military defense purposes, the "optical" use of windows was not part of architectural theory and practice. Wajcman maintains that the architectural window is "blind" and that the gaze is not the principal object of architecture but of painting. ("Gaze" therefore implies voyeurism and all of its vagaries.) Without disputing such an assertion, it would be interesting to verify whether the architectural knowledge that applies to a palace's façade, from the early Italian Renaissance to the baroque period, was ever able to evade questions regarding such things as the horizontal division of floors with the *piano nobile*, the harmonic repetition of aedicules and arches, the choice of orders for columns or pilasters, and so on.[24] Because architecture belongs to a regime of luxury that exposes itself in order to impose an order on society (both visual-aesthetic and rational-technical), buildings are defined through their exterior surfaces. One speaks of the façade, or even the "face" of a building, defined by

André Félibien as "the side turned frontward through which one enters, or a considerable part of what presents itself to anyone who is looking at it."[25] Since architecture refers to the image of a human body, it would be more precise to allude to a visage; however, it would be a visage devoid of a gaze. One can rarely, if ever, say that architecture "gazes back."

Without eyes that look, façades pierced by rows of windows are like a visage without a gaze—that is, the architectural window is blind.[26] Of course, one could always look through the window. Nevertheless, one should distinguish between an optical window and an architectural one, attempt to parse the two distinct scopic regimes, and understand their dissimilarities. During the classical and modern periods, the architectural window often resembled the blind face of power; it remained all the more so with the introduction of the glazed curtain wall in the twentieth century. Within architecture, then, is a type of disembodied "subject." A now classic example of an optical window is seen in Alfred Hitchcock's *Rear Window* (1954), in which a wheelchair-bound photographer (James Stewart), his leg immobilized by a plaster cast and thus unable to respond to his girlfriend's desire (Grace Kelly), uses a potent telephoto lens to observe the lives of his neighbors. Here the subject is reduced to his own eye enhanced by a prosthesis, his energy encapsulated in scopic pulsions.

8.6
Window of Renaissance palace in Florence; in Julien Guadet, *Éléments et théorie de l'architecture*, 5th ed. (Paris: Librairie de la Construction Moderne, 1910), vol. 1, fig. 200. Courtesy Prof. Martin Bressani, McGill University.

Fig. 200. — Fenêtre d'un palais à Florence.

Behind the Victorian conception of private and public lay a topography upon which the juridical existence of habitation was based. Thresholds, sheltered by a variety of custodians and janitors, were thus complex filters, sieves that let the outside come inside. In France, for instance, the first legal disposition that insured the nonviolability of the domicile was passed in 1791.[27] During the first half of the nineteenth century, the expression "wall of private life" assumed its legal and social significance. The French term *intérieur* no longer referred to the interiority of the human heart or soul, but to what, in its midst, guaranteed the conditions for happiness and comfort. Nevertheless, before long the new media of communication—books, newspapers, and magazines—moved into domestic spaces and the tendrils of a planetary knowledge penetrated those sedate rooms, even before the spread of technologies such as the telephone and electricity.[28] As the home became the place of conflicting passions, it emerged as the fortress of English "privacy" (or of German *Gemütlichkeit*), while conversely also becoming a microcosm crisscrossed by mobile borders. In domestic spaces the public and the private engaged in confrontations, a state of warfare that led to André Gide's famous exclamation in 1897: "Families, I hate you! Shut-in homes, closed doors, jealous possessions of happiness."[29] The dividing line between public and private spheres formed an active battleground, one that was constantly shifting and readjusting as society's norms changed and evolved. For example, the telephone was perceived as an unbearable infringement by some, while at the same time it ushered in personalized and individualized information—the tendrils became tentacles.

Today, thresholds rarely constitute a barrier to public space, if they ever did; nor are they conceivable as an obstacle to permeability. For clues to this border condition, one has to reread Georg Simmel's 1909 essay "Bridge and Door," in which he asserts that human nature is constituted by both separation and unification.[30]

8.7
Adolf von Menzel (1815–1905), *The Balcony Room*,
1845, oil on cardboard, 58.0 × 47.0 cm. Courtesy
of Nationalgalerie, Staatliche Museen, Berlin, Germany
(Photo: Joerg P. Anders, Berlin) / Art Resource, NY.

8.8
Gustave Caillebotte (1848–1894), *Interior with Woman at the Window*, 1880, Private Collection. Photo: Scala/White Images / Art Resource, NY.

Paradoxically, a human being is an inhabitant of confines, a creature living enduringly on the frontier; yet, at the same time, he has no secure limits by which to enclose himself. It is the human prerogative to decide, in the face of nature, whether to bond or to cut oneself off, and one way of acting will always presuppose the other. This binomial entity of separation/union is best compared to the two banks of a river: separate, only to be united by a bridge. Overcoming this separation, a bridge also symbolizes the extension of human willpower in space. By spanning via an overpass, one connects, and reconnects, what was separated. A human being inhabits thresholds. The door offers the means to settle within, but it is also what permits one to step out, to cross the border, to unsettle. The sedentary notion of lodging should never be thought without the prospect of a nomadic dislodgment.

Simmel had previously mapped reciprocal states of unity and exclusion in his 1902 essay "The Picture Frame: An Aesthetic Study," a seminal investigation on the nature of framing an artwork.[31] Here, the frame, by the very materiality of its border, is thought as a device that helps the work of art to exclude anything exterior while offering a concentration in its interior. The frame guarantees the possibility of an autonomous existence for an artwork by inscribing it in a place that will resist the continuous "exosmosis" and "endosmosis" that occur in a living cell. For Simmel, nothing should battle with the secondary position of the frame in relation to the painting; instead, everything (matter, color, form, and shape) should maintain the frame as a *parergon* (subordinate work or accessory), a probable echo of Immanuel Kant's considerations on the status of the artwork (*ergon*, main work). Any attempt to weaken the essence of the framing—by opening up the encircling border, by transforming the frame into a piece of furniture, or by using the shape of architectural elements (such as pilasters or pediments) to build the frame—is condemned, inasmuch as it would abate its "parergonality."[32] A subversion or inversion of this hierarchy could derive from an artist's choice or stratagem, or even be the result of a regressive strategy.

This happens because the frame, like the door, is situated in an unstable position, acting as an intermediary between the artwork and its surroundings—with which it is united; from which it is separated. For Simmel, the artwork's frame is a metaphor for the border between social groups, thus showing that the true function of framing is "closing"[33] the object "off against the surrounding world and holding it together."[34] Simmel also analogizes the simultaneous wholeness of a work of art (inclusive of its harmony with its surroundings) to the difficulties encountered by collective social entities, whose members have the contradictory aspirations of both belonging to a group and laying claim to the status of autonomous individuals. Simmel's oeuvre offers a complex theory of the passage and the border that will influence his pupils, such as Georg Lukács, Ernst Bloch, and Siegfried Kracauer, as well as Walter Benjamin's work on dialectical images. For both Simmel and Benjamin, the border reveals itself through an "in-between" condition. Any threshold or marginal zone induces a reciprocal state—it looks two ways at once.

Ethereal Spaces

At the end of the nineteenth century, with the electrification of houses and the proliferation of telephone lines, energy itself invaded the interior. Transparency was not so much a matter of making use of metal and glass in construction as it was a question of how energies would be figured and represented. Around 1900, ether was known as the imponderable medium thought to fill all space and to serve as the vehicle for the transmission of light waves; in the popular imagination, ether was synonymous with space.[35] The interior was now a permeable space where bodies acted within force fields. Henceforth, architecture's scope would

8.9
Window, Great Britain, nineteenth century, from "Get
rid of all disagreeable views from your windows,"
McCaw, Stevenson & Orr's, Glacier Window Decoration,
advertisement, 1890. Courtesy of John Johnson
collection, Bodleian Library, Oxford.

provide both separation and penetrability, becoming what biology has termed a membrane. In a cell, the surface membrane permits the organism to find homeostasis, a balance between solidity and permeability that insures the conditions for processes such as osmosis. In 1926, following this logic, Siegfried Ebeling published *Space as Membrane*, in which he conceived of the house as a multicellular, hollow space whose surfaces were free of anything that would impede the flow of metabolic energies.[36] At last, architecture instantiated the ether, and by embodying invisible forces it acquired an ethereal character. Not by chance, "Ethernet" was the name given to local area networks (LANs) by Bob Metcalf at Xerox PARC (Palo Alto Research Center) in 1973, an invention that still governs the basis of communication in our techno-bodied existence, propagating our thoughts, feelings, and desires at the planetary scale.[37] During the same period, Gilles Deleuze appropriated a biological theory of individuation and differentiation from Gilbert Simondon's seminal work on the philosophy of science and technology, which helped him to define the notion of "body-without-organs." On the basis of Simondon's work, Deleuze founds a theory of limits that overcomes the dualism between interiority and exteriority, yet allows him to maintain that the skin's surface is the most profound condition, and that the living lives at the limit of itself, because Life's characteristic polarities are situated at the level of the membrane. Noting that Simondon writes an admirable chapter on "Topology and Ontogenesis," Deleuze insists on the importance of Simondon's thesis: "The living being grows from the interior to the exterior, with the whole content of its interior in contact 'topologically' with the content of interior space."[38] Simondon offers a description of the processes of individuation and succeeds in exploring preindividual strata as the repository of singularities (in biology, for instance). An individual, according to Simondon (and Deleuze), is not a stable being, but the

result of processes, operations, and forms—a confluence of differential energies between affects, percepts, and emotions (all
traits of sensory experience versus intellection per se).

It is the very notion of limit that must be questioned. According to Paul Virilio, in his book *The Lost Dimension* (1984), limits are no longer defined by the façades of buildings, nor by the
surfaces of plots of land, but by the interface between man and
machine. The previous conception of private and public, or the
differentiation between house and street, is replaced by a new
"electronic topology" in which the grid of the numerical image re-
news the older divisions, such as the division of urban plots, with
an overexposure that cancels the sharp distinction between proximity and distance. The study of the man/machine interface has
led to a generalization of cybernetics. From control of machines
via self-regulating systems to the configuration of a body as an
information compound itself, we have moved into simulating
sensory responses for virtual environments and toward an ability to re-create the world (albeit a phantom world of partly motor
and partly emotive intersubjectivity). At present, our windows on
the world appear as multiple, portable, and nomadic screens: TVs,
LCD monitors or projectors, laptops, camcorders, digital cameras, wireless camera phones, PDAs and smart phones, touch devices, MP3 players, GPS screens, and interactive game consoles
with motion-sensitive controllers. At the moment, as industrial
and interaction designer Bill Moggridge points out, "Designers of
digital technology products no longer regard their task as designing a physical object . . . but as planning the user's interactions."
Today, cell phones show their ugly "face," revealed through layers of complexity and inconsistency. According to designers, this
user-unfriendliness is caused by the number of actors in the
game: from the fragmented state of cellular infrastructures to
the variety in the design of handsets, from the conflicting interactions of service providers to the scalability problems of Web

access. Indeed, superimposed layers are responsible for bad interactive design.[39]

Music streaming through the ether into tiny, elegant machines: Do these appliances do more harm than good? Are such sense-enhancing technologies—from the iPod to wireless Internet—the visible outcroppings of a total upheaval in the way the world is framed? State and corporate strategies of control are utterly unsympathetic, but the artifice could offer the means for opening new doors to perception. On the positive side, one can attend festivals of videos produced by cell phone cameras. On the negative side, due to the invasive technology of mobile phones, one risks being overwhelmed by acoustical attacks. Great success has been achieved by portable audio contraptions inasmuch as they manipulate sounds that are very close to us and to our thoughts, affects, and percepts. Headphones have created a private auditory universe in which sound literally moves through the body. Nevertheless, the enactment of an auditory privatization also offers the ingredients for conflict, a battleground on which sound, music, and noise will struggle. Perhaps due to the lack of an accepted etiquette regarding its use, the technology of mobile phones exasperatingly obliges everyone to listen to private chatter in public places. As Michael Bull notes, "Mobile phones are a case in point, confounding the separation of public and private spheres and our shifting and often contradictory relationship to them."[40] Accordingly, the only defense against noise is not silence, but more noise. Furthermore, because digital sound technologies are becoming more and more realistic, domestic spaces are increasingly divided into multiple listening and watching modules.[41]

In the realm of audio devices, one must acknowledge that Apple's iPod is the first cultural consumer icon of the twenty-first century. Not only is the design of the iPod refined and simple—even simpleminded but the user interface software is even smarter. A successor to Sony's Walkman, this stylish device offers private sonic spheres created by the personal playlist. In its miniaturization, technology acquires a magical touch, placing a vast digital world in one's hand. While carrying their own personal jukebox, users are surrounded by enveloping acoustics and move rhythmically through the space of the city, wrapped in their auditory bubbles. While one is continuously assaulted by noise, this portable implement creates a mobile zone of immunity and security.[42] Nomadic devices are the support of our way of life; they are endowed with a fascinating life of their own, probably extending the contours of our egotistical spheres, running experiments in which the body is the main node for technological mediation. From Kircher's resonating devices to Hermann von Helmholtz's physiology of sound to Thomas A. Edison's phonograph, it is possible to sketch a brief archaeology of the audiovisual, reaching today's architectural acoustics and audio devices.[43]

Marshall McLuhan was right to call media the extensions of the human nervous system, although he was not aware of the physiological research that was investigated in Carl Ludwig's kymograph (blood pressure), Étienne-Jules Marey's sphygmograph (pulse), Hermann von Helmholtz's physiology of the eye and ear, Angelo Mosso's ergograph (muscle's work), or Charles Féré's graphical representation of the phenomenon of psychomotor induction. For instance, Féré, a colleague of the neurologist Jean-Martin Charcot, conducted experiments on human subjects in which he measured physiological response to various forms of simulation and then attempted to quantify the relative strength or weakness of dynamogenic or inhibitory effect. Most relevant are his optical experiments, in particular those involving color. Following the graphical method of Marey's physiological studies, Féré's dynamographs are evidence of how visual representations became the abstract and quantified reactions of the body as a composite set of physical systems: "When rays of red light strike our eyes, our entire body sees red, as dyna-mometric reactions prove."[44] Overcoming any natural function, Féré's work is part of a larger instrumental relocation of vision from a disembodied and punctual system of images to an interplay of forces and motor reactions. Seeing is shifted to a completely nonoptical terrain. The retina is compounded with a neuromotor system triggered externally. Sensation and movement become a single event. Interestingly, Friedrich Nietzsche was a careful reader of Féré's work. In *The Will to Power*, he alludes to physiological states native to artists: "One must think of this condition as a compulsion and urge to get rid of the exuberance of inner tension through muscular activity and movements of all kinds; then an involuntary coordination between this movement and the processes within (images, thoughts desires)—as a kind of automatism of the whole muscular system impelled by strong stimuli from within. . . . Every inner movement (feeling, thought, affect) is accompanied by vascular changes and consequently by changes in color, temperature and secretion."[45]

Of all the technological and sensory transformations of electronic media, probably those concerning sound are the most radical.[46] To balance the hypertrophy of the eye, one has to recall the disembodiment of ear and voice. Sound recording requires duration, a fourth dimension that the visual arts do not trace. To store sound events requires a kind of inscription that traces time's serial flow.[47] Whether one is concerned with the visual, the acoustic, or the digital, it is possible to draw a chart of our sonic environment.[48] This would radically relocate the window/eye issue from a public/private question to the realm of the auditory. However, our digital world is audiovisual, and the two perceptive domains are blurred. Film, telephony, phonography, television, and the interface with computer screens are all connected psychotechnical practices. Nomadic devices offering portable audio/video capabilities help remap the limits of the public and the private.

Möbius Effect

The nomadic contrivances of our life are seductively alive today, stretching the contours of our egotistic spheres. As such, these pervasive, portable devices deeply transform our way of life. The philosopher Jean-Louis Déotte envisions three main stages in the process of such technological mutations, phases which are labeled under headings defined by the work of three major twentieth-century thinkers: Benjamin, Foucault, and Deleuze.[49] The three paradigms consist, respectively, in the prosthetic device, the control regime, and the nomadic flow. None of them has a chronological existence (or explanation), nor do they show any significant, diachronic logic; simply, they coexist in our post-utopian societies.

First, with Benjamin one comes to grips with a theory of the apparatus and equipment (photo and cinema), which exposes how the cameraman puts himself in the position of a surgeon, inasmuch as both operators implement practices that are conceptually close to the nature of a prosthetic equipment. For Benjamin, as with Dziga Vertov's *Man with a Movie Camera* (1929), "The magician maintains the natural distance between himself and the person treated. . . . The surgeon does exactly the reverse: he greatly diminishes the distance from the patient by penetrating the patient's body. . . . Magician is to surgeon as painter is to cinematographer. The painter maintains in his work a natural distance from reality, whereas the cinematographer penetrates deeply into its tissue. . . . *Hence, the presentation of reality in film is incomparably the more significant for people of today, since it provides the equipment-free aspect of reality they are entitled to demand from a work of art, and does so precisely on the basis of the most intensive*

8.10
Anonymous, nineteenth century, futuristic
representation of the video telephone in the year
2000, French engraving, c. 1900, Private Collection.
Photo: Snark / Art Resource, NY

interpenetration of reality with equipment."[50] Today the apparatus carried by the artist Hiroo Iwata—his *Floating Eye* (2000)—offers an illustration of such a prosthetic extension of the eye.[51]

In the second place, Foucault's theory of the device (*dispositif*) used Jeremy Bentham's Panopticon as its acme, and investigated the rules of vision and the regimes of visuality of various heterotopias, ultimately confronting one with an archaeology of the optical window, which permits the articulation of two heterogeneous series: that of knowledge (*savoir*) in the social sciences, and that of power (*pouvoir*).[52] More recently, in *What Is An Apparatus?*, Giorgio Agamben demonstrated that the concept of device (or apparatus) belongs to the field of economy in the Aristotelian sense, one that was appropriated by early Catholicism and scholasticism. For Agamben, any apparatus (including confession, penance, prison, or even cell phones) leads to a process of inexorable subjugation: "Apparatus . . . is first of all a machine that produces subjectifications, and only as such is it also a machine of governance."[53]

Third, the concepts of desiring machines and of nomadic disposition are defined by Deleuze (with Félix Guattari) in the famous chapter twelve of *A Thousand Plateaus*.[54] Nomadic subjects are free to roam across "un-striated," smooth spaces, where no aprioristic, artificial limits or barriers have been plotted on the land. The liberation of fluxes and flows in movement permits one to exit the old landscape and open up a new territory, wherein old subjectivities collapse. Moreover, the nomadic reality offers a "high-speed" condition, even if one remains motionless. Perhaps the best example of such a nomadic condition was Toyo Ito's 1985 installation *Dwelling for Tokyo Nomad Women*, or his *Electronic Tent* (1989).[55] With Ito, Tarzan literally tends to a "garden of microchips" in the "media forest."[56] For Deleuze, "Nomads are always in the middle . . . [they] have neither past nor future, they have only becomings. . . . Nomads have no history,

they only have geography."[57] Any emphasis on temporality has switched into spatial issues, while a planetary awareness has expanded, becoming topographical, and, with the rise of networks, even topological.

In *Cartographies schizoanalytiques* (1989), Félix Guattari outlines a system comprising four ontological "functions." To be precise, Guattari uses the term *foncteurs*, a neologism he crafts to evoke a merging of *fonction* (function) and *facteur* (factor). These *foncteurs* are based on the intersection of the virtual, the actual,[58] the real, and the possible, and they are capable of articulating complex relationships between technical and machinic Phyla (Φ), Universes of (incorporeal) values (U), Fluxes in the energy-space-time continuum (F), and (existential) Territories as chaosmic incarnations (T).[59] To put it in simpler terms, Guattari's *foncteurs* correspond to four ontological functions, respectively: machine-like discursivity, incorporeal complexity, discursivity in energy-space-time, and chaosmic incarnation. Inspired by the theories of Simondon and Deleuze, Guattari's intersections explain how the operation of "heterogenesis" constitutes an entropic phase in the formation of self-organizational crystals.[60] Later, in his book *Chaosmosis* (1992), Guattari returns to

8.11
Hiroo Iwata, *Floating Eye*, 2000, installation, Ars Electronica Festival, Linz (Austria), 2000. Courtesy the artist.

the concept of machinic heterogenesis: "Beneath the diversity of beings, no univocal ontological plinth is given, rather there is a plane of machinic interfaces. Being crystallizes through an infinity of enunciative assemblages associating actualized, discursive components (material and indicative Fluxes, machinic Phylums) with non-discursive, virtual components (incorporeal Universes and existential Territories)."[61] *Foncteurs* refers to functions that are "functive" (another neologism, which indicates components of functions). Guattari continues:

> In order to establish an intensive bridge between these actual and virtual functions (foncteurs) we are inclined to postulate the existence of a deterministic chaos animated by infinite velocities. It is out of this chaos that complex compositions, which are capable of being slowed down in energetico-spatio-temporal coordinates or category systems, constitute themselves. . . . By making assemblages of enunciation open, chaotically determined, the concatenation of the four ontological functions (foncteurs) of Universe, machinic Phylum, Flux and Territory, preserve their pragmatic processuality.[62]

Dismissing all universalist visions (cybernetics, for instance), Guattari's hypothesis of production (machine, language, art, flux, and so on) presents an interesting attempt to preserve in every individual the insecurity and the uncertainty that characterize all creation. In this concept of creation, the machine is considered in all its multiple levels, be they scientific, theoretical, aesthetic, or informational. This is no longer universal or systemic discursivity, but a multiplicity of partial subjectivities revealed in a state of heterogenesis. The use of such operators implies an ethical and political position, because these operators reformulate a possible praxis in the domain of affects, percepts, or concepts.[63] Heterogenesis provides an explanation for the complex relationships that we as individuals maintain with the multiple nomadic machines invading our bodies and our souls. Along the same conceptual lines, the animation of the body will henceforth depend on multiple connections, which perform experiments using the body as a primary node for technological mediation. Likewise, the body's vitality depends on prosthetic and aesthetic links to silicon-based, machine-like phyla.[64]

Today, one's quotidian experience is effectively characterized by the notion of a virtual "ambient reality," an expression that evokes the capacity to remain in contact with people by using different Web-based networks—a social practice that helps one to live a somewhat disembodied connectedness. Through television, cable, the Internet, and other media, there is the possibility of a further eroticization of social relations, which could be hindered by a perverted (even malevolent) use of the media. Moreover, because of security issues, the so-called nomadic apparatuses (such as tablet computers and smart phones) could also become tools of sedentarization and control, since they enhance and confirm the social identity of an individual, beyond the communal context of its use. The success of reality TV shows and of online sites such as MySpace, Facebook, YouTube, Second Life, Twitter, and LinkedIn reveals a passion for self-exhibition, thus marking a new threshold that leads from the era of the "intimate" to that of the "extimate."[65] The relation between intimate and extimate is of a quasi-topological nature, a situation in which the interior is turned into an exterior, like a Möbius strip, a closed, non-orientable surface with only one side and only one boundary. This kind of surface can lead to considerations on networks, the world's tools for a Guattaro-Deleuzian deterritorialization, or what Pierre Lévy has termed the "Möbius effect." He explains that today, only in the realm of the real do things have defined limits. Lévy argues that virtuality is one of four modes of existence, along with reality, possibility, and actuality. Virtualization forces one to rethink classical identity. Virtualization adds to, but does not replace, the real, the possible, and the actual. Virtualization is always heterogenesis, becoming other, openness to alterity. Today, processes of virtualizing address three different fields: the corporal body, the text, and the environment.[66]

Capturing fleeting moments between exhibitionism and voyeurism, artists, photographers, and cinematographers (such as Nicholas Barker) stage in their images the world's ongoing paneroticization.[67] They also attempt to explore the intimate/extimate arrangements, exposing the secret and opening the hidden, shamelessly displaying the abject.[68] Nevertheless, instead of a further rise of individualism, which some believe is related to use of the Internet, some sociologists have found novel types of attraction and binding that can coagulate groups while crossing old barriers, a phenomenon that could be termed a form of neotribalism. Yet again, what appears to be on the rise is a series of interactions, pregnant with (dark?) Dionysian motivations, which will have potent social effects. On the positive side, such new forms of subjectivity might, in turn, lead to a densification of everyday life, to a more fluid kind of sociability, perhaps giving back to the term *aesthetics* its original meaning—that of shared emotions.

NOTES

1 A TOPOLOGY OF EVERYDAY CONSTELLATIONS

1. Charles Baudelaire, "Mon cœur mis à nu," XXI, in Baudelaire, *Œuvres complètes* (Paris: Gallimard, 1975), 689; quoted in Walter Benjamin, *The Arcades Project*, trans. Howard Eiland and Kevin McLaughlin (Cambridge, MA: Belknap Press of Harvard University Press, 1999), 445.

2. Samuel Beckett, *The Unnamable*, in *The Beckett Trilogy: Molloy, Malone Dies, The Unnamable* (London: Picador, 1979), 352.

3. Benjamin, *The Arcades Project*, 462–463, 471–472.

4. Jacques Derrida, *Of Hospitality: Anne Dufourmantelle Invites Jacques Derrida to Respond*, trans. Rachel Bowlby (Stanford: Stanford University Press, 2000).

5. See the debate with Michel Foucault in Michelle Perrot, ed., *L'impossible prison* (Paris: Seuil, 1980), 42. My translation.

6. Gilles Deleuze, "The Rise of the Social," in Deleuze, *Two Regimes of Madness: Texts and Interviews 1975–1995*, ed. David Lapoujade, trans. Ames Hodges and Mike Taormina (Los Angeles: Semiotext(e), 2006), 121.

7. Ibid.

8. Ibid.

9. Friedrich Nietzsche, *The Birth of Tragedy* and *The Genealogy of Morals*, trans. Francis Golffing (New York: Doubleday, 1956), 209.

10. Ibid.

11. Ibid.

12. Ibid., 210.

13. Giorgio Agamben, *What Is an Apparatus? and Other Essays*, trans. David Kishik and Stefan Pedatella (Stanford: Stanford University Press, 2009), 1–24.

14. See François Dosse, *History of Structuralism*, trans. Deborah Glassman (Minneapolis: University of Minnesota Press, 1997), vol. 1, *The Rising Sign, 1945–1966*, vol. 2, *The Sign Sets, 1967–Present*.

15. Claude Lévi-Strauss, *Structural Anthropology* [*Anthropologie structurale*, 1958], trans. Claire Jacobson and Brooke Grundfest Schoepf (New York: Basic Books, 1963), 283.

16. Ibid., 289.

17. Claude Lévi-Strauss, *The Way of Masks*, trans. Sylvia Modelski (London: Jonathan Cape, 1983), 174; quoted in Janet Carsten and Stephen Hugh-Jones, eds., *About the House: Lévi-Strauss and Beyond* (Cambridge: Cambridge University Press, 1995), 6–7.

18. André Lalande, *Vocabulaire technique et critique de la philosophie* (Paris: Quadrige/Presses Universitaires de France, 1972), 1:392–398; Jacqueline Russ, ed., *Dictionnaire de philosophie* (Paris: Armand Colin, 1995), 149.

19. Peter Sloterdijk, *La Domestication de l'Être. Pour un éclaircissement de la clairière*, trans. Olivier Mannoni (Paris: Éditions Mille et Une Nuits, 2000), 71. My translation.

20. Pierre Bourdieu, *Outline of a Theory of Practice*, trans. Richard Nice (Cambridge: Cambridge University Press, 1977), 89.

21. Janet Carsten and Stephen Hugh-Jones, introduction to *About the House: Lévi-Strauss and Beyond*, 19.

22. Gaston Bachelard, *The Poetics of Space*, trans. Maria Jolas (Boston; Beacon Press, 1964, 1969, 1992), xxxii.

23. Ibid.

24. Michel Serres, "Discours et parcours," in Claude Lévi-Strauss et al., *L'identité* (Paris: Bernard Grasset, 1977), 25–39, esp. 29–30. My translation.

25. Ibid., 30.

26. See Adrian Forty, "Type," in *Words and Buildings: Vocabulary of Modern Architecture* (London: Thames and Hudson, 2000), 304–311.

27. Giulio Carlo Argan, "Tipologia" (1960), in *Enciclopedia universale dell'arte* (Venice/Rome: Istituto per la collaborazione culturale; Florence: Sansoni, 1958–1972); Argan, "Sul concetto di tipologia architettonica," in Erwin Gradmann et al., eds., *Festschrift für Hans Sedlmayr* (Munich: Beck, 1962), republished in Argan, *Progetto e destino* (Milan: Il Saggiatore, 1965), 75–81; Argan, "On the Typology of Architecture," trans. Joseph Rykwert, *Architectural Design*, no. 33 (December 1963): 564–565; now in Kate Nesbitt, ed., *Theorizing a New*

Agenda for Architecture: An Anthology of Architectural Theory, 1965–1995 (New York: Princeton Architectural Press, 1996), 242–246.

28. Alan Colquhoun, *Modernity and the Classical Tradition: Architectural Essays, 1980–1987* (Cambridge, MA: MIT Press, 1989), 247–248; Forty, "Type," 311.

29. Talcott Parsons, *The Social System* (Glencoe, IL: Free Press, 1951); and Parsons, *Structure and Process in Modern Societies* (Glencoe, IL: Free Press, 1960); see also Bryan S. Turner, ed., *The Talcott Parsons Reader* (Malden, MA: Blackwell, 1999).

30. "Sociological Theory," The Society for Social Research, Department of Sociology at the University of Chicago, <http://ssr1.uchicago.edu/PRELIMS/Theory/parsons.html> (accessed September 15, 2011).

31. Félix Ravaisson, *De l'Habitude* (1838; Paris: Payot & Rivages, 1997), preface by Frédérick de Towarnicki, 11–12.

32. Félix Ravaisson, *Of Habit*, preface by Catherine Malabou, trans. Clare Carlisle and Mark Sinclair (London: Continuum, 2008), 25.

33. Ibid.

34. Ibid.

35. Gilles Deleuze, *Difference and Repetition*, trans. Paul Patton (New York: Columbia University Press, 1994), 70.

36. Preface to Ravaisson, *Of Habit*, ix.

37. Deleuze, *Difference and Repetition*, 73.

38. Preface to Ravaisson, *Of Habit*, xvii.

39. Marcel Proust, *In Search of Lost Time, Swann's Way*, trans. Lydia Davis (New York: Viking, 2003); see also Proust, *Swann's Way, Remembrance of Things Past*, vol. 1, trans. C. K. Scott Moncrieff (New York: Henry Holt, 1922). Now online: Proust, "Swann's Way: Remembrance of Things Past, Volume One" Project Gutenberg, March 21, 2009, <http://www.gutenberg.org/files/7178/7178-h/7178-h.htm> (accessed September 10, 2011).

40. Friedrich Nietzsche, *The Gay Science* (1882–1887), trans. Walter Kaufmann (New York: Random House, 1974), 236–237.

41. Deleuze, *Difference and Repetition*, 225.

42. Ibid., 94.

43. Ibid.

44. Ibid., 36.

45. Ibid.

46. Ibid., 37.

47. Ibid., 224.

48. Ibid., 225 and 229.

49. Samuel Butler, *Life and Habit* (London: A. C. Fifield, 1877), 79.

50. Ibid., 80.

51. Ibid., 82. See also Samuel Butler, *La vie et l'habitude*, trans. Valéry Larbaud (Paris: Éditions de la 'Nouvelle Revue Française,' 1922), 86–87.

52. Deleuze, *Difference and Repetition*, 73.

53. Ibid., 75.

54. Ibid., 77–78.

55. Samuel Beckett, *Proust* (New York: Grove Press, 1931), 7–8.

56. Ibid., 8.

57. Ibid., 4–5. Robert Smithson included this quotation in his article "Quasi Infinities and the Waning of Space," *Arts Magazine* (November 1966): 41, n. 1; also in *Robert Smithson: The Collected Writings*, ed. Jack Flam (Berkeley: University of California Press, 1996), 37. The article reveals significant connections, crucial in Smithson's disclosure of his obsession about the relationship between past, future, and technology in his art.

58. Beckett, *Proust*, 8.

59. François-Bernard Michel, *Proust et Beckett: deux corps éloquents: essai* (Arles: Actes Sud, 2011), 136–137, 177–178.

60. Benjamin, *The Arcades Project*, 544.

61. Ibid., 331.

62. Ibid., 473.

63. Ibid., 462–463.

64. Deleuze, *Difference and Repetition*, 94.

65. Edmond and Jules de Goncourt, "Bachaumont," in their *Portraits intimes du XVIIIe siècle* (Paris: E. Dentu, 1857); cited in Jean-Louis Cabanès, *Les frères Goncourt: art et écriture* (Talence: Presses Universitaires de Bordeaux, 1977), 436. My translation.

66. Edmond de Goncourt and Jules de Goncourt, *Journal des Goncourt. Mémoires de la vie littéraire, premier volume, 1851–1861* (Paris: G. Charpentier, 1887), 1852

entry. My translation. <http://www.gutenberg.org/files/14799/14799-0.txt> (accessed February 2, 2012).

67. Remy de Gourmont, *Le Deuxième Livre des masques* (Paris: Mercure de France, 1924), 259; cited in Benjamin, *The Arcades Project*, 545.

68. Benjamin, *The Arcades Project*, 545.

69. Ibid.

70. Ibid., 224.

71. Ibid. Such a scaling down will find its true achievement with the theories of Minimum Dwelling (*Existenzminimum*), as applied in housing developments (*Siedlungen*) in Germany during the Weimar period, where minimal floor space requirements were defined systematically.

72. Benjamin, *The Arcades Project*, 461.

73. Ibid.

74. Ibid., 460.

75. Ibid., 458.

76. Louis Aragon, *Paris Peasant*, trans. Simon Watson Taylor (London: Jonathan Cape, 1971), 24.

77. See Johann Friedrich Geist, *Arcades, the History of a Building Type* (Cambridge, MA: MIT Press, 1983).

78. Aragon, *Paris Peasant*, 28.

79. See Lydia Marinelli, ed., *Die Couch: vom Denken im Liegen* (Munich: Prestel, 2006).

80. Benjamin, *The Arcades Project*, 392.

81. Named after its scholarly journal *Annales d'histoire économique et sociale*.

82. Philippe Ariès, ed., *À propos de l'histoire de l'espace privé* (Berlin: Institute for Advanced Studies, 1984), typescript of the colloquium.

83. Norbert Elias, "Details Are Infinite," in *À propos de l'histoire de l'espace privé*, 217–220.

84. Ibid. See Philippe Ariès, Georges Duby, et al., eds., *A History of Private Life* (Cambridge, MA: Belknap Press of Harvard University Press, 1987–1991), 5 vols.

85. Jean-François Lyotard, *The Postmodern Condition: A Report on Knowledge* (1979), trans. Geoff Bennington and Brian Massumi (Minneapolis: University of Minnesota Press, 1999), xxiv–xxv, 37–38.

86. Alain (pseudonym of Émile-Auguste Chartier), *Entretiens chez le sculpteur* (1934–1937; Paris: Gallimard, 1969), 79. My translation.

87. Alfred de Musset, *La Confession d'un enfant du siècle* (Paris: Félix Bonnaire, 1836), 2 vols., chapter IV, 18, <http://www.ibibliotheque.fr/confession-d-un-enfant-du-siecle-alfred-de-musset-mus_confession/lecture-integrale/page18> (accessed February 2, 2012).

88. Ernest Renan, "La poésie de l'Exposition," in *Essais de morale et de critique* (Paris: Michel-Lévy frères, 1859), 373; cited in Benjamin, *The Arcades Project*, 197.

89. Renan, "La poésie de l'Exposition," 363; cited in Benjamin, *The Arcades Project*, 554.

90. Ibid.

91. Ibid.

92. Georg Simmel, *Philosophie des Geldes* (Leipzig: Duncker und Humblot, 1901), 491–494; cited in Benjamin, *The Arcades Project*, 226–227.

93. Ibid.

94. Ibid., 226.

95. Georg Simmel, *The Philosophy of Money*, trans. Tom Bottomore and David Frisby (London: Routledge, 1990), 476–484.

96. Albert O. Hirschman, *Shifting Involvements: Private Interest and Public Action* (Princeton: Princeton University Press, 1982), 76–86.

97. Victor Hugo, *Choses vues (1830–1885)*, ed. Hubert Juin (Paris: Gallimard, 1972), vol. 1, 229. My translation.

98. Rainer Maria Rilke, *The Notebooks of Malte Laurids Brigge*, trans. John Linton (London: Hogarth Press, 1930), 43–44.

99. Walter Benjamin with Asja Lacis, "Naples," *Frankfurter Zeitung*, 1925; in Benjamin, *Selected Writings, vol. 1, 1913–1926*, ed. Marcus Bullock and Michael W. Jennings (Cambridge, MA: Belknap Press, 1996), 416.

100. Ibid., 419.

101. Ibid., 420.

102. Ibid., 416.

103. Ibid., 420.

104. Ibid., 417.

105. Benjamin, *The Arcades Project*, 221.

106. Sigfried Giedion, *Bauen in Frankreich* (Berlin: Klinkhardt & Biermann, 1928), 85; cited in Benjamin, *The Arcades Project*, 423.

107. Giedion, *Bauen*, 89; cited in Benjamin, *The Arcades Project*, 423.

108. Benjamin, *The Arcades Project*, 840.

109. Ibid., 531.

110. Ibid.

111. Ibid., 532.

112. Benjamin, "Oskar Walzel, Das Wort kunstwerk," in *Gesammelte Schriften*, 3:51; quoted in Jean-Michel Palmier, *Walter Benjamin: le chiffonnier, l'ange et le petit bossu* (Paris: Klincksieck, 2006), 446. My translation.

113. Benjamin, *The Arcades Project*, 463.

114. Benjamin, "On the Concept of History" (1940), in Benjamin, *Selected Writings*, vol. 4, 1938–1940, trans. Harry Zohn, ed. Howard Eiland and Michael W. Jennings (Cambridge, MA: Belknap Press of Harvard University Press, 2003), 396.

115. Gilles Deleuze, *The Fold: Leibniz and the Baroque*, trans. Tom Conley (Minneapolis: University of Minnesota Press, 1993), 158.

116. Ibid.

117. Gilles Lipovetsky and Jean Serroy, *L'Écran global: culture-médias et cinéma à l'âge hypermoderne* (Paris: Seuil, 2007).

118. Jacques Derrida, *The Specters of Marx: The State of the Debt, the Work of Mourning and the New Internationale*, trans. Peggy Kamuf (London: Routledge, 1994), 3–8.

119. Michel Foucault, *Maurice Blanchot: The Thought from Outside*, trans. Jeffrey Mehlman and Brian Massumi (New York: Zone Books, 1987), 23–24; first published as "La Pensée du dehors," *Critique*, no. 229 (June 1966): 521–546.

120. Foucault, *Maurice Blanchot*, 24.

121. Deleuze, *The Fold*, 120.

122. Beckett, *The Unnamable*, 352.

2 FIGURING THE INVISIBLE

1. Hermann Muthesius, "Die Werkbund-Arbeit der Zukunft," in *Der Werkbund-Gedanke in den germanischen Ländern* (Jena: Eugen Diederichs Verlag, 1914), 32–49: "Es ist das Eigentümliche der Architektur, daß sie zum Typischen drängt. Die Typisierung aberverschmäht das Außerordentliche und sucht

das Ordentliche." Hanno-Walter Kruft, *A History of Architectural Theory: From Vitruvius to the Present*, trans. Ronald Taylor, Elsie Callander, and Antony Wood (New York: Princeton Architectural Press, 1994), 371, 582.

2. See Giulio Carlo Argan, "On the Typology of Architecture" (1965), in Kate Nesbitt, ed., *Theorizing a New Agenda for Architecture* (New York: Princeton Architectural Press, 1996), 240–246.

3. Gottfried Semper, *Der Stil in den technischen und tektonischen Künsten, oder praktische Aesthetik, ein Handbuch für Techniker, Künstler und Kunstfreunde*, vol. 1, *Die textile Kunst, für sich betrachtet und in Beziehung zur Baukunst* (Frankfurt am Main: Verlag für Kunst und Wissenschaft, 1860); vol. 2, *Keramik, Tektonik, Stereotomie, Metallotechnik, für sich betrachtet und in Beziehung zur Baukunst* (Munich: F. Bruckmann, 1863); 2nd ed. (Munich: F. Bruckmann, 1878–1879); Semper, *Style in the Technical and Tectonic Arts; or, Practical Aesthetics*, trans. Harry Francis Mallgrave and Michael Robinson (Los Angeles: Getty Research Institute, 2004).

4. Eugène-Emmanuel Viollet-le-Duc, *Histoire de l'habitation humaine depuis les temps préhistoriques jusqu'à nos jours* (Paris: Hetzel & Cie., 1875), 20; Viollet-le-Duc, *The Habitations of Man in All Ages*, trans. Benjamin Bucknall (Boston: James R. Osgood and Co., 1876), 8–23. Viollet-le-Duc owned a copy of Semper's *Der Stil*: see *Catalogue des livres composant le bibliothèque de feu M. E. Viollet-le-Duc* (Paris: A. Labitte, 1880).

5. Léon Poliakov, *The Aryan Myth: A History of Racist and Nationalist Ideas in Europe*, trans. Edmund Howard (New York: Basic Books, 1974), 189–190, 193.

6. Henry Martin, *Histoire de France depuis les temps les plus reculés jusqu'en 1789*, vol. 1 (1837), 4th ed. (Paris: Furne, Jouvet, 1874), 2; quoted in Poliakov, *The Aryan Myth*, 34–35.

7. Georges Cuvier, *Le règne animal* (Paris: Déterville, 1817), 94; Jules Michelet, *Rome*, introduction to the 1831 edition; from the anthology *Michelet, 1798–1874*, ed. Lucien Febvre (Paris: Traits, 1946), 95–96, 154; cited in Poliakov, *The Aryan Myth*, 199.

8. Jakob Grimm, *Geschichte der deutschen Sprache* (Leipzig: S. Hirzel, 1868), 3rd ed., vol. 1, iv and 113–122 (chap. VIII, "Einwanderung"); quoted in Poliakov, *The Aryan Myth*, 198–199.

9.   Poliakov, *The Aryan Myth*, 206–207.

10. Eugène-Emmanuel Viollet-le-Duc, *Histoire d'un dessinateur, comment on apprend à dessiner* (Paris: Bibliothèque d'éducation et de récréation, 1879).

11. Eugène-Emmanuel Viollet-le-Duc, *Dictionnaire raisonné de l'architecture française du XIe au XVIe siècle*, 10 vols. (Paris: B. Bance; A. Morel, 1854–1868).

12. See Baron Georges Cuvier, *Britannica Concise Encyclopedia*, <http://www.britannica.com/EBchecked/topic/147625/Georges-Baron-Cuvier> (accessed January 10, 2012).

13. François Duchesneau, *Genèse de la théorie cellulaire* (Paris: Vrin, 1987), 21; and Laurent Baridon, *L'imaginaire scientifique de Viollet-le-Duc* (Paris: Éditions L'Harmattan, 1996), 101–105.

14. Viollet-le-Duc, *Histoire d'un dessinateur*, 34.

15. Martin Bressani, "Notes on Viollet-le-Duc's Philosophy of History: Dialectics and Technology," *Journal of the Society of Architectural History* 48, no. 4 (December 1989): 327–350; Bressani, "Opposition et équilibre: le rationalisme organique de Viollet-le-Duc, " *Revue de l'Art* 112 (1996): 28–37.

16. Jean-Jacques Rousseau, *Julie ou La Nouvelle Héloïse*, ed. René Pomeau (Paris: Garnier, 1988), 127–130.

17. Viollet-le-Duc, *Dictionnaire raisonné*, 6:214–300.

18. Ibid., 6:255–257.

19. Arthur, comte de Gobineau, *Essai sur l'inégalité des races humaines* (Paris: P. Belfond, 1967).

20. Viollet-le-Duc, *The Habitations of Man in All Ages*, 42–43.

21. See Jacques Gubler, "Une maison, histoire et contrepoint," in *Viollet-le-Duc et la montagne*, ed. Pierre A. Frey and Lise Grenier (Grenoble: Glénat, 1993), 34–42.

22. Baridon, *L'imaginaire scientifique de Viollet-le-Duc*, 107–117.

23. *Der Vorgeschichtliche Mensch: Ursprung und Entwicklung des Menschengeschlechtes: für Gebildete aller Stände*, ed. Wilhelm Baer; second edition, ed. Friedrich von Hellwald (Leipzig: O. Spamer, [1880]), 63, 159, 179.

24. Franz Carl Müller-Lyer, *Die Entwicklungsstufen der Menschheit. Eine Gesellschaftslehre in Überblicken und Einzeldarstellungen*, 2 vols. (Munich: J. F. Lehmann, 1910–1912); Müller-Lyer, *The History of Social Development*, trans. Elizabeth Coote Lake and E. J. Lake (New York: Alfred A. Knopf, 1921), 146.

25. Ministère de l'instruction, *Enquête sur les conditions de l'habitation en France. Les maisons-types*, ed. and intro. Alfred de Foville, 2 vols. (Paris: E. Leroux, 1894–1899); vol. 2 with an essay by Jacques Flach, 2:2.ii.

26. Ibid., xiv–xv.

27. Ibid., xl.

28. Frank E. Manuel, *The Prophets of Paris* (Cambridge, MA: Harvard University Press, 1962), 103–148, esp. 121.

29. Ibid., 123–129, 142.

30. Ibid., 115–118.

31. Zeev Sternhell, *La droite révolutionnaire: les origines françaises du fascisme, 1885–1914* (Paris: Seuil, 1978), 21. On typology, see Françoise Arnault, *Frédéric Le Play, De la métallurgie à la science sociale* (Nancy: Presses Universitaires de Nancy, 1993), 87–99.

32. See Frédéric Le Play, "Family types. Patriarchal, Stem, Unstable," in *La Réforme sociale* (Tours: Mame, 1872), 352–358; Le Play, *On Family, Work, and Social Change*, ed. Catherine Bodard Silver (Chicago: University of Chicago Press, 1982), 259–262.

33. Edmond Demolins, *Les grandes routes des peuples; essai de géographie sociale, comment la route crée le type social*, 2 vols. (Paris: Firmin-Didot et Cie., 1901–1903).

34. Edmond Demolins, *À quoi tient la supériorité des Anglo-saxons* (Paris: Firmin-Didot et Cie, 1897); Demolins, *Anglo-Saxon Superiority: To What It Is Due*, trans. Louis B. Lavigne (New York: R. F. Fenno & Company, 1899).

35. Lion Murard and Patrick Zylberman, *L'hygiène dans la République. La santé publique en France ou l'utopie contrariée (1870–1918)* (Paris: Fayard, 1996), 73–76.

36. See Louis Bonnier and Paul Juillerat, *Une institution nécessaire: le casier sanitaire des maisons* (Paris: J. Rousset, 1906).

37. Paul Juillerat and Louis Bonnier, *République française. Préfecture du département de la Seine. Direction des affaires municipales. Rapport à M. le préfet sur les recherches effectuées au bureau du casier sanitaire pendant l'année 1908 [1909, 1910, 1915–1916–1917], relatives à la répartition de la tuberculose et du cancer dans les maisons de Paris*, 4 vols. (Paris: Imprimerie de Chaix, 1909–1918).

38. Paul Juillerat and Louis Bonnier, *L'hygiène du logement* (Paris: C. Delagrave, 1909).

39. Cesare Lombroso and Gina Lombroso-Ferrero, *Criminal Man* (New York: Putnam, 1911); Cesare Lombroso and Giuseppe Ferrero, *The Female Offender* (New York: D. Appleton, 1895).

40. Adolphe Quételet, *Anthropométrie, ou mesure des différentes facultés de l'homme* (Brussels: C. Muquardt, 1870).

41. Alphonse Bertillon, *La photographie judiciaire* (Paris: Gauthier-Villars, 1890). See also Henry T. F. Rhodes, *Alphonse Bertillon. Father of Scientific Detection* (New York: Greenwood Press, 1968), 102–109.

42. David de Giustino, *Conquest of Mind: Phrenology and Victorian Social Thought* (London: Croom Helm, 1975).

43. Johann Gaspar Spurzheim, *The Physiognomical System of Drs. Gall and Spurzheim*, 2nd ed. (London: Baldwin, Cradock, and Joy, 1815); and Spurzheim, *Phrenology, in Connexion with the Study of Physiognomy* (Boston: Marsh, Capen & Lyon, 1833).

44. Claudio Pogliano, "Entre forme et fonction: une nouvelle science de l'homme," in Jean Clair, ed., *L'âme au corps. Arts et sciences, 1793–1993* (Paris: Gallimard, 1993), 238–265.

45. See John D. Davies, *Phrenology, Fad and Science: A Nineteenth-Century American Crusade* (New Haven: Yale University Press, 1955).

46. O. S. Fowler, *A Home for All, or, The Gravel Wall and Octagon Mode of Building* (New York: Fowler and Wells, 1854); repr. Fowler, *The Octagon House: A Home for All* (New York: Dover Publications, 1973).

47. On André Godin (1817–1888), see Thierry Paquot and Marc Bédarida, eds., *Habiter l'utopie: le familistère Godin à Guise* (Paris: La Villette, 2004).

48. Victor Considérant, *Description du phalanstère et considérations sociales sur l'architectonique* (1834; 1840; 2nd ed., Paris: Librairie sociétaire, 1848; repr. Paris: Guy Durier, 1979).

49. Jean-Baptiste André Godin, *La richesse au service du peuple. Le familistère de Guise* (Paris: Librairie de la Bibliothèque démocratique, 1874; repr. Neuilly: Guy Durier, 1979).

50. Jean-Baptiste André Godin, *Solutions sociales* (Paris: A. Le Chevalier 1871), 501.

51. Cesare Lombroso, *The Man of Genius* (New York: C. Scribner's Sons, 1891).

52. Peter Strasser, "Cesare Lombroso: l'homme délinquant ou la bête sauvage au naturel," in Clair, *L'âme au corps*, 352–359.

53.   Adolphe Quételet, *Sur l'homme* (Paris: Bachelier, 1835; 1836); Quételet, *A Treatise on Man and the Development of His Faculties* (Edinburgh: William and Robert Chambers, 1842).

54.   Quételet, *A Treatise on Man*, 96–103; see also Philippe Comar, "Les chaînes de l'art," in Clair, *L'âme au corps*, 394–404.

55.   Marta Braun, *Picturing Time: The Work of Étienne-Jules Marey (1830–1904)* (Chicago: University of Chicago Press, 1992).

56.   Paul Richer, *Canon des proportions du corps humain* (Paris: C. Delagrave, 1893).

57.   Giovanni Morelli, *Della pittura italiana, studii storico-critici* (Milan: Treves, 1897).

58.   Oskar Schlemmer, László Moholy-Nagy, and Farkas Molnár, *Die Bühne im Bauhaus* (1924; repr., Mainz/Berlin: Kupferberg, 1965).

59.   Roger-Henri Guerrand, *Le logement populaire en France: sources documentaires et bibliographie, 1800–1960* (Paris: École Nationale Supérieure des Beaux-Arts, 1979), 97.

60.   Paul Weindling, *Health, Race and German Politics between National Unification and Nazism, 1870–1945* (Cambridge: Cambridge University Press, 1989).

61.   Wilhelm Heinrich Riehl, *Die Naturgeschichte des Volkes als Grundlage einer deutschen Social-Politik*, 3 vols. (Stuttgart/Tübingen/Augsburg: J. G. Cotta, 1854–1856).

62.   Wilhelm Heinrich Riehl, *The Natural History of the German People*, ed. David J Diephouse (Lewistown, NY: Edwin Melten Press, 1990), 324.

63.   Ibid., 306–309.

64.   Ibid., 312.

65.   Riehl, *Natural History*, 318–323.

66.   Friedrich von Hellwald, *Culturgeschichte in ihrer natürlichen Entwicklung bis zur Gegenwart*, 2nd ed., 2 vols. (Augsburg: Lampart & comp., 1876–1877); von Hellwald, *Kulturgeschichte in ihrer natürlichen Entwickelung bis zur Gegenwart*, 2 vols. (Leipzig: Friesenhahn, 1896). Originally, the German spelling *Culturgeschichte* (cultural history) was used, but later the form *Kulturgeschichte* was universally adopted.

67.   Ernst Haeckel, *Kunstformen der Natur* (Leipzig and Vienna: Bibliographischen Instituts, 1899–1904); Haeckel, *Art Forms in Nature: The Prints of Ernst Haeckel* (Munich: Prestel, 1998).

68. The "Sealed [*ungeöffnet*] Site of a Stone Age Funerary Barrow, or Tumulus [*Grabhügel*] near Waldhusen (Lübeck, Germany)," in von Hellwald, *Kulturgeschichte*, between 48 and 49; and "Germanic Warrior of the Iron Age," between 200 and 201.

69. Friedrich von Hellwald, *Haus und Hof in ihrer Entwicklung mit Bezug auf die Wohnsitten der Völker* (Leipzig: Schmidt, 1888).

70. *Der Vorgeschichtliche Mensch*, 67.

71. Louis Büchner, *Force and Matter: Empirico-Philosophical Studies*, ed. J. Frederick Collingwood (London: Trübner & Co., 1864).

72. Ludwig Büchner, *Die Darwin'sche Theorie in sechs Vorlesungen* (Leipzig: T. Thomas, 1868), Fr. trans., *Conférences sur la théorie darwinienne*, trans. Auguste Jacquot (Paris: C. Reinwald, 1869), 132; quoted by Poliakov, *The Aryan Myth*, 273.

73. August Meitzen, *Siedlung und Agrarwesen der Westgermanen und Ostgermanen, der Kelten, Römer, Finnen und Slaven*, 4 vols. (Berlin: W. Hertz, 1895). Both works by Friedrich von Hellwald and by August Meitzen are criticized by Jacques Flach, professor at the Collège de France. See his "Étude sur les origines et les vicissitudes historiques de l'habitation en France," in *Enquête sur les conditions de l'habitation en France. Les Maisons-types* (Paris: E. Leroux, 1899), 2:1–97, esp. 7, 17.

74. Hermann Muthesius, *The English House*, ed. Dennis Sharp (London: Frances Lincoln, 2007).

75. Hermann Muthesius, *Style-Architecture and Building-Art: Transformations of Architecture in the Nineteenth Century and Its Present Condition*, ed. Stanford Anderson (Santa Monica: Getty Center, 1994), 6; Laurent Stalder, *Hermann Muthesius (1861–1927). Das Landhaus als kulturgeschichtlicher Entwurf* (Zurich: Gta Verlag, 2008).

76. Lawrence A. Joseph, *Henri Cazalis: sa vie, son œuvre, son amitié avec Mallarmé* (Paris: A. G. Nizet, 1972).

77. Cazalis was the doctor and confidant of Guy de Maupassant (and brought the writer to a clinic after his suicide attempt).

78. Jean Lahor [Henri Cazalis], *W. [William] Morris et le mouvement nouveau de l'art décoratif*, conference held in Geneva, January 13, 1897 (Geneva: C. Eggimann,

1897). See also Lahor, "William Morris et l'art décoratif en Angleterre," *Revue encyclopédique* (August 15, 1894): 349–359.

79. Gabriel de Tarde, *Les lois de l'imitation*, 2nd ed. (1895; repr., Paris and Geneva: Resources Slatkine, 1979), 409.

80. Lahor, *W. Morris*, 59.

81. See also Jean Lahor, *L'art nouveau, son histoire, l'art nouveau étranger à l'Exposition, l'art nouveau au point de vue social* (Paris: Lemerre, 1901).

82. Lahor, *L'art nouveau*, n.p.

83. Ibid.

84. Gustave Le Bon, *Les civilisations de l'Inde* (Paris: Firmin-Didot, 1887); Le Bon, *Psychologie des foules* (Paris: F. Alcan, 1895); Le Bon, *The Crowd: A Study of the Popular Mind* (New York: Macmillan, 1896), 139; Le Bon, *The Crowd* (New Brunswick, NJ: Transaction, 1995).

85. Le Bon, *The Crowd* (1896), 134. Le Bon is quoted, for example, in Georges Sorel, *Les illusions du progrès*, 2nd ed. (Paris: Marcel Rivière, 1911), 332.

86. Le Bon, *The Crowd* (1896), 143–145.

87. Ruth Schwartz Cowan, *Sir Francis Galton and the Study of Heredity in the Nineteenth Century* (New York: Garland, 1985).

88. Poliakov, *Aryan Myth*, 264–266.

89. Lapouge's book was translated in Germany in 1939. Georges Vacher de Lapouge, *L'Aryen. Son rôle social. Cours libre de Science Politique professé à l'Université de Montpellier (1889–1890)* (Paris: Albert Fontemoing Éditeur, 1899); Lapouge, *Der Arier und seine Bedeutung für die Gemeinschaft; Freier Kursus in Staatskunde, gehalten an der Universität Montpellier, 1889–1890* (Frankfurt am Main: M. Diesterweg, 1939).

90. Mike Hawkins, *Social Darwinism in European and American Thought, 1860–1945* (Cambridge: Cambridge University Press, 1997).

91. Lahor, *L'art nouveau*, n.p.

92. Ibid.

93. Henri Cazalis, *La science et le mariage, étude médicale* (Paris: O. Doin 1900), Bibliothèque Nationale de France, Paris, signed copy by Cazalis sent to Maurice Barrès; see Maurice Barrès, *Les déracinés* (Paris: Fasquelle, 1897).

94. Jean Lahor, *L'art pour le peuple: à défaut de l'art par le peuple* (Paris: Larousse, 1902).

95. Henri Cazalis, *Quelques mesures très simples protectrices de la santé et de la race* (Paris: Doin, 1904).

96. Jean Lahor, *Les habitations à bon marché et un art nouveau pour le peuple* (Paris: Larousse, 1903); 2nd ed. (Paris: Larousse, 1904); 3rd ed. (Paris: Larousse, 1905).

97. Ibid., 3rd ed., 37–38.

98. See Léon Benouville, *Exposition universelle de 1900, section française, groupe XII, classe 69. Meubles de luxe et à bon marché. Comité d'admission. Rapport de M. Léon Benouville* (Paris: Librairies Imprimeries réunies, 1899).

99. Lahor, *Les habitations à bon marché*, 89.

100. Lahor, *L'art pour le peuple*, 25. On Cazalis's [Lahor's] orientalism, see René Petitbon, *Les sources orientales de Jean Lahor* (Paris: A. G. Nizet, 1962).

101. F. Müller-Lyer, *The History of Social Development*, 349. I replaced the expression "the idea of culture progress," which appears in the translation, with "the idea of cultural progress." See also Walter Gropius, "Die soziologischen Grundlagen der Minimalwohnung für die städtische Industriebevölkerung," *Die Justiz* 5 (1929).

102. Catharine Esther Beecher, *Letters to the People on Health and Happiness* (New York: Harper & Brothers, 1855). See also Catharine Esther Beecher, *Physiology and Calisthenics: For Schools and Families* (New York: Harper & Brothers, 1856).

103. Gisela Moeller, *Peter Behrens in Düsseldorf. Die Jahre von 1903 bis 1907* (Weinheim: VCH, 1991).

104. Paul Schultze-Naumburg, *Die Kultur des Weiblichen Körpers als Grundlage der Frauenkleidung* (Leipzig: Verlag Eugen Diederichs, 1901), with 133 illustrations by J. V. Cissarz; 2nd ed. (Jena: E. Diederichs, 1922).

105. Paul Schultze-Naumburg, *Kunst und Kunstpflege* (Leipzig: Diederichs, 1901); and *Häusliche Kunstpflege* (Jena: Diederichs, 1905). Later, Schultze-Naumburg published a major work on town and country houses, designed in the Biedermeier style: Paul Schultze-Naumburg, *Der Bau des Wohnhauses* (Munich: G. D. W. Callwey, 1924), 2 vols. See Norbert Borrmann, *Paul Schultze-Naumburg, 1869–1949. Maler, Publizist, Architekt . . .* (Essen: Verlag Richard Bacht GmbH, 1989).

106. Mark M. Anderson, *Kafka's Clothes: Ornament and Aestheticism in the Habsburg Fin de Siècle* (New York: Oxford University Press, 1992), 61. Later, Schultze-Naumburg extends his concept of reform to the landscape; see Paul Schultze-Naumburg, *Die Gestaltung der Landschaft durch den Menschen*, 3rd ed. (Munich: Callwey, 1928), three volumes bound in one.

107. See Count Harry Kessler, *The Diaries of a Cosmopolitan. 1918–1937*, trans. and ed. Charles Kessler (London: Weidenfeld and Nicolson, 1971), 390.

108. Hans Surén, *Der Mensch und die Sonne* (Stuttgart: Verlag die Dieck & Co, 1924).

109. Hans Surén, *Deutsche Gymnastik: Vorbereitende Uebungen für den Sport—Frottierübungen, Atemgymnastik, Massage—Körperpflege—Verhalten im Licht-, Luft- und Sonnenbad* (Oldenburg: Stalling, 1925).

110. Hans Surén, *Mensch und Sonne: Arisch-olympischer Geist* (Berlin: Scherl, 1936).

111. Max Adolphi and Arno Kettmann, *Tanzkunst und Kunsttanz aus der Tanzgruppe Herion* (Stuttgart: Ernst Heig, 1927). See Karl Toepfer, *Empire of Ecstasy: Nudity and Movement in German Body Culture, 1910–35* (Berkeley: University of California Press, 1997).

112. Toepfer, *Empire of Ecstasy*, 67–68.

113. On German naturism, see Anna Bramwell, *Ecology in the 20th Century: A History* (New Haven: Yale University Press, 1989), 177–194.

114. Siegfried Kracauer, "Das Ornament der Masse," *Frankfurter Zeitung* 71 (June 9–10, 1927); Kracauer, "On Mass Ornament," in Kracauer, *The Mass Ornament: Weimar Essays*, ed. Thomas Y. Levin (Cambridge, MA: Harvard University Press, 1995), 75–86.

115. Ernst Jünger, "Die totale Mobilmachung," in *Krieg und Krieger*, ed. Ernst Jünger (Berlin: Junker und Dünnhaupt, 1930); Jünger, *Die totale Mobilmachung* (Berlin: Junker und Dünnhaupt, 1934).

116. Gilles Deleuze, "The Rise of the Social," postscript to Jacques Donzelot, *The Policing of Families*, trans. Robert Hurley (Baltimore: Johns Hopkins University Press, 1997).

117. Borrmann, *Paul Schultze-Naumburg*, illustration 278.

118. Paul Schmitthenner, "Das fabrizierte Fachwerkhaus (system Schmitthenner)," *Wasmuth Monatshefte für Baukunst* (1929): 376–378, 400. See Vittorio Magnago Lampugnani and Romana Schneider, eds., *Moderne Architektur*

in *Deutschland 1900 bis 1950. Reform und Tradition* (Stuttgart: Verlag Gerd Hatje, 1992), 245–262. On *Fachwerk* constructions, see Bernd Becher and Hilla Becher, *Framework Houses* (Cambridge, MA: MIT Press, 2001).

119. Paul Schmitthenner, *Das Deutsche Wohnhaus* (Stuttgart: Konrad Wittwer, 1932), reprint: *Das Deutsche Wohnhaus . . .* (Stuttgart: Deutsche Verlags-Anstalt, 1984); and Paul Schmitthenner, *Gebaute Form: Variationen über ein Thema*, ed. Elisabeth Schmitthenner (Stuttgart: Alexander Koch, 1984).

120. Ernst Jünger, *Der Arbeiter. Herrschaft und Gestalt* (Hamburg: Hanseatische ver-lagsanstalt, 1932); Jünger, *Le travailleur*, trans. Julien Hervier (Paris: Christian Bourgois, 1989); Ernst Jünger, "The Worker: Domination and Form," in Anton Kaes, Martin Jay, and Edward Dimendberg, eds., *The Weimar Republic Sourcebook* (Berkeley: University of California Press, 1994), 159–164.

121. Ernst Jünger, *Storm of Steel*, trans. Michael Hofmann [*In Stahlgewittern*, 1920, rewritten 1924] (London: Allen Lane, 2003).

122. Walter Benjamin, "Theories of German Fascism," in Benjamin, *Selected Writings*, vol. 2, *1927–1934*, ed. Michael W. Jennings, Howard Eiland, and Gary Smith, trans. Rodney Livingstone et al. (Cambridge, MA: Belknap Press of Harvard University Press, 1999), 313.

123. Ibid., 318.

124. Walter Benjamin, "The Work of Art in the Age of Its Technological Repro-ducibility," in Benjamin, *Selected Writings*, vol. 3, *1935–1938*, ed. Howard Ei-land and Michael W. Jennings, trans. Edward Jephcott, Howard Eiland, et al. (Cambridge, MA: Belknap Press of Harvard University Press, 2002), 121.

125. Ibid., Benjamin's emphasis.

126. Jünger, *Le travailleur*, 147–155. See also Ernst Jünger, *Typus, Name, Gestalt* (Stuttgart: E. Klett, 1963).

3 DREAM HOUSE

1. Charles Baudelaire, *Les Fleurs du mal*, CXXI, "La Mort des amants," in Baude-laire, *Œuvres complètes* (Paris: Gallimard, 1975), 127; cited by Marcel Proust, *Chroniques* (Paris: Éd. de la NRF, 1927), 224–225; Walter Benjamin, *The Ar-cades Project* [*Das Passagen-Werk*], trans. Howard Eiland and Kevin McLaugh-lin (Cambridge, MA: Belknap Press of Harvard University Press, 1999), 217.

2. Walter Benjamin, *Das Passagen-Werk*, ed. Rolf Tiedemann (Frankfurt am Main: Suhrkamp, 1982), 2 vols.

3. See Benjamin, *The Arcades Project*, 389.

4. Ibid.

5. Theodor Reik, *Der überraschte Psychologe; über erraten und verstehen unbewusster Vorgänge* (Leiden: A.W. Sijthoff, 1935), 130–132; Reik, *Surprise and the Psycho-analyst: On the Conjecture and Comprehension of Unconscious Processes* (London: K. Paul, Trench, Trubner & Co., Ltd., 1936); see Benjamin, *The Arcades Project*, 402.

6. See Benjamin, *The Arcades Project*, 402.

7. Ibid., 389.

8. Ibid., 220.

9. Bertolt Brecht, "Aus einem Lesebuch für Städtebewohner" (1926–1927), in Brecht, *Manuel pour habitants des villes* (Paris: L'Arche, 2006), 54–64.

10. Walter Benjamin, "The Destructive Character" (1931), in Benjamin, *Selected Writings*, vol. 2, part 2, 1931–1934, ed. Michael W. Jennings, Howard Eiland, and Gary Smith, trans. Edmund Jephcott (Cambridge, MA: Belknap Press of Harvard University Press, 1999), 542.

11. Benjamin, *The Arcades Project*, 406.

12. Charles Baudelaire, "The Painter of Modern Life" (1863), in *The Painter of Modern Life and Other Essays*, trans. and ed. Jonathan Mayne (London: Phaidon Press, 1964), 9.

13. Ibid.

14. Ibid., 11.

15. Ibid., 9.

16. Ibid., 11.

17. Charles Baudelaire, "Les Fenêtres," *Le Spleen de Paris*, XXXV, in Baudelaire, *Œuvres complètes*, ed. Claude Pichois, 2 vols. (Paris: Gallimard/La Pléiade, 1975), 1:339. See Baudelaire, *Paris Spleen*, trans. Louis Varèse (New York: New Directions, 1947), 77.

18. Baudelaire, "The Painter of Modern Life," 36.

19. Ibid.

20. Arnold van Gennep, *The Rites of Passage* (1909), trans. Monika B. Vizedom and Gabrielle L. Caffe (Chicago: University of Chicago Press, 1961).

21. Benjamin, *The Arcades Project*, 494.

22. Ibid.

23. Jacques Leenhardt, "Le passage comme forme d'expérience: Benjamin face à Aragon," in Heinz Wismann, ed., *Walter Benjamin et Paris* (Paris: Cerf, 1986), 169.

24. Rita Bischof and Elisabeth Lenk, "L'intrication surréelle du rêve et de l'histoire dans les Passages de Benjamin," in Wismann, *Walter Benjamin et Paris*, 179–199.

25. Benjamin, "Surrealism: The Last Snapshot of the European Intelligentsia," in Benjamin, *Selected Writings*, 2:208.

26. Benjamin, *The Arcades Project*, 88.

27. Walter Benjamin, "On Some Motifs in Baudelaire," in Benjamin, *The Writer of Modern Life: Essays on Charles Baudelaire*, ed. Michael W. Jennings, trans. Howard Eiland et al. (Cambridge, MA: Belknap Press of Harvard University Press, 2006), 170–210.

28. Pierre Mabille, preface to "L'éloge des préjugés populaires," *Minotaure* 2, no. 6 (Winter 1935): 2; cited in Benjamin, *The Arcades Project*, 501.

29. Mabille, preface to "L'éloge des préjugés populaires," 2; cited in Benjamin, *The Arcades Project*, 396.

30. Ibid.

31. Ibid., 389.

32. Benjamin, *The Arcades Project*, 389.

33. Louis Aragon, *Une vague de rêves* (1924; Paris: Seghers, 2006); cited in Benjamin, "Surrealism," 208.

34. *The Correspondence of Walter Benjamin, 1910–1940*, ed. Gershom Scholem and Theodor W. Adorno, trans. Manfred R. Jacobson and Evelyn M. Jacobson (Chicago: University of Chicago Press, 1994), 497.

35. Ibid.

36. Ibid.

37. Benjamin, "Surrealism," 210.

38. Ibid.

39. Bischof and Lenk, "L'intrication surréelle," 184.

40. Benjamin, *The Arcades Project*, 393.

41. Ibid., 462–464.

42. Benjamin, "Surrealism," 217.

43. Ibid.

44. Beatrice Hanssen, ed., *Walter Benjamin and the Arcades Project* (London: Continuum, 2006), 8; Benjamin, "Surrealism," 217.

45. Ibid.

46. Benjamin, *The Arcades Project*, 405.

47. Ibid., 157.

48. Ibid., 154.

49. Alfred Gotthold Meyer, *Eisenbauten, ihre Geschichte und Aesthetik* (Esslingen: P. Neff, 1907); Meyer, *Construire en fer: histoire et esthétique*, ed. Philippe Duboy (Gollion/Paris: Infolio, 2005).

50. Sigfried Giedion, *Bauen in Frankreich, Eisen, Eisenbeton* (Leipzig: Klinkhardt & Biermann, 1928); Giedion, *Construire en France, en fer, en béton*, trans. Guy Ballangé (Paris: Éditions de la Villette, 2000); Giedion, *Building in France, Building in Iron, Building in Ferro-concrete*, trans. J. Duncan Berry (Santa Monica: Getty Center for the History of Art and the Humanities, 1995).

51. Letter from Walter Benjamin to Sigfried Giedion, February 15, 1929, courtesy of Laurent Stalder (GTA Archives, ETH Zurich: Sigfried Giedion library, Zurich).

52. Giedion, *Bauen*, 1–2; cited in Benjamin, *The Arcades Project*, 407.

53. Giedion, *Bauen*, 15; cited in Benjamin, *The Arcades Project*, 390.

54. Benjamin, *The Arcades Project*, 391.

55. Giedion, *Bauen*, 3; cited in Benjamin, *The Arcades Project*, 391.

56. Ibid., 390.

57. Ibid., 391.

58. Ibid.

59. See Ernst Bloch, *Erbschaft dieser Zeit* (1935; Frankfurt am Main: Suhrkamp, 1985); Bloch, *The Heritage of Our Times*, trans. Neville and Stephen Plaice (Cambridge, UK; Malden, MA: Polity, 2009); quote from Bloch, *Héritage de ce temps*, trans. Jean Lacoste (Paris: Payot, 1978), 202.

60. Benjamin, *The Arcades Project*, 391.

61. Ibid.

62. Ibid.

63. Maxime Du Camp, *Paris, ses organes, ses fonctions et sa vie dans la seconde moitié du XIXe siècle*, 6 vols. (Paris: Hachette, 1869–1876), 1:241; cited in Benjamin, *The Arcades Project*, 153.

64. Giedion, *Bauen*, 34; cited in Benjamin, *The Arcades Project*, 40.

65. Giedion, *Bauen*, 43; cited in Benjamin, *The Arcades Project*, 214.

66. Marcel Proust, *Remembrance of Things Past*, vol. 1, trans. C. K. Scott Moncrieff (New York: Random House, 1925), 489–490; cited in Benjamin, *The Arcades Project*, 561.

67. Benjamin, *The Arcades Project*, 154.

68. Ibid., 88.

69. Ibid., 423.

70. For several representations of Paris dwelling sections, see Jean-Pierre Babelon, ed., *Le Parisien chez lui au XIXe siècle: 1814–1914* (Paris: Archives nationales, 1976), 14–43.

71. Alain-René Le Sage, *Le diable boiteux* (1707; 2nd ed. 1726), ed. Béatrice Didier (Paris: Flammarion, 2004); Luis Vélez de Guevara, *El diablo cojuelo* (1641), ed. Ángel R. Fernández González and Ignacio Arellano (Madrid: Editorial Castalia, 1988).

72. See the unsigned illustration in the 1759 edition of Alain-René Le Sage's *Le diable boiteux*, republished in *Le diable boiteux par monsieur Le Sage*, new ed. (Amsterdam: Pierre Mortier, 1789), woodcut, p. 112.

73. Cutaway of a residential building in Paris, drawing by Bertall, lithograph by Lavieille, published in *Le diable à Paris: Paris et les Parisiens* (text by Balzac, E. Sue, G. Sand, et al.), series of lithographs with legends by Gavarni and vignettes by Bertall (Paris: J. Hetzel, 1845–1846), 2 vols., and in *L'Illustration* (January 11, 1845): 293.

74. Benjamin, *The Arcades Project*, 406.

75. Johann Friedrich Geist, *Passagen, ein Bautyp des 19. Jahrhunderts* (Munich: Prestel, 1979), 32, our translation; See Geist, *Arcades, the History of a Building Type*, trans. Jane O. Newman and John H. Smith (Cambridge, MA: MIT Press, 1983).

76. Rainer Maria Rilke, *The Notebooks of Malte Laurids Brigge*, trans. and ed. Michael Hulse (London: Penguin, 2009).

77. Benjamin, *The Arcades Project*, 407.

78. Ibid., 532.

79. Charles Asselineau, *Mélanges tirés d'une petite bibliothèque romantique* (Paris: R. Pincebourde, 1866); Asselineau, *Bibliographie romantique*, 2nd ed. (Paris: P. Rouquette, 1872).

80. Gretel Adorno and Walter Benjamin, *Correspondance: 1930–1940*, ed. Christoph Gödde and Henri Lonitz, trans. Christophe David (Paris: le Promeneur, 2007), 170.

81. Benjamin, "Central Park," in *The Writer of Modern Life: Essays on Charles Baudelaire*, 134–169, see 134.

82. Charles Baudelaire, *Correspondance*, ed. Claude Pichois, 2 vols. (Paris: Gallimard/Bibliothèque de la Pléiade, 1973), 1:338–341. Pierre Bouvier's translation.

83. Benjamin, *The Arcades Project*, 205.

84. Baudelaire, *Correspondance*, 1:338–341. Pierre Bouvier's translation.

85. Benjamin, *The Arcades Project*, 207.

86. Ibid.

87. Ibid., 209.

88. Baudelaire, *Correspondance*, 1:338–341. Pierre Bouvier's translation.

89. Benjamin, *The Arcades Project*, 259. See Dr. René Laforgue, *L'Échec de Baudelaire: étude psychanalytique sur la névrose de Charles Baudelaire* (Paris: Denoël et Steele, 1931), 201–204. Laforgue, a controversial figure, was a founder of the Société Psychanalytique de Paris. See Laforgue, *The Defeat of Baudelaire*, trans. Herbert Agar (London: Hogarth Press, 1932).

90. Emmanuel Pernoud, *Le Bordel en peinture: l'art contre le goût* (Paris: A. Biro, 2001); Baudelaire, "The Painter of Modern Life," 395–422.

91. Baudelaire, "The Ideal," in *The Flowers of Evil*, trans. Cyril Scott (London: Elkin Mathews, 1909), 19.

92. Benjamin, "Central Park," 134.

93. Michel Butor, *Histoire extraordinaire, essai sur un rêve de Baudelaire* (1961; Paris: Gallimard, 1988), 29, 57, 217. Pierre Bouvier's translation.

94. Benjamin, *The Arcades Project*, 210.

95. Ibid., 409.

96. Ibid.

97. Ibid.

98. Benjamin, "Surrealism," 209.

99. Ibid., 212.

100. Walter Benjamin, "Experience and Poverty," trans. Rodney Livingstone, in Benjamin, *Selected Writings*, 2:734.

101. Benjamin, "Surrealism," 209.

102. Ibid.

103. Walter Benjamin, "Karl Krauss," trans. Edmund Jephcott, in Benjamin, *Selected Writings*, 2:438.

104. Paul Scheerbart, *Glasarchitektur* (Berlin: Verlag der Sturm, 1914); Scheerbart, *Glass architecture*, ed. Dennis Sharp, trans. James Palmes (New York: Praeger, 1972); Scheerbart, *L'architecture de verre*, trans. Pierre Galissaire (Strasbourg: Circé, 1995).

105. Gretel Adorno and Walter Benjamin, *Correspondance*, 124, 135, 137; Dominique Vellay, *La Maison de verre: le chef-d'œuvre de Pierre Chareau* (Arles: Actes Sud, 2007).

106. Benjamin, *The Arcades Project*, 158.

107. Baudelaire, "Quelques caricaturistes français," in Baudelaire, *Œuvres complètes*, 2:558–559. Pierre Bouvier's translation.

108. Ibid.

109. J. J. Grandville, *Un Autre monde* (Paris: H. Fournier, 1844), pl. 106.

110. Ibid., pl. 243.

111. Ibid., pl. 53.

112. Benjamin, *The Arcades Project*, 200–201.

113. Walter Benjamin, "Paris, the Capital of the Nineteenth Century," in Benjamin, *Selected Writings*, vol. 3, 1935–1938, trans. Howard Eiland (Cambridge, MA: Belknap Press of Harvard University Press, 2002), 37.

114. Annie Renonciat, *J. J. Grandville* (Paris: Delpire, 2006); Renonciat, *La vie et l'œuvre de J. J. Grandville*, ed. Claude Rebeyrat (Paris: ACR Édition, 2000).

115. Benjamin, "Dream Kitsch: Gloss on Surrealism," trans. Howard Eiland, in Benjamin, *Selected Writings*, 2:3–5.

116. Benjamin, "Paris, the Capital of the Nineteenth Century," 37.

117. Ibid.

118. Mario Perniola, *Le sex-appeal de l'inorganique*, trans. Catherine Siné (Paris: L. Scheer, 2003).

119. Marleen Stoessel, "Dans le demi-jour: le même et le semblable," in Wismann, *Walter Benjamin et Paris*, 437.

120. Benjamin, *The Arcades Project*, 213.

4 THE WAVE

1. Hannah Arendt, *Walter Benjamin, Bertolt Brecht: Zwei Essays* (Munich: R. Piper, 1971), 54. My translation.

2. Walter Benjamin, *Fragments philosophiques, politiques, critiques, littéraires*, ed. Rolf Tiedemann and Hermann Schweppenhäuser, trans. Christophe Jouanlanne and Jean-François Poirier (Paris: Presses Universitaires de France, 2001), 189.

3. Rainer Maria Rilke, *Auguste Rodin* (New York: Archipelago Books, 2004), 41.

4. See, for example, Roger-Henri Guerrand, *L'art nouveau en Europe*, preface by Louis Aragon (Paris: Plon, 1965; repr. Paris: Perrin, 2009).

5. Rainer Maria Rilke, *Die neue Kunst in Berlin*, written for the reopening of Berlin's Keller & Reiner Art Gallery, later published in the *Wiener Rundshau*. See Rainer Maria Rilke, "L'art nouveau à Berlin," in *Œuvres en prose, Récits et essais*, ed. Claude David (Paris: Gallimard, 1993), 691–694.

6. Rainer Maria Rilke, "Notes sur la mélodie des choses," *Œuvres en prose*, 692.

7. Rainer Maria Rilke, "Sur l'art, I," *Œuvres en prose*, 678.

8. Rainer Maria Rilke, *Duino Elegies: and, The Sonnets to Orpheus*, part II, 12th and 1st sonnets, our translation; see Rilke, "The Sonnets to Orpheus," trans. Robert Hunter (1993), <http://www.hunterarchive.com/files/poetry/sonnet stoorpheus.html>.

9. See Peter Sloterdijk, "Air/condition," in *Sphären III—Schäume, Plurale Sphärologie* (Frankfurt: Suhrkamp, 2004). See also Sloterdijk, "Air/Condition," in *Terror from the Air*, trans. Amy Patton and Steve Corcoran (Cambridge, MA: MIT Press, 2009), 71–106.

10. Walter Benjamin, "Curriculum, VI," quoted in Jean-Michel Palmier, *Walter Benjamin, le chiffonnier, l'Ange et le Petit Bossu* (Paris: Klincksieck, 2006), 134.

11. Hannah Arendt, "Walter Benjamin," in Arendt, *Vies politiques* (Paris: Gallimard, 1986), 270–271. See also Arendt, "Walter Benjamin," in Arendt, *Men in Dark Times* (New York: Harcourt Brace Jovanovich, 1983).

12. Walter Benjamin, *The Arcades Project*, trans. Howard Eiland and Kevin McLaughlin (Cambridge, MA: Belknap Press of Harvard University Press, 1999), 552.

13. Palmier, *Walter Benjamin*, 59–60.

14. Benjamin, *Fragments*, 245–246.

15. Palmier, *Walter Benjamin*, 61.

16. Bruno Tackels, *Walter Benjamin. Une vie dans les textes. Biographie* (Arles: Actes Sud, 2009), 43–44; regarding the photo of nudists bathing at Haubinda, see Esther Leslie, *Walter Benjamin* (London: Reaktion Books, 2007), 21.

17. Marino Pulliero, *Le désir d'authenticité. Walter Benjamin et l'héritage de la* Bildung *allemande. Biographie* (Paris: Bayard, 2005), 30–31.

18. Ibid., 473. See also John Alexander Williams, *Turning to Nature in Germany. Hiking, Nudism and Conservation, 1900–1940* (Stanford: Stanford University Press, 2007), esp.123–145.

19. Bruno Tackels, *Walter Benjamin. Une vie dans les textes. Biographie*, 45.

20. Palmier, *Walter Benjamin*, 107–110.

21. Benjamin, *Fragments*, 113.

22. Michael Hau, *The Cult of Health and Beauty in Germany: A Social History, 1890–1930* (Chicago: University of Chicago Press, 2003).

23. Benjamin, *Fragments*, 190.

24. Ibid., 188–190.

25. Gershom Scholem and Theodor W. Adorno, eds., *The Correspondence of Walter Benjamin, 1910–1940*, trans. Manfred R. Jacobson and Evelyn M. Jacobson (Chicago: University of Chicago Press, 1994), 350, 353.

26. Walter Benjamin, "Paris, the Capital of the Nineteenth Century," in Benjamin, *The Writer of Modern Life: Essays on Charles Baudelaire*, ed. Michael Jennings (Cambridge, MA: Belknap Press of Harvard University Press, 2006), 30–45.

27. Walter Benjamin, *Berlin Childhood around* 1900, trans. Howard Eiland (Cambridge, MA: Belknap Press of Harvard University Press, 2006), 98.

28. Theodor W. Adorno, *Kierkegaard: Construction of the Aesthetic* (Minneapolis: University of Minnesota Press, 1989), 40–46.

29. Charles Baudelaire, *Œuvres complètes*, ed. Claude Pichois, 2 vols. (Paris: Gallimard/La Pléiade, 1975), 1:558.

30. Honoré de Balzac, *Les Employés* (1849; Paris: Gallimard, 1985), 105.

31. Karl Marx, *Capital*, vol. 1, trans. Ben Fowkes (New York: Vintage Books, 1977), 163–164.

32. Benjamin, *The Arcades Project*, 197, 657–658.

33. Old Nick (pseudo. of Émile Daurand Forgues), J. J. Grandville (Jean-Ignace-Isidore Gérard, alias), *Petites misères de la vie humaine* (Paris: H. Fournier, 1843).

34. Charles Baudelaire, *Paris Spleen: Little Poems in Prose* [*Spleen de Paris*], trans. Keith Waldrop (Middletown, CT: Wesleyan University Press, 2009). See "Double Bedroom," 9–11; cited in Benjamin, *The Arcades Project*, 553.

35. See Baudelaire, "The Soup and the Clouds," in *Paris Spleen*, 86.

36. Benjamin, *The Arcades Project*, 558.

37. Ibid., 557.

38. Adolf Loos, *Ornament and Crime: Selected Essays*, ed. Adolf Opel and Michael Mitchell (Riverside, CA: Ariadne Press, 1997).

39. Benjamin, *The Arcades Project*, 226.

40. Ibid., 559.

41. Ibid., 556.

42. Marleen Stoessel, "Dans le demi-jour: le même et le semblable," in Heinz Wismann, ed., *Walter Benjamin et Paris* (Paris: Cerf, 1986), 438.

43. Salvador Dalí, "L'âne pourri," in *Le Surréalisme au service de la révolution* (Paris: J. Corti, July 1930), no. 1, p. 12; cited in Benjamin, *The Arcades Project*, 547.

44. André Breton, article in *Minotaure: Revue artistique et littéraire*, no. 3–4 (1933); reprinted, Breton, *Point du jour* (Paris: Gallimard, 1934), 234–236; cited in Benjamin, *The Arcades Project*, 549.

45. Benjamin, *The Arcades Project*, 657.

46. Ibid., 186.

47. Ibid., 195.

48. Dalí, "L'âne pourri"; cited in Benjamin, *The Arcades Project*, 547.

49. Dalí, ibid.; cited in Benjamin, *The Arcades Project*, 547.

50. Dolf Sternberger, "Jugendstil. Begriff und Physionomie," *Die neue Rundschau* 45, no. 2 (September 9, 1934): 255–271; cited in Benjamin, *The Arcades Project*, 550.

51. Ibid.

52. Ibid., 549.

53. Ibid., 550.

54. Henrik Ibsen, *The Master Builder: A Drama in Three Acts*, trans. John W. Arctander (Minneapolis: W. Kriedt, 1893).

55. Stoessel, "Dans le demi-jour," 438.

56. Benjamin, *The Arcades Project*, 557.

57. Friedrich Nietzsche, *Also sprach Zarathustra: ein Buch für alle und keinen* (Leipzig: Insel-Verlag, 1908); Henry van de Velde, *Récit de ma vie*, vol. 1, *1863–1900: Anvers, Bruxelles, Paris, Berlin*, with commentary by Anne Van Loo (Brussels: Versa; Paris: Flammarion, 1992), 197.

58. Henry van de Velde, *Récit de ma vie*, vol. 2, *1900–1917: Berlin, Weimar, Paris, Brussels*, with commentary by Anne Van Loo (Brussels: Versa; Paris: Flammarion, 1995), 153–158.

59. Van de Velde, *Récit de ma vie*, 2:352–363.

60. Lieven de Cauter, "The Birth of Pleinairism from the Spirit of the Interior," in Françoise Aubry and Jos Vandenbreeden, eds., *Horta: Art nouveau to Modernism* (Ghent: Ludion, 1996), 13–26; Leon Ploegaarts, "Van de Velde and Nietzsche," in Alexandre Kostka and Irving Wohlfarth, eds., *Nietzsche and "An Architecture of Our Minds"* (Los Angeles: Getty Research Institute, 1999).

61. Van de Velde, *Récit de ma vie*, 2:113.

62. Van de Velde, *Récit de ma vie*, 1:249.

63. See Claude Quiguer, *Femmes et machines de 1900: lecture d'une obsession modern style* (Paris: Klincksieck, 1979), 26; and Patrick Waldberg, *Éros modern' style* (Paris: Jean-Jacques Pauvert, 1964).

64. *Der Kuss* (engraving), *Pan* 4, no. 2 (July-August-September 1898): 117.

65. Stanford Anderson, *Peter Behrens and a New Architecture for the Twentieth Century* (Cambridge, MA: MIT Press, 2000), 27–43.

66. Otto J. Bierbaum, "Faunsflötenlied für Peter Behrens," in *Irrgarten der Liebe* (Berlin/Leipzig: Tusel Verlag, 1901), 352; cited in Quiguer, *Femmes et machines de 1900*, 90.

67. Linda Dalrymple Henderson, "Vibratory Modernism: Boccioni, Kupka, and the Ether of Space," in Bruce Clarke and Linda Dalrymple Henderson, eds., *From Energy to Information: Representation in Science and Technology, Art, and Literature* (Stanford: Stanford University Press, 2002), 126–149.

68. Henry van de Velde, "Die Linie," *Die Zukunft* 40, no. 49 (September 6, 1902): 385–388; van de Velde, *Zum neuen Stil*, ed. Hans Curjel (Munich: Piper, 1955), 181.

69. Christoph Asendorf, "Bodies in Force Fields: Design between the Wars," in Clarke and Henderson, *From Energy to Information*, 195–212.

70. Dolf Sternberger, *Panorama oder Ansichten vom 19. Jahrhundert* (Hamburg: Claassen, 1938), 33; cited in Benjamin, *The Arcades Project*, 558. According to Adorno, the content of Sternberger's book "was stolen from [Ernst] Bloch, from Benjamin, and from himself," and his "conceptual structure is incredibly mediocre." In Gretel Adorno and Walter Benjamin, *Briefwechsel 1930–1940*, ed. Christoph Gödde and Henri Lonitz (Frankfurt am Main: Suhrkamp, 2005).

71. Sternberger, *Panorama*, 33; cited in Benjamin, *The Arcades Project*, 559; Georg Simmel, "Die Grosstädte und das Geitesleben," in Margarete Susman and Michael Landmann, eds., *Brücke und Tür; Essays des Philosophen zur Geschichte, Religion, Kunst und Gesellschaft* (Stuttgart: K. F. Koehler, 1957), 227. Incidentally, the idea became popular at the time that neural life (*das Nervenleben*) would behave similarly to electric grids in large cities, and that failures and short circuits would lead to neurasthenia or other neuropathologies. See Andreas Killen, *Berlin Electropolis: Shock, Nerves, and German Modernity* (Berkeley: University of California Press, 2006).

72. Adorno's letters about Benjamin's "Paris, the Capital of the Nineteenth Century," now in Walter Benjamin, *Selected Writings*, vol. 3, 1935–1939, ed. Howard Eiland and Michael W. Jennings (Cambridge, MA: Belknap Press of Harvard University Press, 2002), 50–67, cit. 60.

73. Quiguer, *Femmes et machines de 1900*, 74.

74. Frank Wedekind, *The First Lulu* (New York: Applause Theater Books, 1994).

75. Quiguer, *Femmes et machines de 1900*, 75.

76. Ibid., 79.

77. Walter Benjamin, "Rückblick auf Stefan George," in Benjamin, *Schriften*, ed. Theodor W. Adorno and Gretel Adorno, 2 vols. (Frankfurt: Suhrkamp, 1955), 2:325; cited in Quiguer, *Femmes et machines de 1900*, 79–80.

78. Quiguer, *Femmes et machines de 1900*, 146.

79. Dolf Sternberger, "Jugendstil. Begriff und Physiognomie," *Die neue Rundschau* 45, no. 2 (September 9, 1934): 255–271; Sternberger, *Über den Jugendstil und andere Essays* (Hamburg: Claassen, 1956), 25–26.

80. Frank Wedekind, *Mine-Haha, or On the Bodily Education of Young Girls* (1903), trans. Philip Ward (London: Hesperus, 2010).

81. Wolfgang de Bruyn, *Fidus. Künstler alles Lichtbaren* (Berlin: Schiler Verlag, 2001).

82. Benjamin, *The Arcades Project*, 557.

83. Quiguer, *Femmes et machines de 1900*, 195.

84. Benjamin, *The Arcades Project*, 556.

85. Ibid., 559.

86. Ibid., 556.

87. See *Max Klinger: die druckgraphischen Folgen* (Heidelberg: Edition Braus, 2007); *Fernand Khnopff, 1858–1921* (Ostfildern-Ruit: Hatje Cantz, 2004); Eva Mendgen, *Franz von Stuck: The Art of Persuasion* (Tettenweis: Franz von Stuck Geburtshaus, 2002).

88. Gabriela Christen, *Ferdinand Hodler—Unendlichkeit und Tod: monumentale Frauenfiguren in den Zürcher Wandbildern* (Berlin: Reimer, 2008).

89. Juliette Laffon, ed., *Isadora Duncan (1877–1927). Une sculpture vivante* (Paris: Paris-Musées, Actes Sud, 2009); Kimerer L. LaMothe, *Nietzsche's Dancers: Isadora Duncan, Martha Graham, and the Revaluation of Christian Values* (New York: Palgrave Macmillan, 2006).

90. Heinrich Vogeler was a painter and architect who gained fame through his drawing *The Beautiful Melusine* (undated), and his painting *Spring* (1898). He was a founder of a colony of artists in Worpswede in the northeast of Bremen which was also frequented by Rilke, who wrote several texts on Vogeler. See Heinrich Vogeler, *Zwischen Gotik und Expressionismus-Debatte: Schriften zur Kunst und Geschichte*, ed. Siegfried Bresler (Bremen: Donat, 2006); Cornelia Baumann and Vera Losse, *Heinrich Vogeler und der Jugendstil* (Cologne: DuMont, 1997).

91. Quiguer, *Femmes et machines de 1900*, 178.

92. Benjamin, *The Arcades Project*, 556.

93. Quiguer, *Femmes et machines de 1900*, 185.

94. Dolf Sternberger, "Jugendstil. Begriff und Physionomie," cited in Benjamin, *The Arcades Project*, 550.

95. Edith Wharton, "The Fullness of Life," in *The Collected Short Stories of Edith Wharton*, ed. R. W. B. Lewis, vol. 1 (New York: Charles Scribner's Sons, 1968).

96. Jacqueline Carroy, "L'hystérique, l'artiste et le savant," in Jean Clair, ed., *L'âme au corps. Arts et sciences, 1793–1993* (Paris : Réunion des musées nationaux, [with] Gallimard/Electa, 1993), 455–456.

97. Quiguer, *Femmes et machines de 1900*, 191.

98. Regine Prange, *Das Kristalline als Kunstsymbol. Bruno Taut und Paul Klee: zur Reflexion des Abstrakten in Kunst und Kunsttheorie der Moderne* (Hildesheim: Olms, 1991).

99. Hubertus Adam, ed., *Hermann Obrist: Skulptur, Raum, Abstraktion um 1900* (Zurich: Scheidegger & Spiess, 2009), 94; Erich Franz, ed., *Freiheit der Linie: von Obrist und dem Jugendstil zu Marc, Klee und Kirchner* (Bönen: Kettler, 2007).

100. Rudolf Herz and Brigitte Bruns, eds., *Hof-Atelier Elvira, 1887–1928: Ästheten, Emanzen, Aristokraten* (Munich: City Museum, 1985).

101. Ann Cooper Albright, *Traces of Light: Absence and Presence in the Work of Loïe Fuller* (Middletown, CT: Wesleyan University Press, 2007); Jo-Anne Birnie Danzker, ed., *Loïe Fuller: getanzter Jugendstil* (Munich: Villa Stuck, 1995).

102. Françoise Aubry, *L'architecture en Belgique: art nouveau, art déco & modernisme* (Brussels: Éd. Racine, 2006); Aubry, *Art nouveau à Bruxelles: de l'architecture à l'ornementalisme* (Brussels: Quo vadis, 2005); Aubry, *Horta, ou La passion de l'architecture* (Brussels: Ludion, 2005).

103. Paul Scheerbart, *Münchhausen und Clarissa, ein Berliner Roman* (Berlin: Oesterheld, 1906).

104. Quiguer, *Femmes et machines de 1900*, 372.

105. Ibid., 391.

106. Benjamin, *The Arcades Project*, 392.

107. Rainer Maria Rilke, *Die frühen Gedichte* (Leipzig: Insel-Verlag, 1922), 1 (epigraph); cited in Benjamin, *The Arcades Project*, 551.

5 THE STORY OF AN IDEA

1. Aldo van Eyck, "Between Here and There, Now and Later," in the "Door-Window" issue, *Forum voor architectuur en darmee verbonden kunsten*, no. 3 (August 1960): 107–117; now in Aldo van Eyck, *Collected Articles and Other Writings, 1947–1998*, ed. Vincent Ligtelijn and Francis Strauven (Amsterdam: SUN, 2008), 291–292.

2. Max Risselada and Dirk van den Heuvel, eds., *Team 10: In Search of a Utopia of the Present, 1953–81* (Rotterdam: NAi, 2005), 43–49; 60–63. Originally, Team 10 was the committee created in 1954 to organize CIAM 10 in Dubrovnik (1956). The last CIAM meeting, the eleventh, also named CIAM '59, was held in Otterlo , The Netherlands (1959).

3. Aldo van Eyck, "The Greater Reality of the Doorstep," in "Orientation, CIAM 10, Dubrovnik, 1956," written in October 1954; now in van Eyck, *Collected Articles and Other Writings*, 191–192.

4. Martin Buber, foreword to Erwin Anton Gutkind, *Community and Environment: A Discourse on Social Ecology* (London: Watts, 1953; New York: Philosophical Library, 1954), vii–ix. Erwin Anton Gutkind (1886–1968) was the architect of the housing development Sonnenhof at Weitlingkiez, near Berlin (1925–1927); in 1956, he was named a professor at the Graduate School of Fine Arts, University of Pennsylvania.

5. Ellen Shoshkes, "Jacqueline Tyrwhitt: A Founding Mother of Modern Urban Design," *Planning Perspectives* 21, no. 2 (April 2006): 179–198.

6. Sigfried Giedion, *Architektur und Gemeinschaft; Tagebuch einer Entwicklung* (Hamburg: Rowohlt, 1956); Giedion, *Architecture, You and Me: The Diary of a Development* (Cambridge, MA: Harvard University Press, 1958); see also Shoshkes, "Jacqueline Tyrwhitt," 186.

7. Aldo van Eyck, "Is Architecture Going to Reconcile Basic Values?," a talk at the 1959 Otterlo Congress, edited by van Eyck in 1961; published in Oscar Newman, *CIAM '59 in Otterlo* (Stuttgart: Kramer Verlag, 1961); now in van Eyck, *Collected Articles and Other Writings*, 204.

8. Team 10, "Team Primer," *Architectural Design* 32, no. 10 (1962): 598; also Shoshkes, "Jacqueline Tyrwhitt," 187–188.

9. Francis Strauven, *Aldo van Eyck: The Shape of Relativity* (Amsterdam: Architectura & Natura, 1998), 243.

10. Aldo van Eyck, "The Story of Another Idea," *Forum* 7, special issue (September 1959): 197–248; now in van Eyck, *Collected Articles*, 220–271. It was followed by the special issue "Threshold and Meeting—The Shape of the In-between," *Forum* 8, ed. Joop Hardy and Herman Hertzberger (October 1959): 249–284.

11. Ibid.

12. Or the "doorstep" (in Alison and Peter Smithson's view). However, the "doorstep" notion of the Smithsons cannot be identified with van Eyck's "in-between." See Dirk van den Heuvel, "Encounters: The Spaces Between; Historical and Theoretical Backgrounds of the Architectural Teachings of Max Risselada and Hans Tupker," in Dirk van den Heuvel, Madeleine Steigenga,

and Jaap van Triest, eds., *Lessons: Tupker/Risselada. A Double Portrait of Dutch Architectural Education 1953–2003* (Amsterdam: Uitgeverij SUN, 2003), 96–153, esp. 111–121.

13. Including those at the Harvard-MIT Joint Center for Urban Studies, formed in 1959; see Shoshkes, "Jacqueline Tyrwhitt," 189–190.

14. Gabriel Marcel, "I and Thou," in Paul Arthur Schilpp and Maurice Friedman, eds., *The Philosophy of Martin Buber* (London: Cambridge University Press, 1967), 41–48.

15. Gaston Bachelard, preface to Martin Buber, *Je et Tu* (1938), trans. Geneviève Bianquis (Paris: Aubier Montaigne, 1969), 13–14.

16. The "Door–Window" issue, *Forum* 3 (August 1960): 107–117; now in van Eyck, *Collected Articles*, 291–292; quoted by Strauven, *Aldo van Eyck*, 357.

17. Van Eyck, "Is Architecture Going to Reconcile Basic Values?," in *Collected Articles*, 203.

18. Jean Wahl, "Martin Buber and the Philosophy of Existence," in Schilpp and Friedman, *The Philosophy of Martin Buber*, 493.

19. "In other words, Buber doesn't do justice to the 'It,' to the things of the world, because he still thinks within the schema bequeathed by Western metaphysics, which tends to capture man's place in terms of object and subject, when, ontologically, 'being' should not be conceived as an object for man, nor should beings be reduced to the subject-object relation." Ernst Simon, "Martin Buber, the Educator," in Schilpp and Friedman, *The Philosophy of Martin Buber*, 543–576; see 576.

20. Maurice Friedman, "The Bases of Buber's Ethic," in Schilpp and Friedman, *The Philosophy of Martin Buber*, 174.

21. Emmanuel Levinas, "Martin Buber and the Theory of Knowledge," in Schilpp and Friedman, *The Philosophy of Martin Buber*, 133–150. As Levinas remarks, Buber accords the intersubjective aspects of the I-Thou relation a privileged status, but the meeting is not just construed as one between human beings and things, but also as a relationship with God. The original distance (*Urdistanz*) that penetrates the between-men sphere also invades the territory "between God and men."

22. Ibid., 149.

23. Michel Foucault, *Dits et Écrits I, 1954–1975*, ed. Daniel Defert and François Ewald (Paris: Gallimard, 2001), 467, 568, 1094.

24. Aldo van Eyck, "There Is a Garden in Her Face," *Forum* 3 (1960–1961): 121; quoted by Strauven, *Aldo van Eyck*, 416; now in van Eyck, *Collected Articles*, 293.

25. Ibid.

26. Daniel Payot, *Le philosophe et l'architecte* (Paris: Aubier Montaigne, 1982), 106, 108, 111.

27. Arnaud Villani, "De l'esthétique à l'esthésique: Deleuze et la question de l'art," in Alain Beaulieu, ed., *Gilles Deleuze, héritage philosophique* (Paris: Presses Universitaires de France, 2005), 97–121; see 107.

28. François Dosse, *History of Structuralism*, trans. Deborah Glassman (Minneapolis: University of Minnesota Press, 1997), vol. 1, *The Rising Sign, 1945–1966*; vol. 2, *The Sign Sets, 1967–present*.

29. Strauven, *Aldo van Eyck*, 417, 351, 417.

30. *Aldo van Eyck: Works*, ed. Vincent Ligtelijn (Basel: Birkhäuser, 1999).

31. Aldo van Eyck, "The Medicine of Reciprocity Tentatively Illustrated," *Forum* (April-May 1961); now in van Eyck, *Collected Articles*, 312–323.

32. Strauven, *Aldo van Eyck*, 418–419.

33. Ibid.

34. Arnold van Gennep, *The Rites of Passage*, trans. Monika B. Vizedom and Gabrielle L. Caffee (London: Routledge, 2004), 15.

35. Ibid., 20.

36. See the introduction by Aldo van Eyck to Joseph Rykwert, "The Idea of a Town," *Forum* 3 (1963); now in van Eyck, *Collected Articles*, 271–272.

37. Rykwert, "The Idea of a Town," 99–148; 121; and n. 199; 134; and n. 218. Later, in another instance, Rykwert will mention van Gennep's volume in the chapter on rites in *On Adam's House in Paradise: The Idea of the Primitive Hut in Architectural History* (New York: Museum of Modern Art, 1972).

38. Richard Noll, *The Jung Cult: Origins of a Charismatic Movement* (1994; Princeton: Princeton University Press, 1997).

39. Strauven, *Aldo van Eyck*, 64.

40. Rykwert, "The Idea of a Town," 3; n. 175 quotes Henri Frankfort's essay about archetypes in the figurative arts.

41. Today, except in Jungian circles and mystic websites, nobody gives credit to the theory that considers archetypes as belonging to each human being's hereditary constitution, biologically embedded in the mind and soul, and revealed under the guise of multiple representations that vary widely from epoch to epoch and place to place.

42. Rykwert, "The Idea of a Town," n. 196, n. 211, n. 212, n. 276.

43. Julien Ries and Natale Spineto, eds., *Deux explorateurs de la pensée humaine: Georges Dumézil et Mircea Eliade* (Turnhout: Brepols, 2003).

44. Rykwert, "The Idea of a Town," 117, n. 137.

45. Ibid., 120, n. 175.

46. Frank McLynn, *Carl Gustav Jung* (New York: St. Martin's Press, 1997); Richard Noll, *The Aryan Christ: The Secret Life of Carl Jung* (New York: Random House, 1997); Aryeh Maidenbaum and Stephen A. Martin, eds., *Lingering Shadows: Jungians, Freudians, and Anti-Semitism* (New York: Random House, 1991); Elisabeth Roudinesco, "Carl Gustav Jung: de l'archétype au nazisme. Dérives d'une psychologie de la différence," *L'infini* 63 (1998): 73–94.

47. Hilary Ballon, "The History of Louis Hautecœur: Classical Architecture and Vichy Politics," in Martha Pollak, ed., *The Education of the Architect* (Cambridge, MA: MIT Press, 1997), 217–222; Caroline Poulain, "L'action de Louis Hautecœur au secrétariat général des Beaux arts (1940–1944)," PhD dissertation, École nationale des chartes, 2001; Antonio Brucculeri, "L'Architecture classique en France et l'approche historique de Louis Hautecœur," PhD dissertation, Université de Paris VIII, 2002.

48. Daniel Dubuisson, *Impostures et pseudo-science: l'œuvre de Mircea Eliade*, preface by Isac Chiva (Villeneuve-d'Ascq: Presses Universitaires du Septentrion, 2005); Florin Ţurcanu, *Mircea Eliade: le prisonnier de l'histoire* (Paris: Éditions la Découverte, 2003); Alexandra Laignel-Lavastine, *Cioran, Eliade, Ionesco: l'oubli du fascisme: trois intellectuels roumains dans la tourmente du siècle* (Paris: Presses Universitaires de France, 2002); Michael Löwy, "Impostures et pseudo-science. L'œuvre de Mircea Eliade," *Archives de sciences sociales des religions* 132 (2005), <http://assr.revues.org/3128?&id=3128> (accessed February 20, 2006).

49. Carlo Ginzburg, "Mythologie germanique et nazisme. Sur un ancien livre de Georges Dumézil," in *Myths, Emblems, Clues*, trans. John Tedeschi and Anne

C. Tedeschi (London: Hutchinson Radius, 1990); Didier Eribon, *Faut-il brûler Dumézil? Mythologie, science et politique* (Paris: Flammarion, 1992); Bruce Lincoln, *Theorizing Myth: Narrative, Ideology, and Scholarship* (Chicago: University of Chicago Press, 1999; 2000); Stefan Arvidsson, *Aryan Idols: The Indo-European Mythology as Science and Ideology* (Chicago: University of Chicago Press, 2006).

50. Russell T. McCutcheon, *Manufacturing Religion: The Discourse of sui generis Religion and the Politics of Nostalgia* (New York: Oxford University Press, 1997).

51. Leo Frobenius, *Kulturgeschichte Afrikas; Prolegomena zu einer historischen Gestaltlehre* (1933; Wuppertal: Peter Hammer Verlag and Frobenius-Institut, Frankfurt, 1998); Leo Frobenius and Douglas C. Fox, *African Genesis* (New York: B. Blom, 1966).

52. Claude Lévi-Strauss, *Tristes tropiques* (Paris: Plon, 1955), 225–277.

53. Rykwert, "The Idea of a Town," 143. For the author, in "our attempts to give form to human environment," we "must look for it inside ourselves: in the constitution and structure of the human person."

54. Joseph Rykwert, *The Idea of a Town: The Anthropology of Urban Form in Rome, Italy and the Ancient World* (Princeton: Princeton University Press, 1976).

55. Koos Bosma, Dorine van Hoogstraten, and Martijn Vos, *Housing for the Millions: John Habraken and the SAR (1960–2000)* (Rotterdam: NAI Publishers, 2000); Toshio Nakamura, ed., *Herman Hertzberger, 1959–1990* (Tokyo: Ēando Yū, 1991); Jaap Hengeveld, *Piet Blom*, with a text by Francis Strauven (Amersfoort: Hengeveld Publicaties, 2008); Dirk van den Heuvel, "Piet Blom's Domesticated Superstructures," in Dick van Gameren et al., eds., *Delft Architectural Studies on Housing (DASH): The Urban Enclave* (Rotterdam: NAI, 2011), 54–70; Dirk van den Heuvel, "The Kasbah of Suburbia," *AA Files*, no. 62 (2011): 82–89; Dirk van den Heuvel, "'A New and Shuffled Order': The Heroic Structuralism and Other Variants," in Tomas Valena with Tom Avermaete and Georg Vrachliotis, eds., *Structuralism Reloaded: Rule-Based Design in Architecture and Urbanism* (Stuttgart: Edition Axel Menges, 2011), 98–109.

56. Arnulf Lüchinger, *Structuralism in Architecture and Urban Planning* (Stuttgart: Krämer, 1981), 16–17.

57. Jean-Claude Milner, *Le périple structural: figures et paradigme* (Paris: Éditions du Seuil, 2002), 179–245, see 182; new edition (Paris: Verdier, 2008), 277–376.

58. Gilles Deleuze, "How Do We Recognize Structuralism?" (1972), in Gilles Deleuze, *Desert Islands and Other Texts, 1953–1974*, ed. David Lapoujade, trans. Michael Taormina (Los Angeles: Semiotext(e); Cambridge, MA: MIT Press, 2004), 170–192. Claude Lévi-Strauss's intention was to devise a scientific method dealing with the humanities (linguistics, ethnology, anthropology). The two volumes of Gilles Deleuze's thesis, *Difference and Repetition* (1968) and *The Logic of Sense* (1969), represent a prolongation of, but also a philosophical rupture with, the pretense of structuralism to be a hard science. Deleuze's essay "How Do We Recognize Structuralism?" (1972) is literally a post-mortem examination, the autopsy of a corpse. Of course, the connection between structuralism and post-structuralism is not an easy matter.

59. As defined by the Shannon/Weaver model. Claude E. Shannon and Warren Weaver, *The Mathematical Theory of Communication* (1949), ed. Richard E. Blahut and Bruce Hajek (Urbana: University of Illinois Press, 1998).

60. Milner, *Le périple structural*, 201–202.

61. "Mission Dakar–Djibouti, 1931–1933," special issue, *Minotaure* 2 (Paris: Albert Skira, 1933).

62. Ruth Benedict, *Patterns of Culture* (1934; Boston: Houghton Mifflin, 2005), ch. 4; Strauven, *Aldo van Eyck*, 380.

63. Aldo van Eyck, "The Pueblos," *Forum* (August 1962); now in van Eyck, *Collected Articles*, 350–370.

64. Strauven, *Aldo van Eyck*, 388; Aldo van Eyck, "Architecture of the Dogon," *Architectural Forum* 115, no. 3 (September 1961): 116–121.

65. Piet Vollaard, *Herman Haan, Architect* (Rotterdam: Uitgeverij 010, 1995); see Karin Jaschke, "Mythopoesis of Place and Culture: Aldo van Eyck, Herman Haan, and the Dogon," in Max Risselada and Dirk van den Heuvel, eds., *Team 10: Keeping the Language of Modern Architecture Alive* (Delft: Faculty of Architecture, Delft University of Technology, 2007), 110–125.

66. Montserrat Palau Marti, *Les Dogon* (Paris: Presses Universitaires de France, 1957).

67. Marcel Griaule, *Dieu d'eau, entretiens avec Ogotemmêli* (Paris: Éditions du Chêne, 1948); Griaule, *Dieu d'eau: entretiens avec Ogotemmêli* (Paris: Fayard, 1966, 1975; repr., Paris: Livre de poche, 1987, 1991, 2005); Griaule, *Conversations with Ogotemmêli: An Introduction to Dogon Religious Ideas*, introduction

by Germaine Dieterlen (London: Oxford University Press, 1965, 1970, 1972, 1978). The only copy in van Eyck's library is the 1966 edition.

68. Paul Parin, Fritz Morgenthaler, and Goldy Parin-Matthey, *Die Weissen denken zuviel, psychoanalytische Untersuchungen bei den Dogon in Westafrika* (Zurich: Atlantis Verlag, 1963); 3rd ed. (Frankfurt am Main: Fischer Taschenbuch Verlag, 1983); *Les Blancs pensent trop, 13 entretiens psychanalytiques avec les Dogon*, trans. Aude Willm (Paris: Payot, 1966); see, for instance, the chapter on "Le complexe d'Œdipe," 428–436.

69. Aldo van Eyck, Paul Parin, and Fritz Morgenthaler, "A Miracle of Moderation," *Forum* 17, no. 3 (1967): 29–50; now in van Eyck, *Collected Articles*, 373–417.

70. Aldo van Eyck, Paul Parin, and Fritz Morgenthaler, "A Miracle of Moderation," *Via* 1 (1968): 96–124; van Eyck, "A Miracle of Moderation," in Charles Jencks and George Baird, eds., *Meaning in Architecture* (London: Barrie & Rockliff and Cresset Press, 1969).

71. Strauven, *Aldo van Eyck*, 386.

72. Ibid., 300, 386; van Eyck, "Is Architecture Going to Reconcile Basic Values?," in *Collected Articles*, 205.

73. The identification of house and city can be traced back to Alberti and Palladio, although Francis Strauven believes that Aldo van Eyck was not aware of such precedents. However, it is likely he had overheard them, since such homologies were a standard part of an architect's education, especially in the 1940s. See Francis Strauven, "Introduction," in Aldo van Eyck, *The Child, the City and the Artist: An Essay on Architecture: the In-between Realm* (manuscript of 1962; Amsterdam: SUN, 2008), 228, n. 4.

74. Strauven, *Aldo van Eyck*, 397–398; see Aldo van Eyck, "Identification of leaf with tree," original text of 1961, presented at the Team 10 meeting, Abbaye de Royaumont, September 1962. Actually, the handwritten diagram was prepared for *Domus* (May 1965); now in van Eyck, *Collected Articles*, 443.

75. Paul Ricœur, "La métaphore vive," in Laurent Lavaud, ed., *L'image* (Paris: Flammarion, 1999), 224.

76. Kenneth Frampton, "The Vicissitudes of Ideology," in Brian Brace Taylor, ed., *Team 10+20, Architecture d'Aujourd'hui*, no. 177, special issue (January-February 1975): 62–66.

77. Alison Smithson, ed., *Team 10 Primer* (London: Studio Vista, 1968), "Doorstep" section, 96–105.

78. See the influential, revised French edition, *Le Sens de la ville*, by Françoise Choay, George Baird, Reyner Banham, Aldo van Eyck, Kenneth Frampton, and Joseph Rykwert, trans. Jean-Paul Martin (Paris: Éditions du Seuil, 1972).

79. Geneviève Calame-Griaule, compte-rendu, *L'Homme* 9, no. 1 (1969): 111–113; she is the author of *La parole chez les Dogon* (Paris: Gallimard, 1965). The periodical *L'Homme. Revue française d'anthropologie* was founded in 1961 by Émile Benveniste, Pierre Gourou, and Claude Lévi-Strauss.

80. Gilles Deleuze and Felix Guattari, *Anti-Oedipus: Capitalism and Schizophrenia*, trans. Robert Hurley, Mark Seem, and Helen R. Lane (1972; Minneapolis: University of Minnesota Press, 1989), 143–144, 160–161.

6 TOWARD A CYBORG ARCHITECTURE

1. Gilles Deleuze, "The Actual and the Virtual," trans. Eliot Ross Albert, in Gilles Deleuze and Claire Parnet, *Dialogues II*, trans. Hugh Tomlinson and Barbara Habberjam (New York: Continuum, 2002), 112–115.

2. Reyner Banham, "The New Brutalism," *Architectural Review* 118 (December 1955): 361; reprinted in Banham, *A Critic Writes: Essays by Reyner Banham*, ed. Mary Banham et al. (Berkeley: University of California Press, 1996), 7–15, esp. 14.

3. Banham, "The New Brutalism," 14; on Reyner Banham, see Nigel Whiteley, "Banham and 'Otherness': Reyner Banham and His Quest for an *architecture autre*," *Architectural History* 33 (1990): 188–221; Jonathan E. Farnham, "Pure Pop for Now People: Reyner Banham, Science Fiction and History," *Lotus International*, no. 104 (2000): 112–131; Nigel Whiteley, *Reyner Banham: Historian of the Immediate Future* (Cambridge, MA: MIT Press, 2002); Laurent Stalder, "'New Brutalism', 'Topology' and 'Image': Some Remarks on the Architectural Debates in England Around 1950," *Journal of Architecture* 13, no. 3 (2008): 263–281; Laurent Stalder, "Air, Light, and Air-conditioning," *Grey Room* 40 (2010): 84–99.

4. Banham, "The New Brutalism," 14 (in French in the text).

5. Reyner Banham, "Stocktaking," *Architectural Review* 127 (February 1960); reprinted in Banham, *Design by Choice*, ed. Penny Sparke (New York: Rizzoli, 1981), 48–55; and Banham, *A Critic Writes*, 61.

6. Reyner Banham, *The Architecture of the Well-Tempered Environment* (London: Architectural Press, 1969), 239–243.

7. On the "Visionary Architecture" exhibition, curated by Arthur Drexler at the Museum of Modern Art in 1960, see "Visionary Architecture at the Museum of Modern Art, New York," *Architectural Design* 31, no. 5 (May 1961): 181–182; and Günter Feuerstein, *Visionäre Architektur, Wien 1958–88* (Berlin: Ernst & Sohn, 1988).

8. Ulrich Conrads and Hans G. Sperlich, *Phantastische Architektur* (Stuttgart: Hatje, 1960); Conrads and Sperlich, *Architecture fantastique* (Paris: Delpire, 1960); Conrads and Sperlich, *The Architecture of Fantasy. Utopian Building and Planning in Modern Times*, ed. Christiane Crasemann Collins and George R. Collins (New York: Praeger, 1962); and "Architectures fantastiques," *Architecture d'Aujourd hui* 33, no. 102 (June-July 1962).

9. Michel Ragon, *Wo leben wir morgen? Mensch und Umwelt, die Stadt der Zukunft* (Munich: Callwey, 1967); Ragon, *Histoire mondiale de l'architecture et de l'urbanisme modernes. 3, Prospective et futurologie* (Tournai: Casterman, 1978).

10. Peter Cook, *Experimental Architecture* (New York: Universe Books, 1970).

11. Albert Dalcq, "Form and Modern Embryology," in Lancelot Law Whyte, *Aspects of Form: A Symposium on Form in Nature and Art* (London: Lund Humphries, 1951); published in collaboration with the Institute of Contemporary Arts (ICA) to coincide with the exhibition "Growth and Form," London, Summer 1951, the title of which was inspired by the new edition of D'Arcy Wentworth Thompson, *On Growth and Form* (1917; Cambridge: Cambridge University Press, 1944).

12. Gilles Deleuze, *Difference and Repetition*, trans. Paul Patton (1968; New York: Columbia University Press, 1994), 250–251.

13. Albert Dalcq, *L'œuf et son dynamisme organisateur* (Paris: Albin Michel, 1941).

14. Gilles Deleuze, *Francis Bacon: The Logic of Sensation*, trans. Daniel W. Smith (1981; London: Continuum, 2003), 41.

15. Gilles Deleuze, *The Logic of Sense*, trans. Mark Lester (1969; New York: Columbia University Press, 1990), 88, 342.

16. Anne Sauvagnargues, *Deleuze et l'art* (Paris: Presses Universitaires de France, 2006), 87–88.

17. Ibid., 90.

18. Erwin Schrödinger, *What Is Life? The Physical Aspect of the Living Cell* (New York: Macmillan, 1945); Schrödinger, *What Is Life?* (Cambridge: Cambridge University Press, 1992); Henri Atlan, *Entre le cristal et la fumée: essai sur l'organisation du vivant* (Paris: Éditions du Seuil, 1979, 1986).

19. See the new edition of the main thesis in Gilbert Simondon, *L'Individuation à la lumière des notions de forme et d'information*, preface by Jacques Garelli (Grenoble: Millon, 2005), 228. This merges "L'Individu et sa genèse physico-biologique," Paris, 1964, and "L'Individuation psychique et collective," published in 1989, a reworking of Simondon's doctoral thesis of 1957.

20. Eric W. Weisstein, "Topology," from MathWorld—A Wolfram Web Resource, <http://mathworld.wolfram.com/Topology.html> (accessed January 25, 2012).

21. On the symbolism of the egg, see Michel Ragon, *Où vivrons-nous demain?* (Paris: Robert Laffont, 1963), 85.

22. Anker Valentina, *Max Bill ou la recherche d'un art logique* (Lausanne: L'Âge d'Homme, 1979) 137, 149, 168, 173.

23. Vittorio Fagone, *Baldessari, progetti e scenografie* (Milan: Electa, 1982).

24. Frederick Kiesler, "Manifeste du Corréalisme," *Architecture d'Aujourd'hui* (June 1949).

25. Chantal Béret, ed., *Frederick Kiesler: artiste et architecte* (Paris: Centre Georges Pompidou, 1996), 176–177.

26. Raymond Loewy, *Never Leave Well Enough Alone* (New York: Simon and Schuster, 1951), 181.

27. Nicolas Schöffer, *La Ville cybernétique* (Paris: Tchou, 1969; repr., Paris: Denoël-Gonthier, 1972).

28. Antoine Picon, *L'Art de l'ingénieur* (Paris: Éditions du Centre Georges Pompidou, 1997), 436–437.

29. See Victoria Newhouse, *Wallace K. Harrison, Architect* (New York: Rizzoli, 1989); John Harwood and Janet Parks, *The Troubled Search: The Work of Max Abramovitz* (New York: Miriam and Ira D. Wallach Art Gallery, Columbia University, 2004).

30. Ragon, *Où vivrons-nous demain?*, 86.

31. Frei Otto, "Villes futures," in "Recherches," special issue, *Architecture d'Aujourd'hui* 34, no. 115 (June-July 1964): 22–25; Winfried Nerdinger, ed., *Frei Otto: Complete Works: Lightweight Construction, Natural Design* (Basel:

Birkhäuser, 2005); Juan Maria Songel, *A Conversation with Frei Otto* (New York: Princeton Architectural Press, 2010), 37.

32. Chantal Béret, ed., *Frederick Kiesler: artiste et architecte*, 79.

33. Ibid.

34. Kenneth Frampton, *Modern Architecture: A Critical History* (1980; New York: Thames and Hudson, 2002), 200–201.

35. Quoted by Roberto Gargiani, *Auguste Perret. La théorie et l'œuvre* (Paris: Gallimard/Electa, 1994), 20; the quotation is from M. Zahar, "L'Architecture vivante. L'œuvre des frères Perret," *Art Vivant* 4, no.7 (1928): 764.

36. Perret's notebook, quoted in Gargiani, *Auguste Perret*, 182.

37. Richard Neutra, *Survival through Design* (New York: Oxford University Press, 1954).

38. Ibid., 12.

39. Ibid., 207.

40. Ibid., 150.

41. Ibid., 153–154.

42. Ibid., 124, 150–151.

43. Ibid., 156.

44. Ibid., 153–154.

45. Barbara Mac Lamprecht, *Richard Neutra: Complete Works*, ed. Peter Goessel (Cologne: Taschen, 2000); Dietrich Neumann, *Richard Neutra's Windshield House* (New Haven: Yale University Press, 2001); Sylvia Lavin, *Form Follows Libido: Architecture and Richard Neutra in a Psychoanalytic Culture* (Cambridge, MA: MIT Press, 2004).

46. Ragon, *Où vivrons-nous demain?*, 100; William D. Earls, *The Harvard Five in New Canaan: Midcentury Modern Houses by Marcel Breuer, Landis Gores, John Johansen, Philip Johnson, Eliot Noyes and Others* (New York: W.W. Norton, 2006); Gordon Bruce, *Eliot Noyes* (New York: Phaidon Press, 2007).

47. See Diane Kanner, *Wallace Neff and the Grand Houses of the Golden State* (New York: Monacelli Press, 2005). Numerous models were built and Airform houses still stand in Pasadena, California. For the technique, see Mary Krumboltz Hurd, *Formwork for Concrete* (Detroit: American Concrete Institute, 1969); Jeffrey Head, *No Nails, No Lumber: The Bubble House of Wallace Neff* (New York: Princeton Architectural Press, 2011).

48. Ragon, *Où vivrons-nous demain?*, 96–98; Silvia Berlessi, "Claude Parent et Ionel Schein . . . ," in Frédéric Migayrou and Francis Rambert, eds., *Claude Parent: L'œuvre construite, l'œuvre graphique* (Orléans: Éditions HYX, 2010), 56–59.

49. Ragon, *Où vivrons-nous demain?*, 96.

50. Reyner Banham, "Stocktaking," *Architectural Review* 127 (February 1960): 93–100; and *A Critic Writes: Essays by Reyner Banham*, 57.

51. Dirk van den Heuvel and Max Risselada, *Alison and Peter Smithson: From the House of the Future to a House of Today* (Rotterdam: Uitgeverij 010, 2004).

52. Robert Kronenburg, *Houses in Motion: The Genesis, History and Development of the Portable Building*, 2nd ed. (London: John Wiley and Sons, 2002); Sean Topham, *Blow-Up: Inflatable Art, Architecture, and Design* (Munich: Prestel, 2002); Topham, *Where's My Space Age? The Rise and Fall of Futuristic Design* (Munich: Prestel, 2003).

53. Conrads and Sperlich, *The Architecture of Fantasy*, 77–80; Ragon, *Où vivrons-nous demain?*, 49 (photo of the model), 113.

54. Arthur Quarmby, *The Plastics Architect* (London: Pall Mall Press, 1974), fig. 209.

55. Banham, "Stocktaking," 93–100; Banham, *A Critic Writes*, 60.

56. Quarmby, *The Plastics Architect*.

57. Frei Otto, "Victor Lundy, contribution à l'architecture pneumatique," *Architecture d'Aujourd'hui* 33, no. 102 (June-July 1962): 86–98.

58. See the "Note on 'Camp'" in Susan Sontag, *Against Interpretation and Other Essays* (New York: Farrar, Straus, Giroux, 1964).

59. Mike Webb, "Furniture Manufacturers' Showrooms," *Architect's Journal* (March 19, 1959): 452–454; republished in *Archigram*, no. 1 (May 1961); the Furniture Manufacturers' Association Building appeared in the first issue of the review *Archigram*; Michael Webb, "Furniture Manufacturers' Association Building Project," The Archigram Archival Project, <http://archigram.westminster.ac.uk/project.php?drwid=2640> (accessed June 6, 2011).

60. Charles Vernon Boys, *Soap Bubbles, Their Color and the Forces Which Mold Them* (London: Society for Promoting Christian Knowledge; New York: Young, 1890; repr., New York: Dover; Garden City, NY: Doubleday Anchor Books, 1959).

61. Eduardo Catalano, *Two Warped Surfaces* (Raleigh: North Carolina State College, School of Design, 1958).

62. Zvi Hecker, Alfred Neumann, and Eldar Sharon, "Centre civique de Bat-Yam, Israël," *Architecture d'Aujourd'hui* 34, no. 115 (June-July 1964): 70–71; "Zvi Hecker: Polyhedric Architecture," exhibition at the Israel Museum, Jerusalem, 1976. Alfred Neumann (Vienna 1900–Quebec 1968) was a student of Peter Behrens, Adolf Loos, and Auguste Perret. He was a visiting professor in the architecture school of Laval University, Quebec, between 1962 and 1964 and a professor and director of the Master's program at Laval University from 1964 to 1968. Zvi Hecker was assistant professor in the architecture school of Laval University from 1969 to 1972.

63. John Borrego, *Space Grid Structures, Skeletal Frameworks and Stressed-Skin Systems* (Cambridge, MA: MIT Press, 1968); Marc Mimram, *Structures et formes: étude appliquée à l'œuvre de Robert Le Ricolais* (Paris: Dunod: Presses Pont et Chaussees, 1983); J. François Gabriel, ed., *Beyond the Cube: The Architecture of Space Frames and Polyhedra* (New York: John Wiley, 1997). Alfred Neumann's work seems to have escaped the authors of this last book; nevertheless it is extremely useful.

64. For a brief description of the basic models of the *m phi system*, see Neumann, "L'Architecture morphologique," *Architecture d'Aujourd'hui* 34, no. 115 (June-July 1964): 72.

65. Alfred Neumann, *L'Humanisation de l'espace, le système m phi* (Boulogne-surmer: Éditions A. A., 1956), preface by Walter Gropius.

66. Alfred Neumann, "Morphologic architecture," *Royal Architectural Institute of Canada Journal* 40, no. 5 (May 1963); extracted in Neumann, "L'Architecture morphologique," 72.

67. Neumann, "L'Architecture morphologique," 72.

68. John Desmond Bernal, "Architecture and Science," *Journal of the Royal Institute of British Architects* (June 26, 1937): 805–812; now in Bernal, *The Freedom of Necessity* (London: Routledge and Kegan Paul, 1949); on Bernal's conference paper, see Andrew Brown, *J. D. Bernal: The Sage of Science* (Oxford: Oxford University Press, 2005), 154–155; on Space Groups, see Eric W. Weisstein, "Space Groups," from *MathWorld—A Wolfram Web Resource*, <http://mathworld.wolfram.com/SpaceGroups.html> (accessed January 25, 2012).

69. Alfred Neumann, "Architecture as Ornament," *Zodiac, a Review of Contemporary Architecture*, no. 19 (Milan: Communità, 1969): 93.

70. Ibid.

71. Ibid.

72. Ibid., 93–94.

73. In the 1990s, Neumann's correspondence on the subject of architectural proportions was donated to the British Architectural Library (BAL), RIBA, London: *Alfred Neumann Papers, 1951–1953*. Includes correspondence with Wells Coates, Renée Diamant-Berger, Matila Ghyka, Sigfried Giedion, Walter Gropius, Le Corbusier, Richard P. Lohse, J. M. Richards, José Luis Sert, and John Voelcker, relating to Neumann's EM-PHI System of architectural proportion. The following two recordings can be found in the BAL catalogue: <http://riba.sirsidynix.net.uk/uhtbin/cgisirsi/NpDekGFs80/MAIN_CAT /293440006/49>. Since January 2010, the Alfred Neumann archives have been housed at Columbia University, in the Avery Architectural and Fine Arts Library, Department of Drawing and Archives: <http://library.columbia.edu /indiv/avery/da.html>.

74. See the research guide prepared by the architect's daughter, Eva Neumann, as part of a proposal to donate the archives. An inventory of Alfred Neumann's books can be found in the research guide, but the volumes were not part of the donation. I would like to thank Eva Neumann for graciously sending me a copy of the document. See also Rafael Segal, "Unit, Pattern, Site: The Space Packed Architecture of Alfred Neumann, 1949–1968" (PhD dissertation, Princeton University, 2011), 589 pages, <http://gradworks.umi .com/34/52/3452627.html> (accessed June 2, 2011).

75. Anne Griswold Tyng, "Geometric Extensions of Consciousness," Graham Foundation for Advanced Study in the Fine Arts, extracts published in *Zodiac, a Review of Contemporary Architecture*, no. 19 (Milan: Communità, 1969), 130–162; *Louis Kahn to Anne Tyng: The Rome Letters, 1953–1954*, ed. Anne Griswold Tyng (New York: Rizzoli, 1997).

76. Ragon, *Où vivrons-nous demain?*, illustration, 145.

77. See Wenzel Hablik, *Drei KristallSchlösschen*, c. 1920, crystal and plasticine, Wenzel Hablik Stiftung, Itzehoe, Germany.

78. Wolfgang Voigt, ed., *Gottfried Böhm* (Berlin: Jovis, 2006).

79. Marie-Ange Brayer, ed., *David Georges Emmerich, architecte-ingénieur: une utopie rationnelle* (Orléans: HYX, 1997), 70–71.

80. David Georges Emmerich, "Constructions autotendantes," *Architecture d'Aujourd'hui* 34, no. 115 (June-July 1964): xlii, xlv.

81. Sabine Lebesque and Helene Fentener van Vlissingen, eds., *Yona Friedman: Structures Serving the Unpredictable* (Rotterdam: NAi Publishers, 1999); Hans Ulrich Obrist, *Yona Friedman* (Cologne: Walther König, 2007).

82. Eckhard Schulze-Fielitz, "Une théorie pour l'occupation de l'espace," *Architecture d'Aujourd'hui* 33, no. 102, "Architectures fantastiques" (June-July 1962): 78–85; Schulze-Fielitz, "Urbanisme spatial," *Architecture d'Aujourd'hui* 34, no. 115 (June-July 1964): 26–27; Rudolf Doernach, Hans J. Lenz, and Eckhard Schulze-Fielitz, "Stadtbausystem," *Bauen + Wohnen* 21, no. 5 (May 1967): 176–178; Eckhard Schulze-Fielitz, *Stadtsysteme. Urban Systems*, trans. William C. Wherrette (Stuttgart: Krämer, 1971–1973); Sabrina van der Ley and Markus Richter, eds., *Megastructure Reloaded: Visionäre Stadtenwürfe der Sechzigerjahre Reflektiert von Zeitgenössischen Künstlern + Visionary Architecture and Urban Design of the Sixties Reflected by Contemporary Artists* (Ostfildern: Hatje Cantz, 2008).

83. Eckhard Schulze-Fielitz, "The Space City" (1960), in Ulrich Conrads, ed., *Programs and Manifestoes on 20th Century Architecture*, trans. Michael Bullock (Cambridge, MA: MIT Press, 1970), 175–176.

84. Nicolas Schöffer, "Intégration de l'architecture dans la sculpture. La ville cybernétique," *Architecture d'Aujourd'hui* 34, no. 115 (June-July 1964): 105–107; Schöffer, *La Ville cybernétique*, 137–138.

85. Ibid.

86. Abraham A. Moles, *Théorie de l'information et perception esthétique* (Paris: Flammarion, 1958).

87. Abraham A. Moles and Elisabeth Rohmer, *Psychologie de l'espace* (Paris: Casterman, 1972), 94.

88. Ibid., 146–147 (authors' italics).

89. Joël Unal, *Pratique de voile de béton en autoconstruction* (Paris: Éditions Alternatives, 1981), introduction by Claude and Pascale Häusermann.

90. *La Bulle et l'architecte*, DVD, dir. Julien Donada (Lussas: Doc net films, 2005); Julien Donada, *Bulles: Conversation avec Pascal Häusermann* (Brussels: Facteur Humain, 2010).

91. Jean-Louis Chanéac, "Étude pour des 'villes-cratères,'" *Architecture d'Aujourd'hui* 34, no. 115 (June–July 1964): 42–43.

92. Jean-Louis Chanéac, *Architecture interdite* (Paris: Éditions du Linteau, 2005).

93. Ragon, *Où vivrons-nous demain?*, 112f.; Kisho Kurokawa, *Metabolism and Symbiosis = Metabolismus und Symbiosis*, ed. Peter Cachola Schmal, Ingeborg Flagge, and Jochen Visscher (Berlin: Jovis, 2005).

94. See Michel Ragon, *Les Cités de l'avenir* (Paris: Éditions Planètes, 1965); Ragon, *Les Visionnaires de l'architecture*, ed. André Parinaud with Jean-Pierre Balladur (Paris: Robert Laffont, 1965); Ragon, *La Cité de l'An 2000* (Paris: Casterman, 1968); Justus Dahinden, *Stadtstrukturen für Morgen* (Stuttgart: Verlag Gerd Hatje, 1971); Justus Dahinden, *Urban Structures for the Future* (London: Pall Mall Press; New York: Praeger Publishers, 1972); Reyner Banham, *Megastructure: Urban Futures of the Recent Past* (New York: Harper & Row, 1976).

95. Michael Webb, "Cushicle," *The Archigram Archival Project*, <http://archigram.westminster.ac.uk/project.php?id=92> (accessed June 8, 2011).

96. Michael Webb, "Cushicle," full-size model, *Archigram*, no. 7 (1966).

97. Pascal Häusermann and D. Bayot-Costy, "Projet d'habitation" and "Prototypes de série," *Architecture d'Aujourd'hui* 34, no. 115 (June–July 1964): 115; see also Georges Peillex, "Pascal Häusermann. Architecture fantastique ou habitation de demain?," *Style*, no. 4 (1962): 74–81; Pascal Häusermann (with architects Bruno Camoletti and Eric Hoechel), "Cellule préfabriquée en matière plastique," *Architecture d'Aujourd'hui*, no. 124 (February–March 1968): 102. "Six ultra-light standardized elements in a polyester sandwich with polyurethane foam between the two faces."

98. David Greene, "Spray Plastic House," *Archigram*, no. 1 (May 1961).

99. Peter Cook and Dennis Crompton, "Plug-in Dwellings," *Archigram*, no. 6 (November 1965). In a similar vein, see Warren Chalk, "Capsule Unit Tower," *Archigram*, no. 4 (May 1964); Warren Chalk, Peter Cook, and Dennis Crompton, "Plug-in City," *Archigram*, no. 5 (November 1964); Ron Herron, "Walking City," *Archigram*, no. 5 (November 1964); Dennis Crompton, "Computer City," *Archigram*, no. 5 (November 1964); David Greene, "Drive-in Housing, 1963–1966," *Archigram*, no. 5 (November 1964); and the Archigram Archival Project Web site, <http://archigram.westminster.ac.uk/index.php>.

100. "François Dallegret in Conversation with Alessandra Ponte"; Laurent Stalder, "François Dallegret's Machine World," in Alessandra Ponte, Laurent Stalder, and Thomas Weaver, eds., *God & Co.: François Dallegret beyond the Bubble* (London: Architecture Association School of Architecture, 2011), n.p.

101. Reyner Banham, "A Home Is Not a House," *Art in America* 53, no. 2 (April 1965): 70–79.

102. Charles Deaton, "Projet d'habitation à Denver, États-Unis," *Architecture d'Aujourd'hui* 34, no. 115 (June-July 1964): xxxiii.

103. John Leland, "Retrofitting the '70s: Rescuing a Vision of a Well Rounded World," *New York Times*, January 4, 2001.

104. Le Balcon de Belledone, built at an altitude of 1,200 meters on the highest slopes of the Chartreuse, between Chambéry and Grenoble; the plan comprised a restaurant and a leisure center with a cantilevered swimming pool in the form of a reinforced concrete shell. See *Architecture Française*, no. 313–314 (September-October 1968): 31–34; and "Pascal Haüsermann," <http://www.museumotel.com/hausermann/hauzi.htm> (accessed January 25, 2012).

105. Barbara-Ann Campbell, *John Lautner* (Cologne: Taschen, 1999).

106. *Coop Himmelb(l)au: Architecture Is Now: Projects, (Un)buildings, Action Statements, Sketches, Commentaries, 1968–1983* (New York: Rizzoli, 1983); *Coop Himmelb(l)au: construire le ciel*, exhibition catalogue (Paris: Centre Georges Pompidou, 1993); Frank Werner, *Covering + Exposing: The Architecture of Coop Himmelb(l)au* (Basel: Birkhäuser, 2000).

107. Quarmby, *The Plastics Architect*, figs. 215–219; Heinrich Klotz, ed., *Haus-Rucker-Co: 1967 bis 1983* (Wiesbaden: Braunschweig & Fried/Vieweg & Sohn, 1984); Dieter Bogner, ed., *Haus-Rucker-Co: Denkräume—Stadträume, 1967–1992* (Klagenfurt: Ritter Verlag, 1992).

108. Kisho Kurokawa, "Capsule Declaration," *SD (Space Design)*, no. 3 (March 1969): 50; republished in Kurokawa, "Capsules and the (re)Movable Home," in *Metabolism in Architecture* (London: Studio Vista/Boulder; Colorado: Westview Press, 1977), 75–85.

109. Reyner Banham, "Monumental Wind-bags," *New Society* 2, no. 290 (April 18, 1968): 569–570; republished in Marc Dessauce, *The Inflatable Moment. Pneumatics and Protest in 1968* (New York: Princeton Architectural Press, 1999), 31–33 (author's italics). See Hadas Steiner, "The Forces of Matter," *Journal* of Architecture 10, no. 1 (2005): 91–109; repr. in Philip Beesley and Sarah Bonnemaison, eds., *On Growth and Form, Organic Architecture and Beyond* (Halifax: Tuns Press and Riverside Architectural Press, 2008), 54–65.

110. An interpretation of the notion of topology that differs from the one attempted here (to our mind, at least) was given in the following book, which is very useful in general: Larry Busbea, *Topologies: The Urban Utopia in France, 1960–1970* (Cambridge, MA: MIT Press, 2007), 23–27, 140–167.

111. Dominique Rouillard, *Superarchitecture, Le futur de l'architecture, 1950–1979* (Paris: Éditions de La Villette, 2004); Lara Schrijver, *Radical Games: Popping the Bubble of 1960s Architecture* (Rotterdam: NAi Publishers, 2009).

112. Dessauce, *The Inflatable Moment*, 88–93; Craig Buckley and Jean-Louis Violeau, eds., *Utopie: Texts and Projects, 1967 to 1978* (Cambridge, MA: MIT Press, Semiotext(e), 2011).

113. Michel de Certeau, *The Practice of Everyday Life*, trans. Steven Rendall (Berkeley: University of California Press, 1984), 152.

114. Sauvagnargues, *Deleuze et l'art*, 88–89.

115. Gilles Deleuze, "On Gilbert Simondon," in Deleuze, *Desert Islands and Other Texts, 1953–1974* (New York: Semiotext(e), 2004), 86–89.

116. Anne Sauvagnargues, *Deleuze: l'empirisme transcendantal* (Paris: Presses Universitaires de France, 2009), 286.

117. Deleuze, *Logic of Sense*, 9.

118. Ibid.

119. Ibid., 11.

120. Ibid., 228.

7 PROSTHETICS AND PARASITES

1. Antonin Artaud, untitled text (1948), in Antonin Artaud, *Œuvres*, ed. Évelyne Grossman (Paris: Gallimard, 2004), 1702, my trans.

2. Antonin Artaud, untitled text (1947), *84*, no. 5/6 (1948), no page; now in: Artaud, *Œuvres*, 1581; cited in Gilles Deleuze, *The Logic of Sense*, ed. Constantin V. Boundas, trans. Mark Lester with Charles Stivale (New York: Columbia University Press, 1990), 88 and 342; cited again in Gilles Deleuze and Félix Guattari, *Anti-Oedipus: Capitalism and Schizophrenia*, trans. Robert Hurley,

Mark Seem, and Helen R. Lane (Minneapolis: University of Minnesota Press, 1983), 8.

3. Antonin Artaud, *Selected Writings*, ed. Susan Sontag, trans. Helen Weaver (Berkeley: University of California Press, 1988), 571.

4. Artaud, untitled, *84*, no. 5/6 (1948), cited in Deleuze and Guattari, *Anti-Oedipus*, 9.

5. Robert Sasso and Arnaud Villani, eds., "Le Vocabulaire de Gilles Deleuze," *Cahiers de Noesis* 3 (Spring 2003): 62.

6. See the interpretation offered by Slavoj Žižek, *Organs without Bodies: On Deleuze and Consequences* (New York: Routledge, 2004), in an attempt at a Hegelian-Lacanian reply to Deleuze's critique.

7. Deleuze and Guattari, *Anti-Oedipus*, 26–27.

8. Gilles Deleuze and Félix Guattari, *A Thousand Plateaus: Capitalism and Schizophrenia*, trans. Brian Massumi (London: Athlone Press, 1988), 30.

9. Michel Guillou, "Le Corps et l'appareil," *Traverses* 14/15 (April 1979): 136, 138.

10. Anthony Vidler, "Homes for Cyborgs," *Ottagono* 96 (September 1990), issue on *Prostheses*, ed. Alessandra Ponte, 37–55; Jacques Guillerme, "Thesis on Prosthesis: The Pretext of Latent Needs," ibid., 105–113; Adrian Forty, "Industrial Design and Prosthesis," ibid., 114–129.

11. Jean-Luc Nancy, "The Intruder," in Nancy, *Corpus*, trans. Richard A. Rand (New York: Fordham University Press, 2008), 161.

12. Jean-Luc Nancy, *L'intrus* (Paris: Galilée, 2000), 40; Nancy, "The Intruder," in *Corpus*, 161.

13. Nancy, *L'intrus*, 40–41.

14. Ibid., 43.

15. Benoît Peeters, *Derrida* (Paris: Flammarion, 2010), 508.

16. Deleuze and Guattari, *Anti-Oedipus*, 45–46.

17. Ibid., 1.

18. Gilles Deleuze, "Deleuze and Guattari Fight Back" (1972), in Deleuze, *Desert Islands and Other Texts, 1953–1974*, ed. David Lapoujade, trans. Michael Taormina (Los Angeles: Semiotext(e); Cambridge, MA: MIT Press, 2004), 219.

19. *Robert Morris* (Paris: Centre Georges Pompidou, 1995), 99.

20. Actually, of his first wife Judy's body. See Bruce Nauman, *Please Pay Attention Please: Bruce Nauman's Words: Writings and Interviews*, ed. Janet Kraynak

(Cambridge, MA: MIT Press, 2003), 129: "Interestingly, Nauman does not correct the misconception regarding *From Hand to Mouth*, which is not a cast of Nauman's body, as is often assumed, but of his first wife, Judy Nauman. In a later interview with Lorraine Sciarra, reprinted in this volume, he is less circumspect, remarking 'It's pretty difficult to make a cast of yourself.'"

21. Joan Simon, ed., *Bruce Nauman* (Minneapolis: Walker Art Center, 1994).

22. Amelia Jones, "The Body in Action: Vito Acconci and the 'Coherent' Male Artistic Subject," in Jones, *Body Art: Performing the Subject* (Minneapolis: University of Minnesota Press, 1998), 103–150.

23. *Rebecca Horn* (New York: Guggenheim Museum, 1993).

24. Paul Schimmel and Lisa Phillips, eds., *Charles Ray* (Los Angeles: Museum of Contemporary Art, 1998).

25. *Orlan* (Paris: Flammarion, 2004).

26. *Cindy Sherman, 1975–1993* (New York: Rizzoli, 1993).

27. Christine van Assche, ed., *Gary Hill* (Paris: Centre Georges Pompidou, 1992); Robert C. Morgan, ed., *Gary Hill* (Baltimore: Johns Hopkins University Press, 2000).

28. Matthew Barney, *Cremaster 4*, video (New York: Barbara Gladstone Gallery; Paris: Fondation Cartier, 1995).

29. Karel Čapek, *Rossum's Universal Robots (R.U.R.): a collective drama in three acts with a comedy prelude*, trans. David Short (1920; London: Hesperus, 2011).

30. Manfred E. Clynes and Nathan S. Kline, "Cyborgs and Space," *Astronautics, Journal of the American Rocket Society* (September 1960): 26–27, 74–76; Chris Hables Gray, ed., *The Cyborg Handbook* (London: Routledge, 1995), 29–33.

31. Nicholas de Monchaux, *Spacesuit: Fashioning Apollo* (Cambridge, MA: MIT Press, 2011).

32. N. Katherine Hayles, *How We Became Posthuman: Virtual Bodies in Cybernetics, Literature, and Informatics* (Chicago: University of Chicago Press, 1999), 50–80, 84–112.

33. Donna J. Haraway, "A Cyborg Manifesto: Science, Technology, and Socialist-Feminism in the Late Twentieth Century" (1985), in Haraway, *Simians, Cyborgs and Women: The Reinvention of Nature* (New York: Routledge, 1991), 177–178.

34. Haraway, "Cyborg Manifesto," 178.

35. Ibid., 1.

36. Paul N. Edwards, *The Closed World: Computers and the Politics of Discourse in Cold War America* (Cambridge, MA: MIT Press, 1997); Andy Clark, *Natural-Born Cyborg, Minds, Technologies and the Future of Human Intelligence* (Oxford: Oxford University Press, 2003).

37. Jean-Luc Nancy, "Corpus" (1990), in Juliet Flower MacCannell and Laura Zakarin, eds., *Thinking Bodies* (Stanford: Stanford University Press, 1994), 31.

38. Nancy, *Corpus*, 89.

39. Ibid.

40. Ibid.

41. William Gibson, *Neuromancer* (New York: Ace Books, 1984), 51.

42. *Les Immatériaux*, catalogue for an exhibition at Centre Georges Pompidou, CCI, March 28–July 15, 1985 (Paris: Centre Georges Pompidou, 1985), 2 vols.

43. Jean-Louis Déotte, "Les Immatériaux de Lyotard (1985): un programme figural," *Revue Appareil* (online), <http://revues.mshparisnord.fr/appareil /index.php?id=797> (accessed October 2, 2010); also John Rajchman, "Les Immatériaux or How to Construct the History of Exhibitions," *Tate's Online Research Journal*, Autumn 2009, <http://www.tate.org.uk/download/file /fid/7271> (accessed January 25, 2012).

44. MVRDV, *METACITY/DATATOWN* (Rotterdam: 010 Publishers, 1999).

45. Georges Teyssot, with Olivier Jacques, "In the Shade of Algorithms," in Andres Lepik and Andre Santer, eds., *J. Mayer H. Metropol Parasol* (Ostfildern: Hatje Cantz Verlag, 2011), 77–83.

46. Arthur Quarmby, *The Plastics Architects* (London: Pall Mall, 1974), fig. 147.

47. Marc Dessauce, *The Inflatable Moment: Pneumatics and Protest in 1968* (New York: Princeton Architectural Press, 1999), fig. 63.

48. Sean Topham, *Blow-Up: Inflatable Art, Architecture, and Design* (Munich: Prestel, 2002), 73–78; Sean Topham, *Where's My Space Age? The Rise and Fall of Futuristic Design* (Munich: Prestel, 2003), 96–98; Marie-Ange Brayer, ed., *Architectures expérimentales, 1950–2000* (Orléans: HYX, 2003), 248–253.

49. Frank Werner, *Covering + Exposing: The Architecture of Coop Himmelb[l]au* (Basel: Birkhäuser, 2000).

50. Marshall McLuhan, *The Gutenberg Galaxy: The Making of Typographic Man* (Toronto: University of Toronto Press, 1962); Marshall McLuhan, *Understanding Media: The Extensions of Man* (New York: McGraw-Hill, 1964); Marshall McLuhan with Quentin Fiore, *The Medium Is the Massage: An Inventory of Effects* (New York: Random House, 1967; repr. Corte Madera, CA: Gingko Press, 2001).

51. Peter Sloterdijk, *Bubbles: Microspherology*, trans. Wieland Hoban (Cambridge: Semiotext(e), 2011). Originally published in German as *Sphären. I. Blasen* (Frankfurt: Editions Suhrkamp, 1998).

52. Peter Sloterdijk, *La domestication de l'être: pour un éclaircissement de la clairière*, trans. Olivier Mannoni (Paris: Éditions Mille et Une Nuits, 2000), 37–40.

53. Martin Heidegger, "Letter on Humanism," in Heidegger, *Basic Writings*, ed. David F. Krell (London: Routledge, 1993), 217–265.

54. Jacques Derrida, *Khôra* (Paris: Galilée, 1993).

55. Sloterdijk, *La domestication de l'être*, 43.

56. Ibid.

57. Ibid.

58. Nancy, *Corpus*, 90.

59. Jacques Derrida, "Faxitexture," in Cynthia Davidson, ed., *Anywhere* (New York: Rizzoli, 1992), 20–33.

60. Michel Serres, *The Parasite*, trans. Lawrence R. Schehr, with a new Introduction by Cary Wolfe (1980; Minneapolis: University of Minnesota Press, 2007), 22, 56.

61. Gilles Deleuze, "The Actual and the Virtual," trans. Eliot Ross Albert, in Gilles Deleuze and Claire Parnet, *Dialogues II* (London: Continuum, 2002), 112–115.

62. Gilles Deleuze, *The Fold: Leibniz and the Baroque*, trans. Tom Conley (Minneapolis: University of Minnesota Press, 1993), 104–107.

63. Serres, *The Parasite*, 126.

64. Ibid., 121.

65. Ibid., 86.

66. Claude E. Shannon and Warren Weaver, *The Mathematical Theory of Communication* (1949), ed. Richard E. Blahut and Bruce Hajek (Urbana: University of Illinois Press, 1998).

67. Serres, *The Parasite*, 67.

68. Ibid.

69. Ibid.

70. Ibid., 121.

71. Ibid., 122.

72. Ibid.

73. Ibid., 123.

74. Ibid., 126.

75. Ibid.

76. Ibid., 127.

77. Ibid.

8 WINDOWS AND SCREENS

1. Franz Kafka, "The Street Window," in *The Metamorphosis, In the Penal Colony, and Other Stories*, trans. Willa and Edwin Muir (New York: Schocken Books, 1961), 39.

2. Speaking to Arturo Schwarz, a remark by the artist (Marcel Duchamp): Jeremy Millar, "Looking through the Large Glass," *Tate, etc.*, no. 7 (Summer 2006), <http://commentart.com/publication/TATE_ETC._Issue_7_-_Summer_2006> (accessed February14, 2012).

3. Gérard Wajcman, *Fenêtre: chroniques du regard et de l'intime* (Lagrasse: Verdier, 2004), 19–21, 35.

4. Anne Friedberg, *The Virtual Window: From Alberti to Microsoft* (Cambridge, MA: MIT Press, 2006), 26–42, 103.

5. Leon Battista Alberti, *On Painting and On Sculpture: The Latin Texts of De pictura and De statua*, ed. and trans. Cecil Grayson (London: Phaidon, 1972), 55.

6. Ingrid D. Rowland, *The Ecstatic Journey: Athanasius Kircher in Baroque Rome* (Chicago: University of Chicago Library, 2000), 41.

7. Ibid., 98.

8. Athanasius Kircher, *Musurgia universalis* (Rome: Francisci Corbelletti, 1650), vol. 2, plate between 302 and 303.

9. Ibid., facing 282. See Joscelyn Godwin, *Athanasius Kircher's Theater of the World* (London: Thames and Hudson, 2009).

10. See Bodo von Dewitz and Werner Nekes, eds., *Ich sehe was, was du nicht siehst!: Sehmaschinen und Bilderwelten: Die Sammlung Werner Nekes* (Göttingen: Steidl, 2002); See Laurent Mannoni, Werner Nekes, and Marina Werner,

Eyes, Lies and Illusions: The Art of Deception: Drawn from the Werner Nekes Collection (London: Hayward Gallery, 2004).

11. See Willey Reveley (after Jeremy Bentham), *General Idea of a Penitentiary, Panopticon, Floor-plan, Section and Front View*, c. 1791, pencil, pen, and watercolor. University College London Library, Bentham papers.

12. Wajcman, *Fenêtre*, 373.

13. Ibid., 447.

14. See *Die Wunderkammer des Sehens: aus der Sammlung Werner Nekes* (Graz: Landesmuseum Joanneum, 2003), 46.

15. Ibid.

16. In archaic French: "Qui laisse s'esbastre sa veue folatre / Quel malheur l'attend? La mort aeternelle [sic]."

17. Wajcman, *Fenêtre*, 372, 374–376, 439–440, 450.

18. Bernard Mandeville, *The Fable of the Bees, or, Private Vices, Publick Benefits*, ed. Frederick Benjamin Kaye (Indianapolis: Liberty Fund, 1988), vol. 1, paragraph 94.

19. Jean-François Harouel, *L'embellissement des villes: l'urbanisme français au XVIIIe siècle* (Paris: Picard, 1993); Philippe Perrot, *Le luxe: une richesse entre faste et confort, XVIIIe–XIXe siècle* (Paris: Seuil, 1995).

20. In French, "luxe de bienséance." See Anne Röver-Kann, *Bienséance: zur asthetischen Situation im Ancien Régime, dargestellt an Beispielen der Pariser Privatarchitektur* (Hildesheim: Georg Olms, 1977); Bettina Maria Köhler, *Die Stadt Paris und das Wohnhaus: Zum "Bâtiment Particulier" in der französischen Architekturtheorie von 1600–1750* (Weimar: Verlag und Datenbank für Geisteswissenschaften, 1994).

21. See Lione Pascoli, *Testamento politico d'un Accademico fiorentino* (Cologne: C. d'Egmond's heirs, 1733); Giovanni Battista Piranesi, *Della magnificenza ed architettura de' Romani* (1761), new ed. (Rome: Reale Accademia degli Antiquari di Londra, 1765); John Gwynn, *London and Westminster improved: illustrated by plans: to which is prefixed, a Discourse on Publick Magnificence* (London: Dodsley, 1766); Pierre Patte, *Mémoires sur les objets les plus importants de l'architecture* (Paris: Rozet, 1769); François-Michel Lecreulx, *Discours sur le goût appliqué aux Arts* (Nancy: Hoener, 1778); Vincenzo Ruffo, *Sull'abbellimento della città di Napoli* (Naples: Michele Morelli, 1789).

22. "D'un état policé": citation from Jacques-François Blondel, *Cours d'architecture*, 6 vols. (Paris, 1771–1777), 2:237. See also Natacha Coquery, *L'hôtel aristocratique: Le marché du luxe à Paris au XVIIIe siècle* (Paris: Sorbonne, 1998); Coquery, *L'espace du pouvoir: de la demeure privée à l'édifice public, Paris, 1700–1790* (Paris: S. Arslan, 2000), 46–58.

23. In French, "édifices particuliers." See Jean-François Cabestan, *La conquête du plain-pied: L'immeuble à Paris au XVIIIe siècle* (Paris: Picard, 2004).

24. See Elisabeth Heil, *Fenster als Gestaltungsmittel an Palastfassaden der italienischen Früh- und Hochrenaissance* (Hildesheim: Georg Olms, 1995); Sabine Lietz, *Das Fenster des Barock: Fenster und Fensterzubehör in der fürstlichen Profanarchitektur zwischen 1680 und 1780* (Munich: Deutscher Kunstverlag, 1982).

25. André Félibien, *Des principes de l'architecture, de la sculpture, de la peinture, et des autres arts qui en dépendent* (Paris: J. B. Coignard, 1676), 187.

26. A typical representation of those blind windows is offered by Jean Marot's engravings of the aristocratic mansion of the Hôtel de la Vrillière in Paris, built by François Mansart from 1635 to 1650. See Jean-Pierre Babelon and Claude Mignot, eds., *François Mansart: le génie de l'architecture* (Paris: Gallimard, 1998).

27. Art. 184, *Code Pénal*.

28. Philippe Ariès and Georges Duby, eds., *Histoire de la vie privée*, 5 vols. (Paris: Seuil, 1985–1987); 4:263, 281, 284–286, 563.

29. André Gide, *Les nourritures terrestres* (1897; Paris: Gallimard, 1921), 72; trans. as *The Fruits of the Earth*: "Families, I hate you! Shut-in homes, closed doors, jealous possessions of happiness." (<http://en.wikiquote.org/wiki/Andr%C3%A9_Gide>, accessed June 30, 2011).

30. Georg Simmel, "Bridge and Door" (1909), trans. Mark Ritter, *Theory, Culture and Society* 11 (February 1994): 5–10; "Brücke und Tür," in Simmel, *Das Individuum und die Freiheit: Essais* (Frankfurt am Main: Fischer Taschenbuch Verlag, 1994), 2–12.

31. Georg Simmel, "The Picture Frame: An Aesthetic Study" (1902), trans. Mark Ritter, *Theory, Culture and Society* 11 (February 1994): 11–17.

32. Jacques Derrida, "Parergon," in Derrida, *The Truth in Painting*, trans. Geoff Bennington and Ian McLeod (Chicago: University of Chicago Press, 1987), 15–147, esp. 60–61.

33. Georg Simmel, "Soziologie des Raumes," in *Aufsätze und Abhandlungen, 1901–1908* (Frankfurt am Main: Suhrkamp, 1995), 132–183; Simmel, "The Sociology of Space," in *Simmel on Culture: Selected Writings*, ed. David Frisby and Mike Featherstone (London: Sage, 1997), 137–170, esp. 141.

34. Ibid.

35. Linda Dalrymple Henderson, "Vibratory Modernism: Boccioni, Kupka, and the Ether of Space," in Bruce Clarke and Linda Dalrymple Henderson, eds., *From Energy to Information: Representation in Science and Technology, Art, and Literature* (Stanford: Stanford University Press, 2002), 126–149.

36. Siegfried Ebeling, *Space as Membrane* (1926), trans. Pamela Johnston, ed. Spyros Papapetros, introduction by Walter Scheiffle (London: Architectural Association, 2010).

37. Caroline A. Jones, "Ether," in Jones, ed., *Sensorium: Embodied Experience, Technology, and Contemporary Art* (Cambridge, MA: MIT Press, 2006), 137–141.

38. Gilles Deleuze, "On Gilbert Simondon," in Deleuze, *Desert Islands and Other Texts, 1953–1974*, ed. David Lapoujade, trans. Michael Taormina (Los Angeles: Semiotext(e); Cambridge, MA: MIT Press, 2004), 86–89; Deleuze quotes Gilbert Simondon's book, *L'individu et sa genèse physico-biologique* (Paris: Presses Universitaires de France, 1964), 260. See also François Dosse, *Gilles Deleuze and Félix Guattari: Intersecting Lives*, trans. Deborah Glassman (New York: Columbia University Press, 2010).

39. Bill Moggridge, *Designing Interactions* (Cambridge, MA: MIT Press, 2007), 315–316, 390.

40. Michael Bull, "Auditory," in Jones, *Sensorium*, 112–114.

41. Yet Wi-Fi (WLAN) has confounded all previous ideas that "ether" has an explicit physical dimension—that is, ether's "bandwidth" seems today to be dissolving all notions of time and space (temporality itself) by moving inward, into neurological time-space.

42. Michael Bull, "iPod," in Jones, *Sensorium*, 156–158.

43. Friedrich A. Kittler, *Discourse Networks 1800/1900*, trans. Michael Metteer with Chris Cullens (Stanford: Stanford University Press, 1990), 346–372.

44. Charles Féré, *Sensation et mouvement. Études expérimentales de psycho-mécanique* (Paris: Alcan, 1887), 13.

45. Friedrich Nietzsche, *The Will to Power*, trans. Walter Kauffmann and R. J. Hollingdale (New York: Vintage Books, 1968), section 811.

46. See John Durham Peters, *Speaking into the Air: A History of the Idea of Communication* (Chicago: University of Chicago Press, 1999), 195–205.

47. Friedrich Kittler, *Gramophone, Film, Typewriter*, trans. Geoffrey Winthrop-Young and Michael Wutz (Stanford: Stanford University Press, 1999), 21–114.

48. John Durham Peters, "Helmholtz, Edison, and Sound History," in Lauren Rabinovitz and Abraham Geil, eds., *Memory Bytes: History, Technology, and Digital Culture* (Durham: Duke University Press, 2004), 177–198.

49. Jean-Louis Déotte, *Qu'est-ce qu'un appareil? Benjamin, Lyotard, Rancière* (Paris: L'Harmattan, 2007).

50. Walter Benjamin, "The Work of Art in the Age of its Technological Reproducibility" (second version, 1936), in Benjamin, *Selected Writings*, vol. 3, *1935–1938*, ed. Marcus Bullock and Howard Eiland, trans. Edmund Jephcott and Harry Zohn (Cambridge, MA: Belknap Press of Harvard University Press, 2002), 115–116.

51. Oliver Grau, ed., *MediaArtHistories* (Cambridge, MA: MIT Press, 2007), 4.

52. Michel Foucault, "Of Other Spaces," in Joan Ockman, ed., *Architecture Culture 1943–1968: A Documentary Anthology* (New York: Rizzoli, 1993, 2000), 420–426.

53. Giorgio Agamben, *What Is an Apparatus? and Other Essays*, trans. David Kishik and Stefan Pedatella (Stanford: Stanford University Press, 2009), 20.

54. Gilles Deleuze and Félix Guattari, *A Thousand Plateaus: Capitalism and Schizophrenia*, trans. Brian Massumi (Minneapolis: University of Minnesota Press, 1987), 351–423.

55. Andrea Maffei, ed., *Toyo Ito: Works, Projects, Writings* (London: Blackwell; Milan: Electa, 2002).

56. Toyo Ito, *Tarzans in the Media Forest*, trans. Thomas Daniell (London: AA Publications, 2011), 102–124.

57. Gilles Deleuze and Claire Parnet, *Dialogues*, trans. Hugh Tomlinson and Barbara Habberjam (New York: Columbia University Press, 1987), 31.

58. Gilles Deleuze, "The Actual and the Virtual," trans. Eliot Ross Albert, in Deleuze and Claire Parnet, *Dialogues II* (London: Continuum, 2002), 112–115.

59. Félix Guattari, *Cartographies schizoanalytiques* (Paris: Galilée, 1989), 210–218.

60. Ibid., 227–232.

61. Félix Guattari, *Chaosmosis: An Ethico-Aesthetic Paradigm*, trans. Paul Bains and Julian Pefanis (Bloomington: Indiana University Press, 1995), 58–59.

62. Ibid., 59.

63. Félix Guattari, "L'hétérogenèse machinique," *Chimères*, no. 11 (1991): 78–97.

64. Caroline A. Jones, "The Mediated Sensorium," in Jones, *Sensorium*, 5–49, esp. 43.

65. Supposedly Jacques Lacan coined the term *extimate* from the notion of *intimité*, "intimacy." The resulting neologism, "extimacy," precisely expresses the way in which psychoanalysis problematizes the opposition between "inside" and "outside." The structure of extimacy is perfectly expressed in the topology of the torus and of the Möbius strip.

66. Pierre Lévy, *Qu'est-ce que le virtuel?* (Paris: Éditions la Découverte, 1995), 22–25; Pierre Lévy, *Becoming Virtual: Reality in the Digital Age*, trans. Robert Bononno (New York: Plenum Trade, 1998).

67. See Nicholas Barker, *Unmade Beds* (Stockport, UK: Dewi Lewis Publishing, 1998), a book based on Barker's film *Unmade Beds* (1997).

68. See Diane Watteau, ed., *Vivre l'intime (dans l'art contemporain)* (Paris: Thalia édition, 2010).

INDEX